Especially for:

_____

From:

_____

Date:

_____

GOD
CALLING

GOD AT
EVENTIDE

GOD
CALLING

GOD AT
EVENTIDE

EDITED BY
A.J. RUSSELL

BARBOUR
PUBLISHING

All scripture quotations, unless otherwise indicated, are taken from the King James Version of the Bible.

Published by Barbour Books, an imprint of Barbour Publishing, Inc., P.O. Box 719, Uhrichsville, Ohio 44683, www.barbourbooks.com

Our mission is to publish and distribute inspirational products offering exceptional value and biblical encouragement to the masses.

Member of the
Evangelical Christian
Publishers Association

Printed in the United States of America.

INTRODUCTION

Very few books, even number-one bestsellers, are read with much passion a decade after their release. In twenty or thirty years, most are largely forgotten.

So there must be something special about a book that is not only read but revered more than seventy years after its first publication. *God Calling* is such a volume.

It began in the fall of 1932 when two British women met to pray and share fellowship with each other, and to write down what they thought God was saying to them through His Son, Jesus Christ. Ultimately, they generated a year's worth of writings, which were then edited for publication by A. J. Russell, a London newspaperman.

The two women, who have always remained anonymous, were "poor, brave [and] courageously fighting against sickness and penury," in Russell's words. "They were facing a hopeless future and one of them even longed to be quit of this hard world for good," he wrote in his original introduction. But then God spoke to their hearts, and *God Calling* was born.

Over the decades, the anonymous friends' work has become one of the most read and beloved daily devotionals of all time. Millions of copies have been printed and sold, read personally, and given as gifts, in Great Britain and the United States. The book has also been translated for use around the world, and followed by a sequel, *God at Eventide*.

Their literary approach—*God Calling* and *God at Eventide* are written as if Jesus Himself is speaking to the reader—resonates with both men and women, of varying ages and cultures. "Open this book at any page and taste its beauty," Russell wrote in the original introduction to *God Calling*. "Dwell lovingly on its tender phrases. Let its wonderful quality sink deep into your spirit."

Both of these marvelous books are presented here in their entirety, with a *God Calling* reading for each morning, and its accompanying *God at Eventide* passage for the end of the day. We hope this volume will provide challenge, encouragement, and inspiration for your Christian walk. Read on to meet your loving Savior.

THE PUBLISHER

Note: The book contains the original unabridged text of both *God Calling* and *God at Eventide,* without editorial changes. That is why you will find no *God at Eventide* reading for February 29.

JANUARY 1

God Calling: Between the Years

Our Lord and our God. We joy in Thee. Without Thy
Help we could not face unafraid the year before us.

I stand between the years. The Light of My Presence is
flung across the year to come—the radiance of the Sun of
Righteousness. Backward, over the past year, is My Shadow
thrown, hiding trouble and sorrow and disappointment.

Dwell not on the past—only on the present. Only use the
past as the trees use My Sunlight to absorb it, to make from it
in after days the warming fire-rays. So store only the blessings
from Me, the Light of the World. Encourage yourselves by the
thought of these.

Bury every fear of the future, of poverty for those dear to
you, of suffering, of loss. Bury all thought of unkindness and
bitterness, all your dislikes, your resentments, your sense of
failure, your disappointment in others and in yourselves, your
gloom, your despondency, and let us leave them all, buried,
and go forward to a new and risen life.

Remember that you must not see as the world sees. I hold
the year in My Hands—in trust for you. But I shall guide you
one day at a time.

Leave the rest with Me. You must not anticipate the gift
by fears or thoughts of the days ahead.

And for each day I shall supply the wisdom and the strength.

God at Eventide: All Is Ready

Write for all things are now ready.

The world is waiting for My Message of Love, and Hope
and Cheer. The very unrest of spirit is a sign. The turning
from the husk of religion is a sign.

Man is no longer lulled by empty phrases and promises

of a better life hereafter. He must know Me before he would wish to spend Eternity with Me. He must know Me here in the storm where he needs strength and rest.

He has been sleeping; now he has been shocked awake. Now he must find Me or fling defiance at Me or school himself into denial, or indifference.

Reason and argument avail nothing. Only by the lives of My followers can man be helped; only by seeing Mine unmoved, at peace, joyful, in a world of sorrow, disillusionment, and mistrust.

Your denial today will not be "I know not the man." The world is indifferent as to whether you profess Me or not. No, it will be your failure to present Me in your life as I am—vital, sustaining, spirit-renewing, your All.

JANUARY 2

God Calling: Arm of Love

You are to help to save others. Never let one day pass when you have not reached out an arm of Love to someone outside your home—a note, a letter, a visit, help in some way.

Be full of Joy. Joy saves. Joy cures. Joy in Me. In every ray of sunlight, every smile, every act of kindness, or love, every trifling service—joy.

Each day do something to lift another soul out of the sea of sin, or disease or doubt into which man has fallen. I still walk today by the lakeside and call My Disciples to follow Me and to become fishers of men.

The helping hand is needed that raises the helpless to courage, to struggle, to faith, to health. Love. Laugh. Love and laughter are the beckoners to faith and courage. Trust on, love on, joy on.

Refuse to be downcast. Refuse to be checked in your upward climb. Love and laugh. I am with you. I bear your burdens. Cast your burden upon Me and I will sustain thee. And then in very lightheartedness you turn and help another with the burden that is pressing too heavily upon him or her.

How many burdens can you lighten this year? How many hearts can you cheer? How many souls can you help?

And in giving you gain: "Good measure, pressed down, and running over." I your Lord have said it.

God at Eventide: Your Resolutions

It is in union with Me that you receive strength to carry out your good resolutions.

Contact with Me brings power for the work I wish you to do, that work for which I know you to be most suited and which you only can do, and do so well.

It is in contact with Me that you are endued with the Grace that I alone can give, enabling you to minister acceptably to those to whom I send you, and those whom I bring to you.

Even among the distractions and manifold interests of the world—live in My Presence, yet daily withdraw yourself to be alone with Me.

JANUARY 3

God Calling: The Way Will Open

But they that wait upon the
Lord shall renew their strength.
ISAIAH 40:31

You must be renewed, remade. Christ, Christ, Christ. Everything must rest on Me. Force is born of rest. Only Love is a conquering force. Be not afraid, I will help you.

Be channels both of you. My Spirit shall flow through

and My Spirit shall, in flowing through, sweep away all the bitter past.

Take heart. God loves, God helps, God fights, God wins. You shall see. You shall know. The way will open. All My Love has ever planned, all My Love has ever thought, you shall see each day unfold. Only be taught. Just be a child. A child never questions plans. It accepts gladly.

God at Eventide: Mutual Need

Abide in Me and I in you.

This year dwell much upon this stupendous Truth. You need to abide in Me this year to share in the Spirit-life of the Universe, in its creative power and energy. Thus you are a part in God's whole.

But I must abide in you, for only so can I express My Love and Power and Truth through you interpreting them in deed, and look, and word.

In these words of Mine you have My twofold nature.

The Strong Protector! so Strong to shield; and offering you, My guest, all provision you need.

And then you have Me in My Humility, one with you, your close Companion, dwelling in you, and dependent on you. Think on these things.

God Calling: Do Not Plan

Shew us Thy Way, O Lord, and let us walk in Thy Paths.
Lead us in Thy Truth and teach us.

All is well. Wonderful things are happening. Do not limit God at all. He cares and provides.

Uproot self—the channel-blocker. Do not plan ahead; the way will unfold step by step. Leave tomorrow's burden. Christ is the Great Burden-bearer. You cannot bear His load and He only expects you to carry a little day-share.

God at Eventide: Your Mandate

Here in this evening hour I draw near to you—and listen. Tell Me of the Peace you know in Me; of the tender confidence in Me that has brought Peace and Safety into your life.

Tomorrow you will go back into the world with My message of Eternal Life. Truths that you are only just beginning fully to grasp, that are bringing you Vision and Joy, you will pass to others, that they may be saved the wasted years that lie behind you. Turn to them as you would to one following you along a dangerous road and warn them against the pitfalls in their way.

Point out to them the beauties of The Way, the sunlit hills ahead, the sunset glories, the streams and flowers of My peaceful glades.

Direct their attention from earth's allures or mirages to Me, your Companion of The Way. Tell them of your Joy in Me. That is your mandate from High Heaven.

JANUARY 5

God Calling: Hoard Nothing

Love Me and do My Will. No evil shall befall you. Take no thought for tomorrow. Rest in My Presence brings Peace. God will help you. Desire brings fulfillment. Peace like a quiet flowing river cleanses, sweeps all irritants away.

You shall be taught, continue these prayer times, even if they seem fruitless. The devil will try by any means to stop them. Heed him not. He will say evil spirits may enter in. Heed him not.

Rest your nerves. Tired nerves are a reflection on, not of, God's Power. Hope all the time.

Do not be afraid of poverty. Let money flow freely. I will let it flow in, but you must let it flow out. I never send money to stagnate—only to those who pass it on. Keep nothing for yourself. Hoard nothing. Only have what you need and use. This is My Law of Discipleship.

God at Eventide: The Healing Hour

As yet you can only dimly see what this evening-time will mean for you.

For a while you shed earth's cares and frets, and know the uplift of soul that comes through planned Communion with Me.

You are renewed, and that renewing is your safeguard from mental and spiritual disintegration.

In this brief time you taste, in contact with Me, something of My Resurrection Life. It is the glorified Christ you know, and to know Him is to partake too of His Risen Life.

Thus health, physical, mental, and spiritual, comes to you and flows from you.

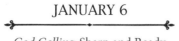

God Calling: Sharp and Ready

Guide me, O Thou Great Jehovah,
Pilgrim through this foreign land.
I am weak but Thou art mighty,
Guide me with Thy powerful Hand.

You must pray. The way will open. God cares and His plans unfold. Just love and wait.

Love is the Key. No door is too difficult for it to open.

What cause have you to fear? Has He not cared for and protected you? Hope on. Hope gladly. Hope with certainty. Be calm, calm in My Power.

Never neglect these times; pray and read your Bible and train and discipline yourself. That is your work—Mine to use you. But My instruments must be sharp and ready. Then I use them.

Discipline and perfect yourselves at all costs. Do this, for soon every fleeting thought will be answered, every wish gratified, every deed used. It is a fearful Power, a mighty Power. Oh! be careful that you ask nothing amiss—nothing that is not according to My Spirit.

All thoughts harmful must be turned out. See how necessary I have made the purity and goodness of your own lives to you. Soon, you shall ask and at once it will come. Welcome the training. Without it I dare not give you this Power.

Do not worry about others' lives. You must perfect yourselves first in My Strength.

God at Eventide: Land of Promise

Imagine the Hope of My Heart that day on the mountainside when I told My followers that to no throne on earth I led them; old forms and negations that had meant so much in the past were to be swept away; motives and impulses were to be all-important.

By the thoughts of his heart was a man to be judged. Prayer was like a son appealing to a father. Love was to be the foundation, the Golden Rule. Tribal, even racial, distinctions were to be ignored and the claims of the whole great family of God were to be met.

To such heights as they had never before scaled I led them, up to Peak-truths they had thought unscalable.

What hopes I had of them as their wonder turned to Vision and they responded to My Message.

What hopes I have today of each of you, My Followers, as you catch sight of your Land of Promise ahead.

JANUARY 7

God Calling: The Secret Pearl

Look upon us with Thy favor, O Lord, while we behold "the land that is very far off" and yet so near to the seeing eye and the listening ear.

Wait. Wonders are unfolding. Tremble with awe. No man can stand upon the threshold of Eternity unshaken. I give unto you Eternal Life. A free gift, a wonderful gift—the Life of the Ages.

Silently comes the Kingdom. No man can judge when It enters the heart of man, only in results. Listen quietly. Sometimes you may get no message. Meet thus all the same. You will absorb an atmosphere.

Cultivate silence. "God speaks in silences." A silence, a soft wind. Each can be a message to convey My meaning to the heart, though by no voice, or even word.

Each word or thought of yours can be like a pearl that you drop into the secret place of another heart, and in some hour of need, lo! the recipient finds the treasure and realizes for the first time its value.

Do not be too ready to *do*, just *be*. I said, "*Be* ye therefore perfect" not "do" perfect things. Try and grasp this. Individual efforts avail nothing. It is only the work of the Universal Spirit—My Spirit—that counts.

Dwell in thought on this more and more; saints have taken a lifetime to grasp it.

God at Eventide: Cleansing Light

I am the True Light that cometh into the world, and men
love darkness rather than Light, because their deeds are evil.

Truly not all men desire My Light. Not all men would welcome its clear shining.

Many shrink from its revelation, preferring the darkness that would hide their deeds, rather than the remorseless Light that would show the evil of which they are ashamed.

Pray for Light, rejoice to have it, welcome its revelation, and so, when in your lives it has done its searching, cleansing work, then bear it yourselves gladly, triumphantly, out into a world that needs so sorely the Light of the World.

JANUARY 8

God Calling: Love Bangs the Door

Life with Me is not immunity *from* difficulties, but peace *in* difficulties. My guidance is often by *shut* doors. Love bangs as well as opens.

Joy is the result of faithful trusting acceptance of My Will, when it seems *not* joyous.

St. Paul, my servant, learnt this lesson of the banged doors when he said "our light affliction, which is but for a moment, worketh for us a far more exceeding and eternal weight of glory." Expect rebuffs until this is learned—it is the only way.

Joy is the daughter of calm.

God at Eventide: Ways of Witness

I call upon you to make Me known—

> *By your unfailing trust in Me.*
> *By your joy, unrepressed by the difficulties of the way.*
> *By your tender concern for the weak and the wandering.*
> *By your acceptance of My Gift of Eternal Life.*
> *By your growth in Spiritual development,*
> *proof of that inner life, which alone can engender it.*

Make Me known, more and more, by your serenity, by unflinching adherence to Truth.

Make Me known by My Spirit within and round you, your conduct and speech ever bearing witness to the Power and the Wonder of My Presence.

So shall all men know that you are My disciple, and that your claim is never for the recognition of the self—but for Me, the Christ-in-you.

JANUARY 9

God Calling: No Strain

Be calm, no matter what may befall you. Rest in Me. Be patient, and let patience have her perfect work. Never think things overwhelming. How can you be overwhelmed when I am with you?

Do not feel the strain of life. There is no strain for My

children. Do you not see I am a Master Instrument-maker? Have I not fashioned each part? Do I not know just what it can bear without a strain? Would I, the Maker of so delicate an instrument, ask of it anything that could destroy or strain?

No! The strain is only when you are serving another master, the world, fame, the good opinion of men—or carrying two days' burden on the one day.

Remember that it must not be.

God at Eventide: A Love-Home

Hush earth's desires that you miss not My Footfall. It brings the strength of a warrior, and the eagerness of a Lover.

Let your heart thrill with the glad, "He comes." Forsake all thought but the thought of Me as I enter. Soul-rest and heart-comfort I bring. Forget all else.

Let Me lift the burden from your shoulders, My burden, borne for you. Here in quiet, we will rest, while you are reinvigorated.

Poor dwelling, you feel, for the King of Kings. Yet I see your Home of Love as Love has made it. I come from locked doors, where youth is trying to live without Me; where old age, ever refusing to answer My pleading and knocking, now hears Me no more, and sits silent and alone.

Comfort Me, My children. Make of your hearts a Love-Home for the Man of Sorrows, still so often despised and rejected of men. Yet I would turn their sorrow into joy.

God Calling: Influence

When you come to Me, and I give you that Eternal Life I give to all who believe in Me, it alters your whole existence, the words you speak, the influences you have.

These are all eternal. They *must* be. They spring from the life within you, My Life, Eternal Life, so that they too live forever. Now, you see how vast, how stupendous, is the work of any soul that has Eternal Life. The words, the influence, go on down the ages forever.

You must ponder on these truths I give you. They are not surface facts, but the secrets of My Kingdom, the hidden pearls of rare price.

Meditate upon them. Work at them in your minds and hearts.

God at Eventide: How Self Dies

Hush your spirit still more in My Presence. Self dies, not by human combat, not necessarily by supplicatory prayer, but by the consciousness of My Presence, and of My Spirit-values. Thus self shrivels into lifelessness, into nothingness.

It is so necessary to dwell with Me, to draw so close to Me in an understanding as complete as it is possible for man to realize.

Do you not see now the need for the training and discipline I have enjoined on you? They are vital in that they attune your being to the consciousness of My Mind and Purpose. When this Mind is in you that is in Me you are able to penetrate the outer courts of the Temple, and in the very Holy of Holies to grasp the meaning that lay behind all I said and did and was.

Sacrifice all for this. Your work has to be inspired. Where can you find inspiration but in My Presence?

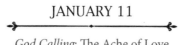

God Calling: The Ache of Love

Use My unlimited stores for your needs and those of others. Seek My wonderful truths and you *shall* find.

There may come times when you sit in silence, when it seems as if you were left alone. Then, I command you to remember I have spoken to you.

You will have the consciousness of My Presence when you hear no voice. Abide in that Presence. "I am the light of the world," but sometimes in tender pity, I withhold too glaring a light, lest, in its dazzling brightness, you should miss your daily path and work.

Not until Heaven is reached do souls sit and drink in the ecstasy of God's revelation to His Own. At the moment you are pilgrims and need only your daily marching orders and strength and guidance for the day.

Oh! Listen to My Voice, eagerly, joyfully. Never crowd it out. I have no rival claimants, and if men seek the babble of the world, then I withdraw.

Life has hurt you. Only scarred lives can really save.

You cannot escape the discipline. It is the hallmark of discipleship. My children, trust Me always. Never rebel.

The trust given to Me today takes away the ache of rejection of My love that I suffered on earth and have suffered through the ages. "I died for you, My children, and could ye treat Me so?"

God at Eventide: *Your* Good News

"How beautiful upon the mountains are the feet of those who bring glad tidings. . .that publish Peace." When you are weary think that yours are the feet of those who bring glad tidings.

This will rob your steps of weariness, will give a Joy and

a spring to your walk.

"Bringeth glad tidings. Publisheth Peace." What a joyful mission. One of gladness and Peace. Never forget this, and the Joy of your message and mission will radiate from you gladdening and transforming.

JANUARY 12

God Calling: Thanks for Trials

You must say "Thank You" for everything, even seeming trials and worries.

Joy is the whole being's attitude of "Thank You" to Me. Be glad. Rejoice. A father loves to see his children happy.

I am revealing so much to you. Pass it on. Each Truth is a jewel. Some poor spirit-impoverished friend will be glad of it. Drop one here and there.

Seek to find a heart-home for each Truth I have imparted to you. More Truths will flow in. Use *all* I give you. Help others. I ache to find a way into each life and heart, for all to cry expectantly, "Even so, come Lord Jesus."

God at Eventide: Bright Shadows

He descended into Hell. . .He ascended into Heaven.

It is good for man to know his Lord is ever with him through every danger, every change, every seeming chance. It is good to walk the dark waters with Me.

I did not make the darkness. It was no artist-design to create a darkness which should make My Light seem the greater radiance.

Willfulness and sin have caused earth's shadows, but I am there to walk the dark places with you. So that even the

22

darkest place may be illumined by the Light of the Sun of Righteousness.

JANUARY 13

God Calling: Friends Unseen

Never despair, never despond. Be just a channel of helpfulness for others.

Have more sympathy. Feel more tenderness toward others. Your lives shall not be all care. *Gold* does not *stay* in the crucible—*only* until it is refined. Already I hear the music and the marching of the unseen host, rejoicing at your victory.

No follower of Mine would ever err or fall, if once the veil were withdrawn which prevents him seeing how these slips delight the evil spirits, and the pain and disappointment of those who long for him to conquer in My Strength and Name, and the ecstasy of rejoicing when victory is won.

My Strength is *the same* as that in which I conquered Satan in the Wilderness—depression and sorrow in the Garden, and even death on Calvary.

Think of that.

God at Eventide: Fight Evil Forces

You are going to be a mighty force against evil because you will be ever-increasingly the agent of Divine Power. Think, when this is so, how could you for one moment imagine that evil could leave you alone? It is to the advantage of evil to thwart you.

Think how those who care for you in the Unseen watch to see you conquer in My strength for My Glory.

The great battles of your world are fought in the Unseen. Fight there your battles and win. More than conquerors through Him Who loves you. Fight with the whole armor of God, ready prepared for you.

Victors through Me. Press on, Victory is in sight.

JANUARY 14

God Calling: Mighty and Marvelous

Glad indeed are the souls with whom I walk. Walking with Me is security. The coming of My Spirit into a life and Its working are imperceptible, but the result is mighty.

Learn of Me. Kill the self. Every blow to self is used to shape the real, eternal, imperishable you.

Be very candid and rigorous with yourselves. "Did *self* prompt that?" and if it did, oust it at all costs.

When I died on the Cross, I died embodying all the human self. Once that was crucified, I could conquer even death.

When I bore your sins in My own body on the Tree I bore the self-human nature of the world. As you too kill self, you gain the overwhelming power I released for a weary world, and you too will be victorious.

It is not life and its difficulties you have to conquer, only the self in you. As I said to My disciples, "I have many things to say to you, but you cannot bear them now." You could not understand them. But as you go on obeying Me and walking with Me and listening to Me, you will, and then you will see how glorious, how marvelous, My revelations are, and My teachings.

God at Eventide: How Joy Comes

The Joy that follows awareness of Guidance has ever been the upholding Joy of My followers.

It is the result of desiring My Will only, in every detail,

and then the realization of the wonderful way I can act for you when you leave the planning to Me.

Truly all things, every detail in each day, do work together for good to those who love Me. My miracle-working power can become operative when there is no "kicking against the pricks," no thwarting of My Will.

Whether you walk here on earth, or are free from earth's limitations in My Heaven, it is Heaven to walk with Me. Man has sought to describe Heaven in terms of music and song. That is but his endeavor to express the ecstasy he knows on earth in Communion with Me, and to anticipate its magnified intensity in Heaven.

JANUARY 15

God Calling: Relax

Relax, do not get tense, have no fear. All is for the best. How can you fear change when your life is hid with Me in God, who changeth not—and I am the same yesterday, today, and forever.

You must learn poise, soul-balance and poise, in a vacillating, changing world.

Claim My power. The same power with which I cast out devils is yours today. Use it. If not, I withdraw it. Use it ceaselessly.

You cannot ask too much. Never think you are too busy. As long as you get back to Me and replenish after each task, no work can be too much. My Joy I give you. Live in it. Bathe your Spirit in it. Reflect it.

I am beside you—the eager Listener, so ready to hear your plea, so ready to say all that your heart needs.

Live more with Me apart, and so there will come an ever-increasing helpfulness to others.

Heart-poise, mental balance, spiritual strength, will be yours in ever more abundant measure. Never feel that you can help others unaided by Me, for therein lies danger.

Your self-importance is destructive of helpfulness, devitalizing because your strength has such limitations. Mine is limitless.

Grow more dependent upon Me, yet more assured that you can do all things through Me.

JANUARY 16

God Calling: Friend in Drudgery

It is the daily strivings that count, not the momentary heights. The obeying of My Will day in, day out, in the wilderness plains, rather than the occasional Mount of Transfiguration.

Perseverance is nowhere needed so much as in the religious life. The drudgery of the Kingdom it is that secures My intimate Friendship. I am the Lord of little things, the Divine Control of little happenings.

Nothing in the day is too small to be a part of My scheme. The little stones in a mosaic play a big part.

Joy in Me. Joy is the God-given cement that secures the harmony and beauty of My mosaic.

Never lose heart. Kill the proud self as you go on, for on that dead self you rise.

On ever with Me. Do not let earth's frets disturb you. Since you cannot follow Me and indulge self, at all costs turn self out directly its claims disturb; so only can you keep spiritual calm.

Not your circumstances but your self is the enemy. A man's foes are those of his own household.

Do others blame you falsely? I was reviled but I reviled not again.

JANUARY 17

God Calling: God's Rush to Give

Silence. Be silent before Me. Seek to *know* and then to do My will in all things.

Abide in My Love, an atmosphere of loving understanding to all men. This is *your* part to carry out, and then *I* surround you with a protective screen that keeps all evil from you. It is fashioned by your own attitude of mind, words, and deeds toward others.

I want to give you all things, good measure, pressed down, and running over. Be quick to learn. You know little yet of the Divine Impatience that longs to rush to give. Does one worrying thought enter your mind, one impatient thought? Fight it at once.

Love and Trust are the solvents for the worry and cares and frets of a life. Apply them *at once*. You are channels, and though the channel may not be altogether blocked, fret and impatience and worry corrode, and in time would become beyond your help.

Persevere, oh! persevere. Never lose heart. All is well.

I am here. Realize My Presence. My love surrounds you; be filled with My Joy.

You are being truly guided though not until you are content to be led as little children do you really live fully in the Kingdom of Heaven.

Life with Me is of childlike simplicity. Simple souls are the great souls, for in simplicity there is majesty.

JANUARY 18

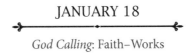

God Calling: Faith–Works

Pray daily for Faith. It is My Gift. It is your only requisite for the accomplishment of mighty deeds. Certainly you have to work, you have to pray, but upon Faith alone depends the answer to your prayers—your works.

I give it to you in response to your prayer, because it is the necessary weapon for you to possess for the dispersion of evil—the overcoming of all adverse conditions, and the accomplishment of all good in your lives, and then you having Faith, give it back to Me. It is the envelope in which every request to Me should be placed.

And yet "Faith without works is dead." So you need works, too, to feed your Faith in Me. As you seek to do, you feel your helplessness. You then turn to Me. In knowing Me, your faith grows—and that faith is all you need for My Power to work.

God at Eventide: Joy of Meeting

So many think of prayer as petition only. It *is* petition. "In everything by prayer and supplication let your requests be made known unto Me."

But prayer is also a glad turning to meet Me for the joy of the meeting, for the rapture of My Presence.

Prayer, too, is preparation for tomorrow's return to those who need you, those to whom My love goes out from you.

JANUARY 19

God Calling: Love Anticipates

Lord, I will seek Thee.

None ever sought Me in vain. I wait, wait with a hungry longing to be called upon; and I, who have already seen your hearts' needs before you cried upon Me, before perhaps you were conscious of those needs yourself, I am already preparing the answer.

It is like a Mother, who is setting aside suitable gifts for her daughter's wedding, before Love even has come into the daughter's life.

The *Anticipatory Love* of God is a thing mortals seldom realize. Dwell on this thought. Dismiss from your minds the thought of a grudging God, who had to be petitioned with sighs and tears and much speaking before reluctantly He loosed the desired treasures. Man's thoughts of Me need revolutionizing.

Try and see a Mother preparing birthday or Christmas delights for her child—the while her Mother-heart sings: "Will she not love that? How she will love this!" and anticipates the rapture of her child, her own heart full of the tenderest joy. Where did the Mother learn all this preparation-joy? From Me—a faint echo this of My preparation-joy.

Try to see this as plans unfold of My preparing. It means much to Me to be understood, and the understanding of Me will bring great joy to you.

I am with you. I will help you. Through suffering to health, through sorrow to joy, through pain to ease, through night to day—you shall be led and comforted.

Without previous experience of dawn and day none could dream that the glorious dawn and fullness of day could follow the blackest night.

Regard this experience not as darkness but as dawn. The first faint glimmers of light are following the black night through which you have passed. The full day is not yet. But hail the *dawn* with Me.

JANUARY 20

God Calling: At One with God

One with Me. I and My Father are one. One with the Lord of the whole Universe!

Could human aspiration reach higher? Could man's demands transcend this? One with Me.

If you realize your high privilege, you have only to think and immediately the object of your thought is called into being. Indeed, well may I have said, "Set your affection on things above, not on things on the earth."

To dwell in thought on the material, when once you live in Me—is to call it into being. So you must be careful only to think of and desire that which will help, not hinder, your spiritual growth. The same law operates, too, on the spiritual plane.

Think Love, and Love surrounds you, and all about whom you think. Think thoughts of *ill-will*, and ill surrounds you, and those about whom you think. Think health—health comes. The physical reflects the mental and spiritual.

I am with you. I am delivering you. But look for deliverance not from circumstances alone, but deliverance from the self-ties that bind you to earth, and that hinder your entrance into the kingdom of service in which there is perfect freedom. All is well.

You shall rise to newness of Life. You cannot fail to rise as you free yourself from the toils and sins and failures that bind you to earth.

No past sin can enchain you. You look to Me and are saved. They are all forgiven. Conquer your faults with My Strength now, and nothing can prevent you from rising, nothing that is past.

JANUARY 21

God Calling: A Crowded Day

Believe that I am with you and controlling all. When My Word has gone forth, *all* are powerless against it.

Be calm. Never fear. You have much to learn. Go on until you can take the most crowded day with a song. "Sing unto the Lord." The finest accompaniment to a Song of Praise to Me is a very crowded day. Let Love be the motif running through all.

Be glad all the time. Rejoice exceedingly. Joy in Me. Rest in Me. Never be afraid. Pray more. Do not get worried. I am thy Helper. "Underneath are the Everlasting Arms." You cannot get below that. Rest in them, as a tired child rests.

God at Eventide: Exceeding Great Reward

I am thy shield and thine exceeding great reward.

Shield from the storm of life. Shield from even the consequences of your own faults and failings. Shield from your weakness. Shield from worry. Shield from fear and sorrow. Shield from the world with its allure and temptations. Not only your shield, but your exceeding great reward.

Not the reward of perfection in your life, for that you could not win here. Not the reward of what you do, or of any merit in yourself. Only the result, or reward of your questing. The satisfaction of your hunger to find Me. Exceeding great reward.

Your reward is the same as that of the greatest saint who has ever lived. Given not as a trophy of victory, not as a recognition of virtue, but given because you are the seeker, and I, your Lord, am the Sought.

JANUARY 22

God Calling: Gray Days

Be not afraid. I am your God, your Deliverer. From all evil, I will deliver you. Trust Me. Fear not.

Never forget your "Thank You." Do you not see it is a lesson? You *must* say "Thank You" on the grayest days. You *must* do it. All cannot be light unless you do. There is gray-day practice. It is absolutely necessary.

My death upon the Cross was not only necessary to save a world, it was necessary if only to train My disciples. It was all a part of their training: My entering Jerusalem in triumph; My washing the disciples' feet; My sorrow-time in Gethsemane; My being despised, judged, crucified, buried. Every step was necessary to their development—and so with you.

If a gray day is not one of thankfulness, the lesson has to be repeated until it is. Not to everyone is it so. But only to those who ask to serve Me well and to do much for Me. A great work requires a great and careful training.

God at Eventide: I Know All

I am the sharer of the secrets of your life. How rich in blessing each experience may be if shared with Me alone.

How often, by much speaking and self-indulgent sharing with others, a jewel or rare beauty may be robbed of its priceless worth to your soul. A bud of Joy and sweet perfume too rashly forced to premature bloom will lose its purity and fragrance.

Even the sharing of past sins and failures may mean self for the time in the foreground, or vitality, so needed for the present, lost. Dwell in the Secret Place of the Most High.

JANUARY 23

God Calling: How Power Comes

Lord, Thou art our Refuge. Our God, in Thee do we trust.
O Master, come and talk with us.

All power is given unto Me. It is Mine to give, Mine to withhold, *but* even I have to acknowledge that I cannot withhold it from the soul that dwells near Me, because it is then not a gift, but passes insensibly from Me to My disciples.

It is breathed in by the soul who lives in My Presence.

Learn to shut yourself away in My Presence—and then, without speaking, you have those things you desire of Me, Strength—Power—Joy—Riches.

God at Eventide: Fear No Evil

I am the Lord of your life, Guardian of your inmost being, the Christ of God. Sheltered in My Hidden Place no harm can befall you. Pray to know this.

Let this Truth become a part of your very consciousness, that where I am no evil can be, and that therefore when you abide in Me and I in you no evil can touch you.

Spiritual Truths take sometimes many years to learn, sometimes they come in a flash of sudden revelation.

JANUARY 24

God Calling: Your Great Reward

You pray for Faith, and you are told to do so. But I make provision in the House of My Abiding for those who turn toward Me and yet have weak knees and hearts that faint. Be not afraid. I am your God. Your Great Reward. Yours to look up and say, "All is well."

I am your Guide. Do not want to see the road ahead. Go just one step at a time. I very rarely grant the long vista to My disciples, especially in personal affairs, for one step at a time is the best way to cultivate Faith.

You are in uncharted waters. But the Lord of all Seas is with you, the Controller of all Storms is with you. Sing with joy. You follow the Lord of Limitations, as well as the God in whose service is perfect freedom.

He, the God of the Universe, confined Himself within the narrow limits of a Baby-form and, in growing Boyhood and young Manhood, submitted to your human limitations, and you have to learn that your vision and power, boundless as far as spiritual things are concerned, must in temporal affairs submit to limitations too.

But I am with you. It was when the disciples gave up effort after a night of fruitless fishing that I came and the nets broke with the overabundance of supply.

I am teaching you, but not always Spiritual Truths that gladden you.

Often, too often, there has to be the word of reproof as I tell you of commands of Mine not obeyed, of resolutions made when in contact with Me that you have failed to keep, of work done for Me in no spirit of Love and Joy, of failure to obtain supply because your attitude (often not your heart) questioned My unlimited supply.

I teach no easy lesson.

I choose no flower-bordered path in which to walk with you, but take heart that I do walk with you as with Peter of old even when he denied Me.

He had seen his sin. He went out and wept bitterly.

JANUARY 25

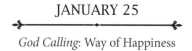

God Calling: Way of Happiness

Complete surrender of every moment to God is the *foundation* of happiness; the *superstructure* is the joy of Communion with Him. And that is, for each, the place, the mansion, I went to prepare for you.

My followers have misunderstood that and looked too often upon that promise as referring only to an After-Life, and too often—far too often—upon this life as a something to be struggled through in order to get the reward and the joy of the next.

Seek to carry out all I say, and such understanding, insight, vision, and joy will be yours as shall pass indeed all understanding. The plans of God are very wonderful—beyond your highest hopes.

Cling to thoughts of protection, safety, guidance.

I am listening. Picture Me, your Lord. Not as one deaf to your entreaties, but rather as One straining with an intensity of Love to catch the first faint cry from one of His children.

Even in the case of those who love Me, how often do I listen in vain for the spontaneous words of Love?

Do not cry to Me only when cares press and you are weary. Speak to Me often. Share with Me all the little happenings, all the frets, all the little glad things.

These not only draw us more closely to each other, but they are to Me compensations for the neglect I suffer from My world.

JANUARY 26

God Calling: Keep Calm

Keep your Spirit-Life calm and unruffled. Nothing else matters. Leave all to Me. This is your great task, to get calm in My Presence, not to let one ruffled feeling stay for one moment. Years of blessing may be checked in one moment by that.

No matter *who* frets you or what, yours is the task to stop all else until absolute calm comes. Any block means My Power diverted into other channels.

Pour forth—pour forth—pour forth—I cannot bless a life that does not act as a channel. My Spirit brooks no stagnation, not even rest. Its Power must flow on. Pass on everything, every blessing. Abide in Me.

See how many you can bless each day. Dwell much in My Presence.

I am your Lord, trust Me in all. Never doubt My keeping Power. Behold Me, the Lord of your life. Gain strength from Me. Remember that Healing, Divine Healing, is not so much a question of praying on your part, and of granting on Mine, as of living with Me, thinking of Me, sharing My Life. That contact makes you whole. Go forward gladly, go forward unafraid.

JANUARY 27

God Calling: Height of the Storm

> *Lord, to whom shall we go?*
> *thou hast the words of eternal life.*
> JOHN 6:68

I am with you both. Go forward unafraid. Health and Strength, Peace and Happiness and Joy—they are all My gifts. Yours for the asking. In the spiritual (as in the material) world there is no empty space, and as self and fears and worries depart out of your lives, it follows that the things of the Spirit, that you crave so, rush in to take their places. All things are yours, and ye are Christ's, and Christ is God's. What a wonderful cycle, because ye are God's.

Be not afraid. Fear not. It is to the drowning man the Rescuer comes. To the brave swimmer who can fare well alone He comes not. And no rush of Joy *can* be like that of a man towards his Rescuer.

It is a part of My method to wait till the storm is at its full violence. So did I with My disciples on the lake. I could have bidden the first angry wave be calm, the first gust of wind be still, but what a lesson unlearned. What a sense of tender nearness of refuge and safety would have been lost.

Remember this—My disciples thought that in sleep I had forgotten them. Remember how mistaken they were. Gain strength and confidence and joyful dependence and anticipation from that.

Never fear. Joy is yours, and the radiant Joy of the rescued shall be yours.

God at Eventide: Help for All

I have not promised My Help to the virtuous only. To the sinner who turns to Me, to the saint who lives with Me, to both alike My miracle-working Power is manifested.

Help, temporal as well as spiritual, truly I bestow, not as a reward of goodness but as a fulfillment of My pledge made to all who believe in Me.

But when one turns to Me I at once plan the rescue craved. If that one hearing My plan, learning of My Purpose, should fail to do his appointed task in that plan, how can My healing of physical, spiritual, or temporal disharmony be manifested?

JANUARY 28

God Calling: Low Ambitions

Fear not. Do not fear to be busy. You are the servant of all. "He that would be the greatest among you, let him be the servant of all."

Service is the word of My disciples. I served indeed, the humblest, the lowliest. I was at their command. My highest powers were at their service.

Be used. Be used by all, by the lowest, the smallest. How best you can serve? Let that be your daily seeking, not how best can you be served.

Look around you. Do the aims and ambitions that man

strives for bring peace, or the world's awards bring heart-rest and happiness? No! indeed, man is at war with man. Those whom the world has most rewarded, with name, fame, honour, wealth, are weary and disappointed.

And yet, to the listening ear, above the jangle of the world's discordant cries, there echoes down the 1900 years My message, "Come unto Me, all ye that are weary and heavy laden and I will give you rest."

And the weary and disappointed who listen and turn to Me find indeed that rest. Joy of the Weary I am, Music to the Heart I am, Health to the Sick, Wealth to the Poor, Food to the Hungry, Home to the Wanderer, Rapture to the Jaded, Love to the Lonely.

There is not *one* want of the soul that I do not supply for the asking, and to you too, I long to be all.

God at Eventide: Your Defender

I am the Gift of God to man. Only so was it possible for man to know God the Father. Only so was it possible for man to know that he had ever an Advocate with God—the Sinless Christ.

There is always One Who understands your case, Whose appeal cannot fail to be heard. He has the right of Sonship. He has a right to plead for you.

If He can plead for offending man, undertaking full responsibility for him, what better Advocate could you have? He knows. He has seen the tears of sorrow, the heartache and temptation. He can plead as none other.

His own temptation was so real that, conqueror as He was, He can yet feel the tenderest pity for the vanquished. He knows how seeming fair evil can appear, and He can estimate the added burden of tainted blood, inherited weakness, and sin.

He gave His only Begotten Son. This *great gift am I*, your

Friend, your Companion. Leave all to Me, your Advocate, trained during My years on earth to plead, never for Myself, but for every one who rests his cause in My Hands.

JANUARY 29

God Calling: I Clear the Path

Wait on the LORD.
PSALM 27:14

I am thy shield. Have no fear. You must know that "All is well." I will never let anyone do to you both, other than My Will for you.

I can see the future. I can read men's hearts. I know better than you what you need. Trust Me absolutely. You are not at the mercy of Fate, or buffeted about by others. You are being led in a very definite way, and others, who do not serve your purpose, are being moved out of your Path by Me.

Never fear, whatever may happen. You are both being led. Do not try to plan. I have planned. You are the builder, *not* the Architect.

Go very quietly, very gently. All is for the very best for you.

Trust me for all. Your very extremity will ensure My activity for you. And having your foundation on the Rock—Christ, Faith in Him, and "being rooted and grounded in Him," and having belief in My Divinity as your Corner Stone, it is yours to build, knowing all is well.

Literally, you have to depend on Me for everything— everything. It was out of the depths that David cried unto Me, and I heard his voice. All is well.

Study the "Overcomeths" in the Revelation to My servant
John, and you will see the tender intimacy with Me promised
as a result of overcoming. To believe is not enough. To believe
in Me does truly involve the possession of Eternal Life, but
that is a trust to use as truly as the talent of My story.

It is not only a something to be enjoyed.

Eternal life is a refreshing, reforming, enriching, uproot-
ing, ennobling Power to be employed to the full by those to
whom I entrust it.

In this My servants so often fail, and so miss the wonder
of Communion with Me. Guard this Truth.

JANUARY 30

God Calling: The Soul at War

No evil can befall you if I am with you. "Ill that He blesses is
our good." Every time of being laid aside is a time of retreat
into the quiet place with Me. Never fear but in that place you
shall find restoration and power and joy and healing.

Plan both of your retreat days now and then—days when
you live apart with Me, and arise rested and refreshed—
physically, mentally, and spiritually, to carry on the work I
have given to you. I will never give you a load greater than
you can bear.

Love, Joy, Peace, welcome these. Let no personal feelings,
no thoughts of self banish these. Singly, they are miracle-
producing in a life, but together, they can command all that
is needed on the physical, mental, and spiritual planes.

It is in these wonder-realm attributes all success lies. You
have to see your inner lives are all they should be, and then
the work is accomplished. Not in rushing and striving on the
material plane, but on the battlefield of the Soul are these
things won.

I come, a truly willing guest. Love always draws. Remember that. Love is the magnetic Power of the Universe. God is *love,* the Power that draws all men by various ways unto Himself.

Remember that your Love, too, being of God, has the same magnetic Power. Love, and you will draw to you those whom you desire to help.

When you fail to do so, search your life. Love is deficient. More love is necessary.

JANUARY 31

God Calling: Suffering Redeems

All sacrifice and all suffering is redemptive: to teach the individual or to be used to raise and help others.

Nothing is by chance.

Divine Mind, and its wonder working, is beyond your finite mind to understand.

No detail is forgotten in My Plans, already perfect.

> *O let me hear Thee speaking*
> *In accents clear and still,*
> *Above the storms of passion,*
> *The murmurs of self-will.*
>
> *O speak to reassure me,*
> *To hasten, or control;*
> *O speak, and make me listen,*
> *Thou Guardian of my soul!*

Softly at even, comes the footfall of your Master. My day has been long and weary. Hearts that I have yearned over and longed for still withstand Me.

I see the aged, desolate without Me. I see the disappointment of men and women, who in Me would find heart-satisfaction which others cannot give them. I see youth crowding Me out of its work-filled, pleasure-filled days. And yet I wait. I knock, I plead, I call, unheard, unheeded, unwanted.

As I was the link between the Father and man, so now must My followers be the links between man and Me.

Human Love, material aid, human understanding and friendship must bind those for whom I yearn.

Channels through which My help can flow to man truly you must be, but also the means through which man finds his groping way to Me.

Evening and Morning

O let me hear Thee speaking
In accents clear and still,
Above the storms of passion,
The murmurs of self-will.

O speak to reassure me,
To hasten, or control;
O speak, and make me listen,
Thou Guardian of my soul!

FEBRUARY 1

God Calling: Another Start

Take courage. Do not fear. Start a new life tomorrow. Put the old mistakes away, and start anew. I give you a fresh start. Be not burdened. Be not anxious. If My forgiveness were for the righteous only and those who had not sinned, where would be its need?

Remember as I said, "To whom much is forgiven, the same loveth much."

Why do you fret and worry so? I wait to give you all that is lovely, but your lives are soiled with worry and fret. You would crush My treasures. I can only bless glad, thankful hearts.

You *must* be glad and joyful.

God at Eventide: All Love Excelling

Softly I approach. Gently My Spirit speaks to your heart.

The mystery of man's communion with Me lies in the beauty and wonder of its aloneness. For the moment the world seems not to exist. Its noise and traffic seem hushed.

There is indeed wonder in that stillness. A faint glimpse is seen in the sudden realization of Love between two human beings. Surprise and wonder. . .the world is for them alone. . .no claim other than their love.

What wonder in the heart of man when he realizes the beauty, tenderness and closeness of Communion with Me!

FEBRUARY 2

God Calling: Practice Love

Watch over and protect us.

Want of Love will block the way. You *must* love all. Those that fret you and those who do not.

Practice Love. It is a great lesson, and you have a great Teacher. You *must* love; how otherwise can you dwell in Me, where nothing unloving can come? Practice this and I will bless you exceedingly, above all you cannot only ask, but imagine.

No limit to My Power. Do all you can and leave to Me the rest. Peace will come and Trust. Fear not, I am your Advocate, your Mediator.

God at Eventide: My Wages

If the world understands you, then you are speaking its language, actuated by its motives, living its life according to its standards. Will you have this?

Remember I said very clearly, "Ye cannot serve God and mammon." If you serve God, then, for your work, you should surely look to God for reward.

So many of My servants serve Me, and yet expect to receive the gratitude and praise, or at least the acknowledgment of the world. Why? You are not doing the work of the world. Why expect its pay?

God Calling: If Men Oppose

Only believe. The walls of Jericho fell down. Was it axes or human implements that brought them down? Rather the Songs of Praise of the people and My Thought carried out in action.

All walls shall fall before you, too. There is no earth-power. It falls like a house of paper at My miracle-working touch. Your faith and My power—the only two essentials. Nothing else is needed.

So, if man's petty opposition still holds good, it is only because I choose to let it stand between you and what would be a mistake for you. If not—a word—a thought—from Me, and it is gone. The hearts of Kings are in My rule and governance. All men can be moved at My wish.

Rest in this certainty. Rely on Me.

God at Eventide: Ambassadors All

If you love Me and long to serve others by showing them what I am like, you will assuredly do so.

Because self will disappear, be cast out.

When self has gone then those who see you will not see the self in you; only the ambassador of your King.

You have here in this seemingly narrow life of yours countless opportunities of overcoming self. Let this be your great task.

God Calling: Drop Your Crutch

Just go step by step. My Will shall be revealed as you go. You will never cease to be thankful for this time when you felt at peace and trustful and yet had no human security.

That is the time of the True learning of trust in Me. "When thy father and mother forsake thee, then the Lord will take thee up." This is a literal dependence on Me.

When human support or material help of any kind is removed, then My Power can become operative. I cannot teach a man to walk who is trusting to a crutch. Away with your crutch, and My Power shall so invigorate you that you shall indeed walk on to victory. Never limit My Power. It is limitless.

God at Eventide: Wise Rest

Rest should play a large part in the lives of My followers, for tiredness and physical strain can cause man to lose his consciousness of My Presence.

Then the Light that banishes evil seems to be withdrawn—never by deliberate act of Mine, but as the result of man's attitude towards Me. Ponder on this.

FEBRUARY 5

God Calling: You Shall Know

Walk with Me. I will teach you. Listen to Me and I will speak. Continue to meet Me, in spite of all opposition and every obstacle, in spite of days when you may hear no voice, and there may come no intimate heart-to-heart telling.

As you persist in this, and make a life-habit of it, in many marvelous ways I will reveal My Will to you. You shall have more sure knowing of both the present and the future. But that will be only the reward of the regular coming to meet Me.

Life is a school. There are many teachers. Not to everyone do I come personally. Believe literally that the problems and difficulties of your lives can be explained by Me more clearly and effectually than by any other.

God at Eventide: The Aching Spirit

Just as I said that those who hungered and thirsted after righteousness would be filled, so I say to you—none ever longed to know Me better and remained unsatisfied. Even with your imperfect knowledge, you are daily realizing how true this is.

Man dwells so much on material things that he fails to grasp the Spiritual laws that never fail.

For all spirit-longing there is fulfillment. I soothe the aching Spirit.

You think I answer your prayer. Yes, but the answer was there, awaiting the prayer.

You will see these simple Truths more and more as you live with Me; truths hidden from the wise but revealed to the little ones of the Kingdom.

God Calling: God's Longing

To the listening ear I speak, to the waiting heart I come. Sometimes I may not speak. I may ask you merely to wait in My Presence, to know that I am with you.

Think of the multitudes who thronged Me when I was on Earth all eager for something. Eager to be healed or taught or fed.

Think as I supplied their many wants, and granted their manifold requests what it meant to Me, to find amid the crowd, some one or two who followed Me just to be near Me, just to dwell in My Presence. How some longing of the Eternal Heart was satisfied thereby.

Comfort Me awhile by letting Me know that you would seek Me just to dwell in My Presence, to be near Me, not even for teaching, not for material gain, not even for a message— but for Me. The longing of the human heart to be loved for itself is something caught from the Great Divine Heart.

I bless you. Bow your heads.

God at Eventide: True Humility

*If I, your Lord and Master, have washed your feet,
you ought also to wash one another's feet.*

How My followers have misunderstood this. They interpret the required attitude to be one of service. In service there can be condescension, there can be a total lack of humility.

I sought to teach a lesson to those who would approach Me to partake of that wonderful Union with Me, vouchsafed to those who worthily eat of My Flesh and drink of My Blood.

I desired to teach them that they must come to Me in the Spirit of humility towards others. No sense of superiority, especially Spiritual superiority. True humility. Learn this lesson in daily Companionship with Me. "For I am meek and lowly of heart."

FEBRUARY 7

God Calling: Light Ahead

Trust and be not afraid. Life is full of wonder. Open child-trusting eyes to all I am doing for you. Fear not.

Only a few steps more and then My Power shall be seen and known. You are, yourselves, now walking in the tunnel-darkness. Soon, you yourselves shall be lights to guide feet that are afraid.

The cries of your sufferings have pierced even to the ears of God Himself—My Father in Heaven, your Father in Heaven. To hear, with God, is to answer. For only a cry from the heart, a cry to Divine Power to help human weakness, a trusting cry, ever reaches the Ear Divine.

Remember, trembling heart, that with God, to hear is to answer. Your prayers, and they have been many, are answered.

God at Eventide: The Way of Progress

Impress upon all that growth is one of the laws of My Kingdom.

However long your span of life on earth, it can never be too long for growth and progress.

Be ever seeking My Will for you. Not a new religion, nor the right religion, but—My Will. Then all will be well and growth will follow.

God Calling: On Me Alone

I am your Lord, your Supply. You *must* rely on Me. Trust to the last uttermost limit. Trust and be not afraid. You must depend on Divine Power *only*. I have not forgotten you. Your help is coming. You shall know and realize My Power.

Endurance is faith tried almost to the breaking point. You must wait and trust and hope and joy in Me. You must not depend on man but on Me—on Me, your Strength, your Help, your Supply.

This is the great test. Am *I* your supply or not? Every great work for Me has had to have this great test-time.

Possess your souls in patience and rejoice. You must wait until I show the way. Heaven itself cannot contain more joy than that soul knows, when, after the waiting-test, I crown it Victor, but no disciple of Mine can be victor, who does not wait until I give the order to start. You cannot be anxious if you *know* that I am your supply.

God at Eventide: Future All Unknown

Probe not into the future. Prophecies are not for you. Be a humble follower in the crowd. Live with Me. Ponder My Words, My Teaching, My Actions.

Soon you will find that more and more opportunities of speaking of Me will present themselves. Do not make them. They will proceed from the pressure of inward growth, and not from outward stress.

FEBRUARY 9

God Calling: The Voice Divine

The Divine Voice is not always expressed in words.
It is made known as a heart-consciousness.

God at Eventide: All Will Be Well

In humble anticipation—wait.

Wait as a servant anticipating orders. Wait as a lover eager to note a need, and to supply it.

Wait for My Commands; wait for My Guidance; wait for My Supply. All will come.

In such a life you may well be of good cheer. Can a life be dull when always there is that watchful expectancy, anticipation of glad surprise, that wonder of fulfillment, that Joy of full supply?

FEBRUARY 10

God Calling: The Lifeline

I am your Savior, your Savior from sins' thralls, your Savior from all the cares and troubles of life, your Savior from disease.

I speak in all to you both. Look to Me for salvation. Trust in Me for help. Did not My servant of old say, "All Thy waves and Thy billows are gone over me?" But not all the waters of affliction could drown him. For of him was it true, "He came from above, He took me, He drew me out of many waters."

The lifeline, the line of rescue, is the line from the soul to God, faith, and power. It is a strong line, and no soul can be overwhelmed who is linked to Me by it. Trust, trust, trust.

Never be afraid.

Think of My trees stripped of their beauty, pruned, cut, disfigured, bare, but through the dark, seemingly dead branches flows silently, secretly, the spirit-life-sap, till, lo! with the sun of Spring comes new life, leaves, bud, blossom, fruit, but oh! fruit a thousand times better for the pruning.

Remember that you are in the hands of a Master-Gardener. He makes no mistakes about His pruning. Rejoice. Joy is the Spirit's reaching out to say its thanks to Me. It is the new life—sap of the tree, reaching out to Me to find such beautiful expression later. So never cease to joy. Rejoice.

God at Eventide: Your Power

In your hands I have placed a wonderful force against evil. You cannot realize as yet the mighty weapon you wield.

Make known the Power of Prayer. A force so wonderful, so miracle-working, that when it is united with a will that seeks only My Will and with a Friendship with Me that calms, enobles and enriches, then nothing can withstand its Power.

FEBRUARY 11

God Calling: The Difficult Path

Your path is difficult, difficult for you both. There is no work in life so hard as waiting, and yet I say wait. Wait until I show you My Will. Proof it is of My Love and of My certainty of your true discipleship, that I give you both hard tasks.

Again, I say wait. All motion is more easy than calm waiting. So many of My followers have marred their work and hindered the progress of My Kingdom by activity.

Wait. I will not overtry your spiritual strength. You are both like two persons, helpless on a raft in mid-ocean. But, lo! there cometh toward you One walking on the waters, like unto the Son of Man. When He comes and you receive Him, it will be with you, as it was with My Disciples when I was on Earth, that straightway you will be at the place where you would be.

All your toil in rowing and all your activity could not have accomplished the journey so soon. Oh, wait and trust. Wait, and be not afraid.

God at Eventide: No Remorse

I seek to save you not only from falling into sin, but from the overwhelming remorse that follows the realization of sin.

I know that for frail man this is too great a burden. So when you let it overwhelm you, you nullify My saving Power.

I seek to save you from oppression and depression too. I bid you leave all to follow Me. That is, leave the sins and the failures of the past.

Out of the shadow into the sunlight of My Love and Salvation you must go.

FEBRUARY 12

God Calling: Meet Me Everywhere

Life is really consciousness of Me. Have no fear. A very beautiful future lies before you. Let it be a new life, a new existence, in which in every single happening, event, plan, you are conscious of Me.

"And this is life eternal, that they might know thee, and Jesus Christ, whom thou hast sent."

Get this ever-consciousness and you have Eternal Life—the Life of the Ages. Be in all things led by the Spirit of God and trust Me in all. And the consciousness of Me must bring Joy. Give Me not only trust but gladness.

God at Eventide: See Me Everywhere Still

See Me in all your daily life.

See Me in the little happenings. Recognize me as the source of every act of kindness and Love.

Feel My Power with you when you face any task or danger. Know My consoling tenderness in every sorrow and disappointment.

I, the Master-Painter, can work into the ordinary colors of beauty until you see the befitting background for the joy and ecstasy of the radiance I give.

FEBRUARY 13

God Calling: Near the Goal

In a race it is not the start that hurts, not the even pace of the long stretch. It is when the goal is in sight that heart and nerves and courage and muscles are strained almost beyond human endurance, almost to the breaking point.

So with you now the goal is in sight, you need your final cry to Me. Can you not see by the nerve and heart rack of the past few days that your race is nearly run? Courage, courage. Heed My voice of encouragement. Remember that I am by your side, spurring you on to victory.

In the annals of heaven, the saddest records are those that tell of the many who ran well, with brave, stout hearts, until in sight of the goal, of victory, and then their courage failed. The whole host of heaven longed to cry out how near the end was, to implore the last spurt, but they fell out, never to know until the last day of revealing how near they were to victory.

Would that they had listened to Me in the silence as you two meet with Me. They would have known. There must be the listening ear, as well as the still, small voice.

God at Eventide: Ever Secure

Abide secure in My friendship.

A friend who knows you through and through; knows all your pitiful attempts at living for Me, your many and tragic failures, your childish misunderstanding of Me and what I would do for you.

Your desire to serve Me, your clinging to Me in the dark hours of helplessness; your stumbling confidence in your efforts to walk alone—I know all.

I have seen your persistent blindness to My guidance; I have seen how you obstruct the answers to your own prayers; I have noted your easy acquiescence to those forces that oppose My loving purposes.

I know all this, and yet I say again: Abide with Me secure in My friendship.

FEBRUARY 14

God Calling: In My Presence

You do not realize that you would have broken down under the weight of your cares but for the renewing time with Me. It is not what I say; it is I, Myself. It is not the hearing Me so much as the being in My Presence. The strengthening and curative powers of this you cannot know. Such knowledge is beyond your human reckoning.

This would cure the poor sick world, if every day each soul or group of souls waited before Me. Remember that you must never fail to keep this time apart with Me. Gradually you will be transformed, physically, mentally, spiritually, into My likeness. All who see you or have contact with you will be, by this intercourse with you, brought near to Me, and gradually the influence will spread.

You are making one spot of Earth a Holy Place, and though you must work and spend yourself ceaselessly because that is for the present your appointed task, yet the greatest work either of you can do, and are doing, is done in this time apart with Me. Are you understanding that?

Do you know that every thought, every activity, every prayer, every longing of the day is gathered up and offered to Me, now? Oh! Joy that I am with you. For this I came to Earth, to lead man back to spirit-converse with his God.

God at Eventide: Thanks for All

Thank Me for all the withholding as well as for the giving. Thank Me for sunshine and rain, for drought and springs of water, for sleep and wakefulness, for gain and loss. Thank Me for all.

Know beyond all doubt, all fear, that all is well. Cling to Me in moments of weakness. Cling still in moments of strength, imploring that you may never feel self-sufficient.

No evil shall befall you, rest in this knowledge.

FEBRUARY 15

God Calling: Inspiration—Not Aspiration

You shall be used. The Divine Force is never less. It is sufficient for all the work in the world. I only need the instruments for Me to use. To know that would remake the world.

The world does not need supermen, but supernatural men. Men who will persistently turn the self out of their lives and let Divine Power work through them. England could be saved tomorrow if only her politicians just let Me use them.

Let inspiration take the place of aspiration. All unemployment would cease. I have always plenty of work to be done and always pay My workpeople well as you will see, as more and more you get the right attitude of thought about the work being Mine only.

God at Eventide: Green Pastures

After each salutary experience of life, each blow it may deal you, separate yourself from the world for a time. Walk in My Green Pastures, and wander with Me beside the Waters of Comfort, until your soul is restored.

This is necessary so that you may readjust yourself to life. For you are a new being; you have had a new experience. Learn a new lesson. Your Union with Me will be the closer for your experience.

This is the time when My Love can whisper new meanings to you, can make the Friendship between us a closer, more holy Union.

Come with your Lover into the stillness of My Green Pastures, and walk with Me beside hushed waters.

FEBRUARY 16

God Calling: Never Ruffled

Even were I never to speak to you, you would be well rewarded for setting apart this time, if you only sat still and longed for Me, if you just drew hungering breaths for Me, as you do for the fresh pure air of the open.

Be still, be calm. Wait before Me. Learn of Me patience, humility, peace. When will you be absolutely unruffled whatever happens? You are slow to learn your lesson. In the rush and work and worry, the very seeking of silence must help.

In bustle so little is accomplished. You must learn to take the calm with you in the most hurried days.

God at Eventide: He Changeth Not

Mark My Changelessness.

If I am truly the same, yesterday, today, and forever, then I am no God of moods as so often man portrays Me. Can you worship a God swayed this way and that at man's demand?

Dwell upon the thought of My Changelessness until you grasp the Truth that only as man changes and comes within the influence of My unchanging Law of Love can he realize and experience the Power and Love I have unchangingly for all mankind.

God Calling: Psychic Powers

Psychic powers are not necessarily Spiritual Powers. Do not seek the spiritual through material means. Could you but see, it is weighing beautiful spirit-wings down with Earth's mud.

Seek *this* time as a time of communion with Me—not as a time to ask questions and have them answered. And meet Me in Communion. It is soul-food that I have provided.

Do not expect a perfect Church, but find in a church the means of coming very near to Me. That alone matters, then the much, that is husk, falls away. Hold it of no account. Grasp the truth and find Me—the true Bread of Life. The lesson of the grain is the lesson of My Church and Me. The real life is all that matters, the outward Church is the husk; but the husk was necessary to present the life-grain to man.

God at Eventide: Practice Peace

Peace must fill your hearts and lives, and then you will find that ills and difficulties and sorrows and changes leave you unmoved. Practice that steadfast immobility, no matter what may threaten.

This spirit of calm trust is the shield that turns aside the darts and stings of adversity. Practice it.

Then you must seek to abide at the heart of the Universe with Me, at the center with Me. There alone is changelessness and calm *with me*.

God Calling: Let Me Do It

Never miss these times. It is not what I reveal to you so much as the linking up of your frail natures with the limitless Divine Powers. Already, forces are set in motion. Only My Will is coming to pass. And now God is blessing you very richly.

You think that there is much to *do* in a crisis like this. There is only *one* thing to do. Link your lives onto the Divine Forces, and then, it is as much My work to see those lives and their affairs run in an orderly right manner as to see that tomorrow's sun rises.

It is not passionate appeal that gains the Divine Ear so much as the quiet placing of the difficulty and worry in the Divine Hands. So trust and be no more afraid than a child would be, who places its tangled skein of wool in the hands of a loving mother and runs out to play, pleasing the mother more by its unquestioning confidence than if it went down on its knees and implored her help, which would pain her the rather, as it would imply she was not eager to help when help was needed.

God at Eventide: The Perfect Pattern

See that thou make all things according to the pattern that was shown thee on the Mount.

Otherwise it would have been better not to have gone up the Mount at all? Take this lesson to heart. In your daily valley-life you must live out what you learn in the alone-time on heights with Me.

The Spirit-pattern is so glorious because it is made to fit your life, specially planned for you.

Obeying the command made Moses the good leader he became. This is the time, then, humbly to see your weakness, to adjust your life to the work of My Kingdom, to prepare to live in all things according to the pattern that was shown you on the Mount.

FEBRUARY 19

God Calling: Endure

Do not forget to meet all your difficulties with love and laughter. Be assured that I am with you. Remember, remember it is the last few yards that tell. Do not fail Me. I *cannot* fail you. Rest in My Love.

How many of the world's prayers have gone unanswered because My children who prayed did not endure to the end. They thought it was too late, and that they must act for themselves, that I was not going to act for them. Remember My words: "He that endureth to the end shall be saved."

Can *you* endure to the end? If so, *you* shall be saved. But endure with courage, with Love and laughter. Oh! My children, is My training too hard?

For you, My children, I will unlock the secret treasures hidden from so many. Not one of your cries is unheard. I am with you indeed to aid you. Go through all I have said to you, and live in every detail as I have enjoined you. As you follow implicitly all I say, success—spiritual, mental, and physical— shall be yours. Wait in silence a while, conscious of My presence, in which you must live to have rest unto your souls, and Power and Joy and Peace.

God at Eventide: Youth Renewed

They that wait upon the Lord shall renew their strength. To discover the Pearl of Great Price is to renew your youth. The Kingdom of Heaven is a kingdom of perennial youth.

God Calling: Claim Your Rights

In every thing by prayer and supplication let your requests be made known unto God."

But do not beg. Rather, come just as a business manager bringing to the owner the needs, checks to be signed, etc., and knowing that to lay the matter before him means immediate supply.

I long to supply, but the asking—or the faith-assurance from you, is necessary, because to you that contact with Me is vital.

God at Eventide: The Secret of Joy

Such rapture is yours. Count it all Joy to know Me, and to delight in Me. The secret of Joy is the longing to have My Will, and the gratification of that longing.

There is nothing in Heaven that transcends the Joy, the ecstasy, of loving and doing My Will. To a soul who realizes this wonder, Heaven is already attained as far as mortals here can attain it. My Will for you is My joyous arranging for you.

The frustration of the Divine Plan is man's tragedy.

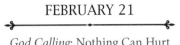

God Calling: Nothing Can Hurt

The way is plain. You do not need to see far ahead. Just one step at a time with Me. The same light to guide you as the Hosts of Heaven know—the Son of Righteousness Himself.

Only self can cast a shadow on the way. Be more afraid of Spirit-unrest, of soul-disturbance, of any ruffling of the Spirit, than of earthquake or fire or any outside forces.

When you feel the absolute calm has been broken—away alone with Me until your heart sings and all is strong and calm.

These are the only times when evil can find an entrance. The forces of evil surround the city of man-soul and are keenly alert for one such unguarded spot through which an arrow can pierce and do havoc.

Remember all that you have to do is to keep calm and happy. God does the rest. No evil force can hinder My Power—only you yourself have power to do that. Think when all God's mighty forces are arrayed to aid you—and your poor, puny self impedes their onward march.

God at Eventide: Wise as Serpents

Each servant of Mine should regard himself as an outpost for My Truths, where he must be prepared to receive My Messages, and to signal them on. This is work of great importance in My Kingdom.

Wherever you go make Me known. That was My Risen injunction, My Commission. Wherever you go establish outposts of My Empire, make contacts for Me. Make Me known to men—sometimes by speech, sometimes in silence.

God Calling: You Must Trust

You *must* trust Me wholly. This lesson has to be learnt. You shall be helped, you shall be led, guided, continually. The children of Israel would long before have entered the Promised Land—only their doubts and fears continually drove them back into the wilderness. Remember always, doubts delay. Are you trusting all to Me or not?

I have told you how to live, and you must do it. My children, I love you. Trust My tender Love. It will never fail you, but you must learn not to fail it.

Oh! could you see, you would understand. You have much to learn in turning out fear and being at peace. All your doubts arrest My work. You must not doubt. I died to save you from sin and doubt and worry. You must believe in Me absolutely.

God at Eventide: Wonder-Work

All work with Me is wonder-work. God working in and through man. This should be the normal work of every Christian's day. For this I came to earth, to show man this could be.

For this I left the earth, so that this should be. Can life offer anything more for you than that you fulfill in yourselves My expectations for My disciples?

Satan frustrates My plan by whispering to My followers a mock humility in which they trace not his evil hand—"They are too weak, too small, too unimportant to do much. . . ."

Away with false humility, which limits not you but Me. Mine is the Power.

God Calling: Secret of Healing

Love the busy life. It is a joy-filled life. I love you both and bid you be of good cheer. Take your fill of joy in the Spring.

Live outside whenever possible. Sun and air are My great healing forces, and that inward Joy that changes poisoned blood to a pure, healthy, life-giving flow.

Never forget that real healing of body, mind, and Spirit comes from within, from the close loving contact of your spirit with My Spirit.

God at Eventide: Conquering and to Conquer

Always seek some conquest, for spiritual growth requires it. In the natural world you see how necessary this striving is, and in the mental and spiritual worlds there must be struggle, too.

So, as you go forward in your spiritual life, you will see always a fresh conquest demanding your effort.

Shun stagnation. Never be discouraged if always you see some fault requiring to be overcome, some obstacle to be surmounted.

Thus you go forth with Me conquering and to conquer.

FEBRUARY 24

God Calling: Share Everything

Silently the work of the Spirit is done. Already Love is drawing others to you. Take *all* who come as sent by Me, and give them a royal welcome. It will surprise you, all that I have planned for you.

Welcome all who come with the love of both your hearts. *You* may not see the work. Today they may not need you. Tomorrow they may need you. I may send you strange visitors. Make each desire to return. Nobody must come and feel unwanted.

Share your Love, your Joy, your Happiness, your time, your food gladly with all. Such wonders will unfold. You see it all but in bud now—the glory of the open flower is beyond all your telling. Love, Joy, Peace, in richest abundance—only believe. Give out Love and all you can with a glad free heart and hand. Use all you can for others, and back will come such countless stores and blessings.

God at Eventide: Always Antagonism

And He passing through the midst of them.

Face evil undaunted, and it will fall back, and let you pass on and do your work for Me.

The maddened crowd had sought to cast Me headlong, but they made way for Me, and through their midst I passed unhindered.

Do not be surprised to find antagonism where you meet evil, because you are a home of My Spirit, and it is My Spirit that arouses the antagonism. Go on your way so quietly, and trust in Me.

In My Strength My follower need not flinch, but, boldly facing evil, will overcome evil with good.

You follow the dauntless Christ.

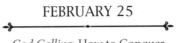

God Calling: How to Conquer

Joy is the sovereign balm for all the ills of the world, the spirit-cure for every ailment. There is nothing that Joy and Love cannot do.

Set your standard very high. Aim at conquering a world, the world all around you. Just say, "Jesus conquers"—"Jesus saves"—in the face of every doubt, every sin, every evil, every fear.

No evil can stand against that, for there is "none other Name under Heaven given among men, whereby men can be saved." To every thought of want or lack, "Jesus saves from poverty," to every fear, "Jesus saves from fear."

Do this to every ill and it will vanish, as night when sun arises.

God at Eventide: The War Within

And he was dumb, because he believed not.

There is physical correspondence to faith and to doubt.

Especially is this so among those who would serve Me. For unlike others, they are not so controlled by the law of physical success or failure, but are under the direct control of the Laws of My Kingdom.

So, in many cases, you may note good health in one ignorant of Me, and ill-health in one of My followers, until he has learned the full control of the physical by the Spiritual. In his case the warring of physical and Spiritual may cause physical ill-health, or unrest.

So do not fret about the physical side, aim increasingly at control by My Spirit.

God Calling: Swift Help

There is nothing lacking in your lives, because really all is yours, only you lack the faith to know it. You are like the King's daughters who sit in rags, and yet around them are stores of all they could desire.

Pray for more faith, as a thirsty man in a desert prays for rain, for water. Swift comes My help, swift and strong. Do you know what it is to feel sure that I can never fail you? As sure as you are that you still breathe? How poor is man's faith! So poor. Do you trust Me as much as you would a friend if that friend came and said he would send you help? Pray daily and most diligently that your faith may increase.

God at Eventide: As from Me

Take every little kindness, every faithful service, every evidence of thought and of Love—as from Me.

As you, and those who live with and for Me, show loving-kindness to others, because you are actuated by My Spirit, so you draw contacts into the circle of My ever-widening Spirit influence.

This is unfailingly so. It is a spiritual law. Though no word of Me may be spoken, yet in this way souls are attracted until at length they find Me, the center and inspiration of all.

Well did I urge My Followers to become fishers of men. No great oratory or personality is needed for this soul-rescue work. Just follow Me as little children.

God Calling: Spirit Sounds

Take time for prayer. Take more time to be alone with Me. So only will you prosper.

Realize that the hearing of Spirit Sounds is more than the hearing of all Earth's noises. I am with you. Let that content you, nay, more, let that fill you with rapture.

Seek sometimes not even to hear Me. Seek a silence of spirit-understanding with Me. Be not afraid. All is well. Dwell much on what I did, as well as what I said.

Remember, I "touched her hand, and the fever left her." Not many words, just a moment's contact, and all fever left her. She was well, whole, calm, able to arise and "minister unto them."

My touch is still a potent healer. Just feel that touch. Sense My Presence, and the fever of work and care and fear just melts into nothingness—and Health, Joy, Peace, take its place.

God at Eventide: My Tireless Search

Share with Me the tireless search for the lost, the ache of disappointment, the sublime courage, the tenderness of complete forgiveness. Share the Joys, the sorrows, the Love, the scorn. I walk the lakeside still, and pause, as, to one and another, I utter the same call I uttered in Galilee, "Come and I will make you fishers of men."

God Calling: Perfect Work

Spend more time alone with Me. A strength and a Joy come from such times that will add much to your friendship and much to your work.

Times of prayer are times of growth. Cut those times short and many well-filled hours of work may be profitless. Heaven's values are so different from the values of earth.

Remember that from the point of view of the Great Worker, one poor tool, working *all* the time, but doing *bad* work, is of small value compared with the sharp, keen, perfect instrument used only a short time but which turns out perfect work.

UPHILL

Does the road wind
uphill all the way?
Yes, to the very end.
Will the journey take
the whole long day?
From morn to night, my friend.
C. G. ROSSETTI

God at Eventide: The Simple Life

The Gift of Eternal Life is a most precious one. Each one who receives it must demonstrate by Joy and Trust and radiancy of Spirit, expressed in being and in bearing, the quality of the Life he possesses.

The other life is existence—just not death.

Power and Joy must radiate from you. These are the expressions of Eternal Life. Life Eternal is to know the Father and Me, His Son, Whom He sent.

"God so Loved the world that He gave His only Begotten Son that whosoever believeth on Him should not perish but have everlasting (i.e., Eternal) Life."

Directly that Life is possessed by a man, all that is not simple, childlike has to go.

Not by complicated devices is My work accomplished.

My followers must be simple and direct. "Let your yea be yea and your nay be nay," I said.

Simplicity is forceful. Simplicity is great. It is a conquering Power.

FEBRUARY 29

God Calling: Draw Near

How little man knows and senses My need! My need of Love and Companionship.

I came "to draw men unto Me," and sweet it is to feel hearts drawing near in Love, not for help, as much as for tender comradeship.

Many know the need of man; few know the need of Christ.

MARCH 1

God Calling: Shower Love

I always hear your cry. No sound escapes Me.

Many, many in the world cry to Me, but oh! how few wait to hear Me speak to them, and yet to the soul, My speaking to it matters so much.

My words are Life. Think then, to hear Me speak is to find Life and healing and strength. Trust Me in all things. Love showered on all brings truly a quick return.

Just carry out My wishes and leave Me to carry out yours. Treat Me as Savior and King, but also with the tender intimacy of One much beloved.

Keep to the rules I have laid down for you, persistently, perseveringly, lovingly, patiently, hopefully, and in faith, and every mountain of difficulty shall be laid low, the rough places of poverty shall be made smooth, and all who know you shall know that I, your Lord, am the Lord.

Shower love.

God at Eventide: Arise from Defeat

It is not upon one battle alone that all depends, or there would be no hope for My failures.

You enter upon a long campaign when you enter My army. Is the battle lost? Acquaint yourself with the cause, discover your weakness, and with dauntless faith, go forth resolved this time to conquer.

No man can conquer who has not learned his weakness, not made ready for the next conflict, and who does not know and claim and trust My strength, always available when summoned, as you have already proved.

MARCH 2

God Calling: Spirit Words

The words that I speak unto you, they are spirit, and they are life."

Just as much as the words I spoke to My disciples of old. This is your reward for not seeking spirit-communication through a medium. Those who do it can never know the ecstasy, the wonder, of spirit-communication as you know it.

Life, Joy, Peace, and Healing are yours in very full measure. You will see this as you go on. At first, you can hardly credit the powers I am bestowing on you.

I sent My disciples out two by two and gave them power over unclean spirits and to heal all manner of diseases.

Wonderful indeed must it have been to St. Peter to feel suddenly that His Lord's power was his.

God at Eventide: Complete in Me

A Rock of Defense. A Joy to the saddened. A Rest to the weary. Calm to the ruffled.

A Companion of the sunlit glades. A Guide through the deserts of life. An Interpreter of experience. A Friend. A Savior.

All these and many more would I be to you. Never a heart's need that I could not soothe and satisfy.

Search the ages. Many men have been many things to other hearts, but never one man to all men, never one man all to one man. This only the Maker of hearts could be.

Not only so, but in Me the soul finds its completion.

MARCH 3

God Calling: Grow Like Me

Think of Me. Look at Me often, and unconsciously you will grow like Me.

You may never see it. The nearer you get to Me, the more will you see your unlikeness to Me. So be comforted, My children.

Your very deep sense of failure is a sure sign that you are growing nearer to Me. And if you desire to help others to Me, then that prayer-desire is answered.

Remember too, it is only struggle that hurts. In sloth, spiritual, or mental, or physical, there is no sense of failure or discomfort, but with action, with effort, you are conscious not of strength but of weakness—at least, at first.

That again is a sign of Life, of spiritual growth.

And remember, My Strength is made perfect in weakness.

God at Eventide: Shining Through

As you grow like Me so My Love must reflect more and more through you, Divinity and Majesty.

Sublime thought, yes, but you doubt if this can be. But God is Love, so God is Majesty. Thus gradually into the lives of those who follow Me there comes My Dignity and Majesty.

Have you not traced it in My closest friends?

MARCH 4

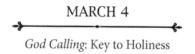

God Calling: Key to Holiness

Draw near to Me, My children. Contact with Me is the panacea for all ills.

Remember that Truth is many-sided. Have much tender Love and Patience for all who do not see as you do.

The elimination of self is the key to holiness and happiness, and can only be accomplished with My help. Study My life more. Live in My Presence. Worship Me.

I said in Gethsemane, "If it be possible let this cup pass." I did *not* say that there was no cup of sorrow to drink. I was scourged and spat upon and nailed to the Cross, and I said, "Father, forgive them; for they know not what they do."

I did *not* say that they did not do it. When My disciple, Peter, urged Me to escape the Cross, I said, "Get thee behind Me, Satan."

When My disciples failed to help the epileptic boy, I said, "This kind cometh not out but by Prayer and Fasting." I did *not* say, "You imagined that he was ill. Nothing is wrong."

When the Bible says, "God has purer eyes than to behold evil," it means to impute evil to His people. He always sees the good in people, but remember that I "beheld the city, and wept over it."

God at Eventide: To the Water's Edge

As God was in the days of Moses, so is He today. Responsive to the prayer of faith. Still ready and willing to make a path through the Red Sea.

Have the faith of Moses, who never faltered in his trust, even with the sea before, the advancing host behind, and no visible way of escape. To the very edge of the waters he led his people.

His task was done. It was for God, his God, in whom he trusted, to act now. Moses waited for, and expected, that act. But to the edge he had to go.

How often man draws back, halts at the thought of the troubled sea ahead. To go further is useless, he says, and gives up.

Or he goes within sight of the sea, and pauses. He must go on, always as far as he can; he must do all his share. God will not. On—to the Edge of the Sea.

Learn from this a mighty lesson. Do all your work, and leave your salvation to God. To say it will be no good is not to go to the edge, and that is to miss the saving Power of God.

The waters shall be divided, and you shall walk through the midst of the sea on dry land. I have said it. I, the Lord. Have I not done this for so many in your own day? For you? Think on these things.

God Calling: Fear Is Evil

Have no fear. Fear is evil and "perfect Love casts out fear." There is no room for fear in the heart in which I dwell. Fear destroys Hope. It cannot exist where Love is or where Faith is.

Fear is the curse of the world. Man is afraid—afraid of poverty, afraid of loneliness, afraid of unemployment, afraid of sickness.

Many, many are man's fears. Nation is afraid of nation. Fear, fear, fear, everywhere. Fight fear as you would a plague. Turn it out of your lives and home. Fight it singly. Fight it together. Never inspire fear. It is an evil ally. Fear of punishment, fear of blame.

No work that employs this enemy of Mine is work for Me. Banish it. There must be another and better way.

Ask Me, and I will show it to you.

God at Eventide: "Share, Share"

I am your Lord. Obey Me in all. You are being surely lead into prosperity and true peace.

Let many share in your every gain. There must be no hoarding in the Christ-life. Not what you can gain, but what you can give. Keep your eyes fixed on Me. Seek to know My Will. Share. Share.

I am a Risen Lord. You cannot live with Me without partaking of My Risen Life. My Kingdom is sharing.

I must share all I have with My followers. So you, too, must share all that I give you—material and Spiritual Blessings—with others.

God Calling: Love and Laugh

Work for Me, with Me, through Me. All work to last must be done in My Spirit. How silently My Spirit works. How gently and gradually souls are led into My Kingdom.

Love and Laughter form the plough that prepares the ground for the seed. Remember this. If the ground is hard, seed will not grow there.

Prepare the ground, prepare it as I say.

God at Eventide: Your Circle Widens

As the circle of your life widens you will feel ever more and more the need of Me. The need indeed to draw from My un-failing resources to gain the help and wisdom required to deal with these new contacts.

Do not refuse them, only let nothing idle or of little worth engross your attention.

As your circle is enlarged, your means to deal with it ad-equately must grow, too.

This is My desire. Ever walk with Me. Learn of Me. Wit-ness for Me, Glorify Me.

MARCH 7

God Calling: Surprises

Many there are who think that I test and train and bend to My Will. I, who bade the disciples take up the cross, I loved to prepare a feast for them by the lakeside—a little glad sur-prise, not a necessity, as the feeding of the multitude may have seemed. I loved to give the wine-gift at the marriage feast.

As you love to plan surprises for those who understand, and joy in them, so with Me. I love to plan them for those who see My Love and tender Joy in them.

Dear to the heart of My Father are those who see not only My tears, the tears of a Savior, but the smile, the joy-smile of a Friend.

God at Eventide: How Firm Your Foundation

As one in a storm needs to dwell in quiet thought upon the firmness of the foundation of his home, so you need in dangers and difficulties of whatever kind to withdraw, and in quiet assurance dwell upon that foundation upon which the house of your life and character is built.

Rest your thoughts on this, on Me. Do not dwell on the channels through which My Help may be directed to you. To do so is indeed to feel at the mercy of wind and weather. You can draw no strength from such.

No, a sense of security can only come from relying on Me, the All-powerful, the Unchanging.

Security engenders Strength, then Peace, then Joy.

"Other foundations can no man lay."

MARCH 8

God Calling: Heaven–Life

The Joy of the Spring shall be yours in full measure. Revel in the earth's joy. Do not you think that Nature is weary, too, of her long months of travail? There will come back a wonderful joy, if you share in her joy now.

Nature is the embodied Spirit of My Thoughts of beauty for this world. Treat her as such—as truly My servant and messenger, as any saint who has ever lived. To realize this will bring to you both new life-joy. Share her joys and travails, and great blessings will be yours.

This is all-important, because it is not only believing certain things *about* Me that helps and heals, but knowing Me, sensing My Presence in a flower, My message in its beauty and perfume.

You can truly live a life not of Earth—a heaven-life here and now. Joy—Joy—Joy.

God at Eventide: New Life

Eternal Life gives a youthful resiliency.

Think of My parable of the wineskins. Those who merely worship Me as a creed are like unto old wineskins.

They cannot accept new truth, new life. It would destroy, not increase their faith.

Those who have My Gift of Eternal, youth-giving Life have the ever-expanding, revitalizing, joy-quality of that Life.

The new wine poured so freely into new bottles. That bracing wine sustains the many who receive it.

MARCH 9

God Calling: Nothing Is Small

Nothing is small to God. In His sight a sparrow is of greater value than a palace, one kindly word of more importance than a statesman's speech.

It is the Life in all that has value and the quality of the life that determines the value. I came to give Eternal Life.

Do not judge of another's capacity by your own.

If the burden another bears presses too heavily, what matter that you could bear that load lightly?

You must learn of Me to judge of the sorrow or strain of another, not with a feeling of superiority, but with one of humble thankfulness.

Would not your burdens have seemed light to Me? But insofar as they pressed heavily upon you so did I judge of them.

That which tore your heart may seem light to another.

Truly I said—Judge not. Only to God can the heart of man be made plain.

Seek My Presence, not only that you may understand Me, but that you may gain the insight to understand more clearly My other children.

MARCH 10

God Calling: Fruit of Joy

You have to hush the heart and bid all your senses be still before you can be attuned to receive Heaven's music.

Your five senses are your means of communication with the material world, the links between your real Spirit-Life and the material manifestations around you, but you must sever all connection with them when you wish to hold Spirit-communication. They will hinder, not help.

See the good in everybody. Love the good in them. See your unworthiness compared with their worth. Love, laugh, make the world, your little world, happy.

As the ripples caused by a flung stone stir the surface of a whole pond, so your joy-making shall spread in ever-widening circles, beyond all your knowledge, all anticipation. Joy in Me. Such Joy is eternal.

Centuries after, it is still bearing Joy's precious fruit.

God at Eventide: Turn It to Good

Never flinch. My standard-bearers must you ever be. Bear your standard high.

Life has its dangers and difficulties, but real as these seem, the moment you see in them a power of evil that will in response to your faith be forced to work in some way for your good, in that moment of recognition evil and danger cease to have any power over you.

This is a wonderful truth. Believe it. Rejoice in it.

MARCH 11

God Calling: Seek Beauty

Draw Beauty from every flower and Joy from the song of the birds and the color of the flowers.

I am with you. When I wanted to express a beautiful thought, I made a lovely flower.

When I want to express to man what I am—what My Father is—I strive to make a very beautiful character.

Think of yourselves as My expression of attributes, as a lovely flower is My expression of thought, and you will strive in all, in Spiritual beauty, in Thought—power, in Health, in clothing, to be as fit an expression for Me as you can.

Absorb Beauty. As soon as the beauty of a flower or a tree is impressed upon your soul, it leaves an image there which reflects through your actions. Remember that no thought of sin and suffering, of the approaching scorn and Crucifixion, ever prevented My seeing the beauty of the flowers.

Look for Beauty and Joy in the world around. Look at a flower until its beauty becomes part of your very soul. It will be given back to the world again by you in the form of a smile or a loving word.

Listen to a bird. Take the song as a message from My Father. Let it sink into your soul. That too will be given back to the world in ways I have said. Laugh more, laugh often. Love more. I am with you. I am your Lord.

God at Eventide: Accept Your Task

Take life as a task; each step of it to be practiced until it can be done perfectly, that is, with patience, with soul harmony, and rest.

Remember the Christ of the humble ways is with you. His "Well done, good and faithful servant," is spoken, not to the great of earth but to the humble bearer of pain and annoyance, to the patient worker in life's ways of service.

So even on the quietest day, and in the lowliest way, mighty opportunities are given you of serving the King of Kings. See that you welcome and do not resent these opportunities.

MARCH 12

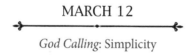

God Calling: Simplicity

Simplicity is the keynote of My Kingdom. Choose simple things always.

Love and reverence the humble and the simple.

Have only simple things here. Your standard must never be the world's standard.

Be gentle to all.

Drink of the Living water, deep draughts from the inexhaustible wells into which the very springs of Eternal Life flow from the Hills of God.

Think thoughts of Love and Beauty. Know no limit to all you can possess and be and do. Live in My Love; surrounded by It, blessed by It, shedding It bountifully on all about you, ever conscious of It being present with you.

You are here to reflect It.

Seek to see the good in all you meet—and in those of whom you hear.

MARCH 13

God Calling: Spiritualism

Wait before Me, gently breathing in My Spirit. That Spirit which, if given a free entrance and not barred out by self, will enable you to do the same works as I did, which being interpreted is, will enable Me to do the same works, and even greater than I did when on Earth—through you.

Spiritualism is wrong. No man should ever be a medium for any spirit other than Mine.

All you should know, all it is well for you to know of My Spirit-Kingdom, I will tell you when and how I see best. The limit is set by your own spiritual development. Follow My injunctions in all things.

Peace—Peace—Peace.

Be happy in Me. Feel that your life is complete in Me. Know the Joy of a friendship in which those who love Me share.

Know a glad contentment in the security of your protected and guided life. Value the Power that Union with Me gives you.

The greatest power that money, fame or position of the world can give, still leaves the possessor but as a child beating helpless hands against an impregnable fortress, as compared with the Power of My Spirit, which can render a follower of Mine himself an invincible, an all-conquering force.

MARCH 14

God Calling: God's Touch

Near, all broodingly near, as some tender mother bird anxious over its young, I am here. I am your Lord, Life of your body and mind and soul—Renewer of your youth.

You do not know all that this time of converse with Me will mean to you. Did not My servant Isaiah say, "They that wait upon the Lord shall renew their strength; they shall mount up with wings as eagles; they shall run, and not be weary; they shall walk, and not faint."

Persevere in all I tell you to do. The persistent carrying out of My commands, My desires, will unfailingly bring you, as far as spiritual, mental, and temporal things are concerned, to that place where you would be.

If you look back over My Words to you, you will see that My leading has been very gradual, and that only as you have carried out My wishes have I been able to give you more clear and definite teaching and guidance.

Man's ecstasy is God's touch on quickened, responsive spirit-nerves. Joy—Joy—Joy.

Be not overcome of evil, but overcome evil with good.

The instruments in your hand for good are invincible against evil, did you but use them.

Every evil you face boldly, in My Spirit, flees at once, ashamed. No evil can look good in the face. Teach to all—that good is stronger than evil. You must answer the challenge of evil.

This spiritual warfare must be ceaselessly waged by My followers. Remember it is not where you are strongest that evil will attack you, but at your weak points. Hence the need to overcome. Be ready to see a weakness in yourself, and attack that until you are victor.

MARCH 15

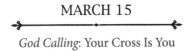

God Calling: Your Cross Is You

Remember, you are only an instrument. Not yours to decide how or when or where you act. I plan all that. Make yourself very fit to do My work. All that hinders your activity must be cured.

Mine is the Cross on which the burdens of the world are laid. How foolish is any one of My disciples who seeks to bear his own burdens, when there is only one place for them—My Cross.

It is like a weary man on a hot and dusty road, bearing a heavy load, when all plans have been made for its carriage. The road, the scenery, flowers, beauty around—all are lost.

But, My children, you may think I did say, "Take up your cross daily, and follow Me."

Yes, but the cross given to each one of you is only a cross provided on which you can crucify the self of yours that hinders progress and Joy and prevents the flow through your being of My invigorating Life and Spirit.

Listen to Me, love Me, joy in Me. Rejoice.

God at Eventide: Guidance *Is* Guidance

Be still before Me. How often in a crisis man rushes hither and thither. Rush is a sign of weakness. Quiet abiding is a sign of strength.

A few quiet actions, as you are led to do them, and all is accomplished wisely and rightly, more quickly and more effectually than could be done by those who rush about and act feverishly.

Guidance IS Guidance, the being led, the being shown the way. Believe this.

Softly across life's tumult, comes the gentle Voice, "Peace, be still." The waves of difficulty will hear. They will fall back. There will be a great calm.

And then the Still, Small Voice of Guidance.

MARCH 16

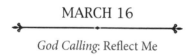

God Calling: Reflect Me

My children, I am here beside you. Draw near in spirit to Me. Shut out the distractions of the world. I am your Life, the very breath of your soul. Learn what it is to shut yourself in the secret place of your being, which is My secret place too.

True it is, I wait in many a heart, but so few retire into that inner place of the being to commune with Me. Wherever the soul is, I am. Man has rarely understood this. I *am* actually at the center of every man's being, but, distracted with the things of the sense-life, he finds Me not.

Do you realize that I am telling you *truths*, revealing them, not repeating oft-told facts. Meditate on all I say. Ponder it. Not to draw your own conclusions, but to absorb Mine.

All down the ages, men have been too eager to say what they thought about My truth, and so doing, they have grievously erred. Hear Me. Talk to Me. Reflect Me. Do not say what you think *about* Me. My words need none of man's explanation. I can explain to each heart.

Make Me real, and leave Me to do My own work. To lead a soul to Me is one thing, to seek to stay with it to interpret mars the first great act. So would it be with human intercourse. How much more then, when it is a question of the soul, and Me, its Maker, and only real Spirit that understands it.

God at Eventide: Perfect Everything

Be ye therefore perfect, even as your Father in Heaven.

That was the aim I set before My disciples when I spoke to them on the Mount.

That is the aim I set before you and every follower of Mine today.

To achieve this you would be as God.

To aim at less would mean an unworthy standard.

To keep your gaze on this as your standard means that your eyes are fixed on the Heights of God, always directed above the difficulties and the lower aims and desires and standards of others round you.

God Calling: No Greater Joy

Withdraw into the calm of communion with Me. Rest—rest, rest in that calm and Peace. Life knows no greater joy than you will find in converse and companionship with Me.

You are Mine. When the soul finds its home of rest in Me, then it is that its real Life begins. Not in years, as man counts it, do we measure in My Kingdom.

We count only from his second birth, that new birth of which I spoke to Nicodemus when I said, "Ye must be born again." We know no life but Eternal Life, and when a man enters into that, then he lives.

And this is Life, Eternal, to know God, My Father and Me, the Son sent by Him. So immature, so childish, so empty is all so-called living before that. I shower Love on you. Pass Love on.

Do not fear. To fear is as foolish as if a small child with a small coin but a rich father fretted about how rent and rates should be paid and what he or she would do about it. Is this work Mine or not? You need to trust Me for everything.

God at Eventide: The Real World

Blessed are they that hear My Voice.

Deaf to My Voice man can so often be. Live, My children, more in the Unseen World. There, in the contemplation of Me, your whole nature becomes sensitive to My faintest whisper.

I have told you, I tell you again, the Unseen World is the real world. Realize more and more as you go through this earth-life that this is only a material-plane parenthesis. The real paragraph, chapter, book of Life is the Spirit-Life.

This point of view will alter your idea of suffering, failure, and the work of life here. It will give you a new view of death. Birth begins the parenthesis, death closes it. Then back to real Life-History. Absorb this.

When you have done so, you will get that same idea about the various periods of your earth-life. Times of struggle, defeat, joy, failure, work, rest, success—treat them all as parts of a parenthesis in the one Eternal Life of *spiritual progress*.

MARCH 18

God Calling: Your Resolutions

Listen, listen, I am your Lord. Before Me there is none other. Just trust Me in everything. Help is here all the time.

The difficult way is nearly over, but you have learnt in it lessons you could learn in no other way. "The kingdom of heaven suffereth violence, and the violent take it by force." Wrest from Me, by firm and simple trust and persistent prayer, the treasures of My Kingdom.

Such wonderful things are coming to you, Joy—Peace—Assurance—Security—Health—Happiness—Laughter.

Claim big, really big, things now. Remember, nothing is too big. Satisfy the longing of My Heart to give. Blessing, abundant blessing, on you both now and always. Peace.

God at Eventide: Joy from Sorrow

I bind up the broken hearts with the cords wherewith men scourged Me in the Judgment Hall, with the whips of scorn wherewith men have mocked My Love and Divinity down the ages.

Symbol, this, of the way in which, out of seeming obstacles stepping-stones can be fashioned, and, out of trials undreamt-of, blessings can be wrought.

Share My Life with its longings and tears, with its Joys unspeakable and its heartaches beyond human description.

Share My Joy.

MARCH 19

God Calling: Courage

I am here. Fear not. Can you really trust Me? I am a God of Power, as well as a Man of Love, so human yet so divine.

Just trust. I cannot, and I will not, fail you. All is well. Courage.

Many are praying for you both.

God at Eventide: Through the Archway

By the obedience of one shall many be made righteous.

Obedience is the keystone of your arch of worship. On it depends your Love and Power.

Through that archway shall many pass into My Holy Place. Once therein their questing souls will pass into My Holy of Holies. Is it too much to ask of you obedience that this may be accomplished?

Do not fret that your life is lived in lowly places. It is not to be lived to impress this earth-plane, but to be so faithful and obedient that those for whom you desire much, shall have THAT much impressed upon them on the spirit-plane.

That much, and more, than you can desire for them.

God Calling: Help from Everywhere

Your foolish little activities are valueless in themselves. Seemingly trivial or of seemingly great moment, all deeds are alike if directed by Me. Just cease to function except through Me.

I am your Lord; just obey Me as you would expect a faithful, willing secretary to carry out *your* directions. Just have no choice but Mine, no will but Mine.

I am dependent on no one agency when I am your supply. Through many channels My help and material flow can come.

God at Eventide: First Place

I do not promise My followers the world's ease and pleasures. I promise those Joys that the world can neither give nor take away.

I promise the heart-rest found in Me alone.

It does not mean that all the beauties and pleasures of the world must be renounced, but that they must be enjoyed only after the treasures and Joys of My Kingdom have been learned, appreciated, and given first place.

MARCH 21

God Calling: All Is Well

Remember My Words to My disciples, "This kind goeth not out but by prayer and fasting." Can you tread the way I trod? Can you drink of My cup? "All is well." Say always, "All is well."

Long though the way may seem, there is not one inch too much. I, your Lord, am not only with you on the journey—I planned, and am planning, the journey.

There are Joys unspeakable in the way you go. Courage—Courage—Courage.

God at Eventide: Simplicity

Be content to do the simple things.

Never think that if you have not the cleverness of the world I cannot use your services.

Pure sparkling wine may be in a silver goblet or in a simple glass, but, to the one who receives, it is the wine that matters, not the vessel, provided that be pure and clean.

It is My truth that matters, not the person that utters it, provided the desire is there to deliver My Message for ME.

True simplicity is found only as you live in Me and act in My Strength; for only in our close companionship can real value be achieved.

Never accept the values of earth. Be content with simplicity.

MARCH 22

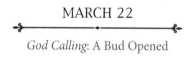

God Calling: A Bud Opened

To Me, your intimate Friend, all Power is given. It is given Me of My Father, and have not My intimate friends a right to ask it?

You cannot have a need I cannot supply. A flower or one thousand pounds, one is no more difficult than the other.

Your need is a spiritual need to carry on My work. All spiritual supply is fashioned from Love. The flower and the thousand pounds—both fashioned from Love to those who need it. Do you not see this?

I thought of you, a bud opened; you converted that into a

cheer for one you love or a smile. That cheer meant increased health. Increased health means work for Me, and that means souls for Me.

And so it goes on, a constant supply, but only if the need is a spiritual one.

God at Eventide: Love's Overflow

I desire the love of man's heart in abundant measure.

Not because God would be adored for Himself and for His own gratification, but because I know that only as the love of man flows out to Me does man attain to his purest and best.

That rush of love, which follows the understanding and realization of My Love for man, sweetens and purifies his whole being.

"Thou shalt love thy neighbor as thyself." The love you give to your neighbor is the overflow of your love to me.

MARCH 23

God Calling: Until Your Heart Sings

I am beside you to bless and help you. Waver not in your prayers. They shall be heard. All power is Mine. Say that to yourself often and steadily.

Say it until your heart sings with the Joy of the safety and power it means to you.

Say it until the very force of the utterance drives back and puts to nought all the evils against you.

Use it as a battle cry—"All power is given unto My Lord," "All power is given unto My Friend," "All power is given unto My Savior," and then you pass on to victory.

Deal with each difficulty as you must.

Then live above it. Say "In Him I conquered." The fight is ever between you and evil, never between you and another. Never make it a personal matter.

If you are fighting with the weapons of the world—envy, resentment, anger—you cannot use those of My Kingdom— Prayer, Love, Peace—which would give you a God-given conquering strength.

It is the endeavor to call both God and mammon to your aid that makes for lack of success. The world looks on in scornful pity, and My followers themselves doubt and wonder.

So often they do not see their own error, but attribute to suffering for My Sake that which may not be according to My Will.

MARCH 24

God Calling: Know Me

I am here. Seek not to know the future. Mercifully I veil it from you.

Faith is too priceless a possession to be sacrificed in order to purchase knowledge. But Faith itself is based on a knowledge of Me.

So remember that this evening time is not to learn the future, not to receive revelation of the Unseen, but to gain an intimate knowledge of Me which will teach you all things and be the very foundation of your faith.

God at Eventide: If It Offends—

Question yourself as to your weakness. What caused

your failure? To continue to bemoan your folly is in itself a weakness. My followers must be strong, not in themselves, but in Me.

The look at Self, however penitent, cannot give strength.

Look unto Me, and, whatever the seeming sacrifice, be ruthless with what hindered or caused you to fall.

MARCH 25

God Calling: Wonders Will Unfold

I am with you. Do not fear. Never doubt My Love and Power. Your heights of success will be won by the daily persistent doing of what I have said.

Daily, steady persistence. Like the wearing away of a stone by steady drops of water, so will your daily persistence wear away all the difficulties and gain success for you and secure your help for others.

Never falter, go forward so boldly, so unafraid. I am beside you to help and strengthen you.

Wonders have unfolded. More still will unfold, beyond your dreams, beyond your hopes.

Say "All is well" to everything. All *is* well.

God at Eventide: Sift Your Motives

Walk in My Ways. Follow the path I have bidden you tread.

Humble yourselves before Me, and keep My laws, so shall you have perfect peace.

I am with you to give you the needed strength. Go forward unafraid. Grow in Grace, and in the knowledge of Me, your Master and your Friend. Count all the learning of earth's wisest as nothing compared with the wisdom that I, your Lord, would show you.

Love and learn. You have much, very much to do for My Kingdom. So seek to become perfect. Sift your motives. All that is unworthy cast aside, uproot its inner growth.

You are freely forgiven. Forgive freely, largely, wonderfully.

MARCH 26

God Calling: Follow Your Guide

I am with you to guide you and help you. Unseen forces are controlling your destiny. Your petty fears are groundless.

What of a man walking through a glorious glade who fretted because ahead there lay a river and he might not be able to cross it, when all the time, that river was spanned by a bridge? And what if that man had a friend who knew the way—had planned it—and assured him that at no part of the journey would any unforeseen contingency arise, and that all was well?

So leave your foolish fears, and follow Me, your Guide, and determinedly refuse to consider the problems of tomorrow. My message to you is trust and wait.

God at Eventide: Keep Step

Go forward, glad indeed.

Walk with Me until your faltering, flagging footsteps learn to keep in step with Me, and gain a firmness and a confidence unknown before.

Walk with Me until a gladsome rhythm reveals the conquest-spirit that you draw from Me, and your whole being thrills with the joy of being, doing and even suffering with Me.

Thus in loving Communion with Me you learn to know my needs and My wishes for others.

"Hear am I, Lord, send me" shows very surely a child-like eagerness, the eagerness of love, even the eagerness for adventure for My cause.

For in My Secret Service there is surely the thrill of *adventure*.

MARCH 27

God Calling: Go Forward

Rest in Me, quiet in My Love, strong in My Power. Think what it is to possess a Power greater than any earthly force. A sway greater, and more far-reaching, than that of any earthly king.

No invention, no electricity, no magnetism, no gold could achieve one-millionth part of all that you can achieve by the Power of My Spirit. Just think for one moment all that means.

Go forward. You are only beginning the new Life together. Joy, Joy, Joy.

God at Eventide: Spirits in Training

Go on along the highway of the Kingdom until all that comes, that touches your outward lives and circumstances, has no power to ruffle your spirit-calm. Make it a delight so to train yourselves.

Why does man rebel at aught that should teach him poise of spirit, whilst in the physical world he welcomes severe exercise that would increase his powers?

The children of this world are surely wiser in their generation than the children of light. If My Children of Light gave to their spirit and character-training all the care that the children of this world give to the body—its feeding, its clothing, its well-being—how rapid would their spiritual progress be!

Yet how little does the body matter compared with the growth of the Spirit. "Fear not them that kill the body, but are not able to kill the soul."

MARCH 28

God Calling: Evil Mountains

Faith and obedience will remove mountains, mountains of evil, mountains of difficulty.

But they must go hand in hand.

God at Eventide: In Eternity Now

Heirs of God. Joint heirs with Me of Eternal Life, if so be that you suffer with Me, that we may also be glorified together.

Glory denotes perfection of character. This can only be learned as you allow discipline to play its part in your life, and also as you entrust your sinful past to Me.

Perfect through suffering. You cannot escape discipline and be truly My disciple.

If you think that life is too short for all you have to do and to conquer, then remember that you have already entered upon *eternity*.

MARCH 29

God Calling: A Life Apart

I reward your seeking with My Presence. Rejoice and be glad. I am your God. Courage and joy will conquer all troubles. First things first.

Seek Me, love Me, joy in Me. I am your Guide. No

perils can affright you, no discipline exhaust you. Persevere. Can you hold on in My strength? I need you more than you need Me. Struggle through this time for My sake. Initiation precedes all real work and success for Me.

Are you ready to live a life apart? Apart with Me? In the world and yet apart with Me? Going forth from your secret times of communion to rescue and save?

God at Eventide: The True Sign

How many believed on My Name after seeing the signs that I did?

Not for the signs, not for the water made wine, not for My miracles will My true follower believe in Me.

No, for something deeper, seen only with the eyes of faith, realized only by a heart of love responding to My Heart of Love. Not of these must it be said, "I do not trust Myself unto them" as I did of those who saw My signs.

I must trust Myself and My Cause to My followers who see me with the eyes of faith. How else can I be loved and known?

They will meet Me, the outcast Savior, when I am performing no mighty deeds, wandering unheeded and unacclaimed through dark and lonely ways, and they will pause, all other pursuit forgotten, and will yet turn and follow Me.

Follow because of some chord in them responsive to the yearning of My Heart for Man, who has shut Me out. Follow, too, because of that in Me which is responsive to the cry of man's hungering soul.

MARCH 30

God Calling: Deliverance

Be calm, be true, be quiet. I watch over you. Rest in My Love. Joy in the very Beauty of Holiness. You are Mine. Deliverance is here for you, but Thankfulness and Joy open the gates.

Try in all things to be very glad, very happy, very thankful. It is not to quiet resignation I give My blessings, but to joyful acceptance and anticipation.

Laughter is the outward expression of joy. That is why I urge upon you Love and Laughter.

God at Eventide: The Love of Your Life

I am beside you. I am with you in all that you do. I control your thoughts, inspire your impulses, guide your footsteps.

I strengthen you, body, mind and spirit. I am the link between you and those who are in the Unseen. I am the Love of your lives. Controller of your destinies. Guardian, advocate, provider, Friend.

Yes, love Me more and more. So will you not only enjoy to the full the treasures and pleasures of My Kingdom, but increasingly those of Nature, My gift to My world.

MARCH 31

God Calling: Love's Offering

I am your Lord, gracious and loving. Rest in My Love; walk in My ways. Each week is a week of progress, steady progress upward. You may not see it, but I do.

I judge not by outward appearances, I judge the heart, and I see in both your hearts one single desire, to do My Will.

The simplest offering by a child brought or done with the one desire to give you pleasure or to show you love, is it not more loved by you than the offerings of those who love you not?

So, though you may feel that your work has been spoiled and tarnished, I see it only as Love's offering. Courage, My children.

When climbing a steep hill, a man is often more conscious of the weakness of his stumbling feet than of the view, the grandeur, or even of his upward progress.

Persevere, persevere. Love and laugh. Rejoice.

God at Eventide: The Wrong Voice

I am the Great Teacher, so ready to explain the simplest lesson to the most ignorant.

It is not for you to seek everywhere explanations of Me and My Kingdom, its laws and its purposes.

Learn of Me. How often I would have spoken to some heart, but the voice of one too eager with explanations about Me crowded Me out.

When Andrew brought Simon to Me *he* was silent to let his brother learn of Me.

The reason for this crowding out of My Voice by My disciples is their unwillingness to believe that I do speak today. So, thinking they worship a silent Christ, they seek to make amends by their much speaking.

> *"To Thee our morning song of praise,*
> *To Thee our evening prayer we raise."*

God Calling: Shut Out from God

Do you not see, My children, that you have not yet learned all? Soon, very soon, you will have mastered your lesson, and then you will truly be able to do all things through Me and My Strength.

Did you not see it with My disciples? Timid, faithless followers, and then, so soon, themselves leaders, healers, conquerors, through Me.

All knowledge was Mine, given Me of My Father, and Mine in manhood's years on Earth. You understand this, My children, I know you do.

Thousands of My servants have gone to their betrayal and death, and others, who knew Me not, with no agony before it.

Had I not been Son of God, bearing man's weight of sin, voluntarily bearing it until of My own free will—for that moment's horror, I was shut out from His sight with man, the sinner, for one short space—had I not been God, had not this been My suffering—then I was but a craven mortal.

God at Eventide: The Time of Resurrection

Spring brings its message of Hope.

Not only does it proclaim the Truth that Nature arises from her time of decay and darkness to a new life. But, My children, it surely speaks to the individual, to nations, to My world, that the time of decay and darkness for them too can pass, and that from conflict and storm, disaster and sin they can spring to a new and gladdening Resurrection-Life.

But Nature obeys My Laws. It is by her obedience that the quickening of new life is succeeded by the beauty of Risen Power.

So, only as man obeys My Will and works according to

My Divine Plan for him can harmony follow chaos, peace follow war, and a reign of Love succeed one of conflict and carnage.

APRIL 2

God Calling: The Priceless Blessing

I am here. Here as truly as I was with My disciples of old. Here to help and bless you. Here to company with you. Do you know, even yet, My children, that this is the priceless blessing of your lives? I forgive you, as you have prayed Me to, for all neglects of My commands, but start anew from today.

Study My words and carry them out unflinchingly, unflinchingly. As you do this, you will find that you are miracle-workers, workers together with Me—for Me. Remember this, not what you *do*, but what you are—that is the miracle-working power.

Changed by My Spirit, shedding one garment of Spirit for a better; in time throwing that aside for a yet finer one, and so on from character to character, gradually transformed into My likeness.

Joy, Joy, Joy.

God at Eventide: Resurrection Preparation

I am the Master of the Universe. Accept My ordered Word. When you do this in joyful sincerity, you link yourself with all creative force of the Universe.

My Spirit can then be operative, first in you and then through you.

My followers forget that the scourging at the pillar, the Divine control ("He answered never a word") and the Cross, the man-rejected, man-forsaken, all these preceded the Resurrection.

Without these there could have been no Resurrection. These steps in Spirit-conquest had to be, before My all-powerful, Divine Spirit could be released to be forever available for those who would hear My Call, and would will to walk in My Way.

APRIL 3

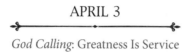

God Calling: Greatness Is Service

My children, I am here, your waiting Lord, ready at your call. I am among you as one that serveth, Meek and Holy, ready to be used and commanded. Remember that is the finest quality of greatness—service. I, who could command a universe—I await the commands of My children. Bring Me into everything.

You will find such Joy as the time goes on in speaking to each other of Me, and together climbing higher. Always humble, meek, and lowly in heart.

Learn this—no position—just a servant.

God at Eventide: See Them Free

If I bore the sins of all in My agonized Heart in the Garden of Gethsemane and on Calvary, then when you seek to punish others whom you despise, you punish and despise Me.

My throwing aside the grave-clothes, and My stepping out into that sunlit Garden on Easter Morn were symbolic of the freedom I had bought for My children, and which they would know in Me.

Are you seeking to bind the grave-clothes round Me? When you recognize a man's sins you must go further always and see him as free, the grave-clothes of sin and limitation cast aside; the stone, that shut out his Vision of Love and God, rolled away; he, the risen man, walking in My Strength, and conquering in My Power.

APRIL 4

God Calling: Divine Efficiency

I am all-powerful and all-knowing, and I have all your affairs in My Hands. Divine efficiency as well as Divine Power is being brought to bear on them. All miracle-work is not the work of a moment as so often men imagine.

My servant Peter was not changed in a flash from a simple fisherman to a great leader and teacher, but through the very time of faithlessness—through the very time of denial—I was yet making him all that he should be. Impetuous spokesman as he always was, ready to lead the other disciples, Peter could never have been the after power he was, had he not learned his weakness. No man can save unless he understands the sinner.

The Peter who was a mighty force for Me afterwards, who, more than all others, founded My Church, was not even first the Peter who said, "Thou art the Christ, the Son of the living God," but the Peter who denied Me. He who had tested My forgiveness in his moment of abject remorse, he could best speak of Me as the Savior.

The Kingdom of Heaven can only be preached by those who have learned to prize the authority of its Kingdom. A many-sided training My apostles need. Oh! joy. Oh, rejoice. I love you. Not one test too much will I lay on you.

God at Eventide: Sharing My Burden

Remember the Truth that you are learning, even now, though dimly.

106

In Eternal Life there are no time-limits. So My sacrifice was for you today, this hour, as truly as ever it was for those who watched Me on Calvary. I am the changeless One. The same yesterday and forever. Sacrificing Myself today, rising today. You then, once you embrace Eternal Life, enter into My Suffering, and help to carry My Cross, as truly today as if you had walked beside Me to Calvary.

APRIL 5

God Calling: Heart's Interpreter

Rest in Me. Seek this evening time just to be with Me. Do not feel you have failed if sometimes I ask you only to rest together in My Presence.

I am with you, much with you both, not only at these times, at all times. Feel conscious of My Presence. Earth has no greater joy than that.

I am the heart's great Interpreter. Even souls who are the nearest together have much in their natures that remain a sealed book to each other, and only as I enter and control their lives do I reveal to each the mysteries of the other.

Each soul is so different—I alone understand perfectly the language of each and can interpret between the two.

God at Eventide: Redeemed

Agony and heartache, pain and loneliness, such as no human being has ever known, were the price of your redemption.

Truly you are not your own.

You are bought with a price. You belong to Me.

You are Mine to use, Mine to love, Mine to provide for.

Man does not understand the infinite Love of the Divine.

Man teaches that as I bought him, so he has to serve, obey and live for me.

He fails to understand that because he is Mine, bought by Me, it is My responsibility to supply his every need. His part is to realize My ownership and to claim My Love and Power.

APRIL 6

God Calling: Easter Joy

I lay My loving Hands on you in blessing. Wait in Love and longing to feel their tender pressure and, as you wait, courage and hope will flow into your being, irradiating all your lives with the warm sun of My Presence.

Let all go this Eastertide. Loosen your hold on earth, its care, its worries, even its joys. Unclasp your hands, relax, and then the tide of Easter Joy will come. Put aside all thought of the future, of the past. Relinquish all to get the Easter Sacrament of Spiritual Life.

So often man, crying out for some blessing, has yet such tight hold on some earth-treasure that he has no hand to receive Mine, as I hold it out in Love. Easter is the wonder-time of all the year. A blessing is yours to take. Sacrifice all to that.

God at Eventide: The Veil Has Gone

*And the veil of the Temple was rent in twain,
from the top to the bottom.*

The veil that had hidden God from the knowledge and sight of man was at last removed.

I, God and man, had torn away the veil separating God the Father, and man, My brother. I came to reveal my Father to man, and I live, ever live, to make intercession to the Father for man. I am the Great Mediator between God and man, the Man, Christ *Jesus.*

APRIL 7

God Calling: Calvary

From the death of My Body on the Cross, as from the shedding of husks in seed-life, springs that New Life which is My Gift to every man who will accept it.

Die with Me to self—to the human life, and then you will know the rapturous Joy of Easter Resurrection.

A Risen Life so glad and free can be yours.

Mary left home and kindred, friends, all, that Easter morning in her search for Me, and not until the "Mary" had been followed by the glad triumphant rapture of her "Rabboni" was her search over.

So with each of you. Man speaks to you too of a buried Christ. Search until you meet Me face-to-face, and My tender uttering of your name awakes your glad "Rabboni."

God at Eventide: Bear Reproach Gladly

Rest unto your souls is found at My Feet. The place of rest is the place of humility.

When you rejoice to serve humbly, when you are content for men to think ill of you, when you can bear reproach and scorn gladly, then what can disturb the gladness of your soul, its rest?

No unrest can assail and hurt the soul that has not its spring in self. That self must be nailed to My Cross, that self must die before you can truly say—"I live, yet not I, but Christ liveth in me."

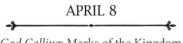

God Calling: Marks of the Kingdom

*Our Savior, we greet Thee. Thy Love and Sacrifice we
would return in our poor faulty measure by Love and sacrifice.*

No gift is poor if it expresses the true Love of the giver. So to
Me your heart's gifts are rich and precious. Rejoice in My glad
acceptance as you bring your Easter offerings.

My children must make a stand. "Come ye out from
among them and be ye separate" was the command. Today in
life and work, in Love and service, My children must be out-
standing. I called a Peculiar People to make known My Name.
My servant Paul said that My followers must be willing to be
deemed "fools" for My Sake.

Be ready to stand aside and let the fashions and customs
of the world go by, when My Glory and My Kingdom are
thereby served. Be known by the Marks that distinguish those
of My Kingdom. Be ready to confess Me before men. To count
all things as loss so that you may gain Me in your lives.

God at Eventide: Stones Rolled Away

And they saw that the stone was rolled away.

How needless their questioning among themselves
had been:

"Who shall roll away the stone?"

Wherever My followers go full of desire to do Me loving
service, they shall find the stones of difficulty, of obstruction,
rolled away.

They came, these faithful women, to the sepulcher with
the spices and ointments they had prepared.

Come, too, with your spices of Love to do Me service,

and you shall find you have been anticipated. I am ever eager in Love to do you service.

APRIL 9

God Calling: Risen Life

Arise, shine; for thy light is come,
and the glory of the LORD is risen upon thee.
ISAIAH 60:1

The Call comes on this My Day for all who love Me, to arise from earth-bands, from sin, and sloth and depression, distrust, fear, all that hinders the Risen Life. To arise to Beauty, to Holiness, to Joy, to Peace, to work inspired by Love and Joy, to rise from death to Life.

Remember that death was the last enemy I destroyed. So with death My Victory was complete. You have nothing then to fear. Sin, too, is conquered and forgiven, as you live and move and work with Me. All that depresses you, all that you fear, are powerless to harm you. They are but phantoms. The real forces I conquered in the wilderness, the Garden of Gethsemane, on the Cross, in the Tomb.

Let nothing hinder your Risen Life. "Risen with Christ," said My servant Paul. Seek to know more and more of that Risen Life. That is the Life of Conquest. Of that Risen Life was it truly said: "I live; yet not I, but Christ liveth in me." Fear and despair and tears come as you stand by the empty Tomb. "They have taken away my Lord, and I know not where they have laid him."

Rise from your fears and go out into the sunlight to meet Me, your Risen Lord.

If by the Spirit you mortify the flesh, you shall live.

This is a further progress-step in My Kingdom. The flesh must hold no pleasure for you that is not held in leash, always under subjection to the Spirit.

It was the utter subjection of the flesh that was manifested in My Silence at the pillar, and in the face of the jibes and insults and blows. It was this complete subjection which meant a Risen Body.

Resurrection-faith is not a matter of belief in Me, and in My Power working a miracle, it is a faith in Me and My Power leading to entire subjection of the body.

The body completely under control of the Spirit is a Risen Body. See now the importance of self-discipline.

APRIL 10

God Calling: Pride Bars the Way

Obedience is one of the keys unlocking the door into My Kingdom, so love and obey. No man can obey Me implicitly without in time realizing My Love, in his turn responding by love to that Love, and then experiencing the joy of the beloved and the lover.

The rough stone steps of obedience lead up to the mosaic of Joy and Love that floor My Heaven. As one on Earth who loves another says, "Where you are is home," so it is in relation with Me. Where I am is My Home—is Heaven.

Heaven may be in a sordid slum or a palace, and I can make My Home in the humblest heart. I can only dwell with the humble. Pride stands sentinel at the door of the heart to shut out the lowly, humble Christ.

I sent no disciple to carry My Healing Power to the Syrophoenician woman's sick daughter, the centurion's servant, or to the ruler's son. My Word was all-sufficient.

All that I needed was the faith of the petitioner. Can you not realize that?

Learn to understand and to ask more of Me. If you do not, then others' bonds are your responsibility.

Loose your own body from all bonds. Remember "the beam and the mote."

As the fault (the beam) is removed from your own eye, giving you the power to remove the mote from your brother's eye, so if you bring your body into subjection, discipline it wholly, you will be enabled to free your brother from bonds that bind him to ill-health.

APRIL 11

God Calling: Hold Your Fort

Remember that My followers are to be a peculiar people, separated from among others. Different ways, a different standard of living, different customs, actuated by different motives. Pray for Love.

Pray for My Spirit of Love to be showered on all you meet. Deal with yourself severely. Learn to love discipline.

Never yield one point that you have already won. Discipline, discipline. Love it and rejoice—rejoice. Mountains can be removed by thought—by desire.

Love and Laugh. To the world, sad faces and depressed spirits speak of a buried Christ. If you want to convince men that I am Risen, you must go through life with Easter gladness. You must prove by your lives that you are Risen with Me.

Men will not learn of My conquest over death by the arguments of theologians, but by the lives of My followers. My Risen followers. If you are still wearing the grave-clothes of gloom and depression, of fear and poverty, men will think of us as tomb-bound still.

No, live in the Spirit of the Garden on that Easter morning. For you, too, I will roll away the stone from the door of the sepulcher. Walk unbound in the Garden with Me, in the Garden of Love, Joy, childlike, boundless Faith—the Garden of Delights.

APRIL 12

God Calling: Golden Opportunity

I am your Guide. Strength and help will come to you; just trust Me wholly.

Fear not. I am evermore ready to hear than you to ask. Walk in My ways and *know* that help will come.

Man's need is God's chance to help. I love to help and save. Man's need is God's golden opportunity for him of letting his faith find expression. That expression of faith is all that God needs to manifest His Power. Faith is the Key that unlocks the storehouse of God's resources.

My faithful servants, you long for perfection and see your bitter failures. I see faithfulness, and as a mother takes the soiled, imperfect work of her child and invests it with perfection because of the sweet love, so I take your poor faithfulness and crown it with perfection.

It is My Pleasure that you wait before Me.

Companionship with Me, with its soul-rest, is all too often sacrificed for petition.

Be content awhile to be silent in My Presence. Draw in the Spiritual Power which will strengthen you to conquer the weaknesses you so deplore.

Life in Me is one of radiance.

Eternal Life is Life refreshed by Living Waters.

There is no stagnation in My Kingdom, in that place prepared for hearts that love Me.

It is a place of Fair Delights.

Claim what you will. It is yours.

APRIL 13

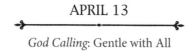

God Calling: Gentle with All

Love and laugh. Make your world the happier for your being in it. Love and rejoice on the gray days.

There are wilderness days for My disciples as well as Mountains of Transfiguration, but on both it is duty, persistently, faithfully done, that tells.

Be gentle with all. Try to see the heart I see, to know the pain and difficulty of the other life, that I know. Try, before you interview anyone, or speak to anyone, to ask Me to act as interpreter between you two.

Just live in the spirit of prayer. In speaking to Me, you find soul-rest. Simple tasks, faithfully done and persisted in, bring their own reward and are mosaics being laid in the pavement of success.

Welcome all who come here. I love you.

It may not be your need I am seeking to supply at a particular moment, but of another through you.

Remember what I have told you before: it is empty vessels I fill, into open hands that I place My supply.

Too often My followers are so busy clutching their foolish possessions that they have no hands to receive the larger blessings, the needed gifts, I am waiting to pass to them, and, through them, to others.

Help all to see the wonderful life that could open out before them. To be Heaven's almoner is the work to which I call each follower Mine.

APRIL 14

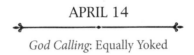

God Calling: Equally Yoked

My children, I guide you always. The walking in the way may not be always carried out, but the guiding is always so sure. God is using you both in marvelous ways. Go on gladly. You will see.

To be a perfect gymnast you must learn balance. It is balance and poise, perfect balance and poise, I am teaching you now. This will give you power in dealing with the lives of others, and that power is already being marvelously manifested.

The vision you both have is the means of clearing the obstacles away. When My disciple sees My purpose ahead, that very sight is the power that clears away every obstacle along that range of vision. You will both have mighty power to do this. Spiritual Light is in itself a miracle-worker.

People waste so much time in seeking to work out what they see. I declare to you that in the seeing My purpose all is done. Truly I said to My disciples, "I have yet many things to say unto you, but ye cannot bear them *now*." But to you, and the twos who gather to hear Me as you do, I can declare those things now, that then I left unsaid.

Is not the message of My servant Paul now plain: "Be ye not unequally yoked together with unbelievers," because My Guidance is intensified immeasurably in power, when the two are one in desire to be with Me—but so few have understood.

God at Eventide: You Can Do This

I will give you rest.

My Gift truly, but the result of your trust.

Train yourself to trust so completely that no tremor even of doubt or fear can enter in.

No fear of the future, no cloud over the present, no shadow of the past.

When the absence of fear is the result of strength for the way gained by contact with Me, and of complete reliance upon My Tenderness and My Power, then you have *My Gift of Rest*.

God Calling: Never Feel Inadequate

Obey My commands. They are steps in the ladder that leads to success. Above all, keep calm, unmoved.

Go back into the silence to recover this calm when it is lost even for one moment. You accomplish more by this than by all the activities of a long day. At all cost keep calm; you can help nobody when you are agitated. I, your Lord, see not as man sees.

Never feel inadequate for any task. All work here is accomplished by My Spirit, and that can flow through the most humble and lowly. It simply needs an unblocked channel. Rid yourself of self, and all is well.

Pray about all, but concentrate on a few things until those are accomplished. I am watching over you. Strength for your daily, hourly task is provided. Yours is the fault, the sin, if it is unclaimed, and you fail for lack of it.

God at Eventide: The Sunlit Way

Know that your Source of joy is something changeless. The hopes of the world are but in material things and when these pass or change their joy fades, hope dies, only dark night remains.

Speak comfort to such. Tell of My Love surrounding you, that My protecting Power is yours. That I can never fail one who trusts in Me. That you can breathe in courage from My Presence as you breathe in air.

Tell the world—that for one who walks a cheerless road with Me, the bare hedge doth blossom as the rose, and life is bathed in sunlit joy.

God Calling: Love Your Servants

Love, love, love. Tender Love is the secret. Love those you are training, love those who work with you, love those who serve you.

Dwell on that thought—God is Love. Link it up with My "I and My Father are one." Dwell on My actions on Earth. See in them Love in operation.

If it was God who so acted, then it was Love, Perfect Love performed those actions, those wonders. Then you, too, must put Love (God) into action in your lives. Perfect Love means perfect forgiveness. Lo, My children, you see that where God is there can be no lack of forgiveness, for that is really lack of love.

> God is Love. . .no judging.
> God is Love. . .no resentment.
> God is Love. . .all patience.
> God is Love. . .all power.
> God is Love. . .all supply.

All you need to have is love to God and man. Love to God ensures obedience to every wish, every command. Love is the fulfilling of all law.

Pray much for love.

God at Eventide: Regain Dominion

Let them have dominion.

Man has lost this dominion because he failed to be guided by My Spirit. He was never meant to function alone. Body, mind, and spirit, he was created by My Father.

The senses were given him to link him to earth, and to create and maintain contact with the world around; but the spirit was definitely his link for guidance and instruction from the world of My Kingdom.

He is a lost soul until he links up in this way, just as a man blind, deaf and dumb would be in a world of sense. This was man's fall. He had this power and lost it.

APRIL 17

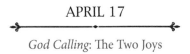

God Calling: The Two Joys

My children, I come. Hearts eager to do My Will, send out a call that ever I find irresistible. I know no barrier then.

Resignation to My Will keeps Me barred out from more hearts than does unbelief. Can anything be such a crime against Love as being resigned? My Will should be welcomed with a glad wonder if I am to do My Work in the heart and life.

In all true discipleship, and in the true spiritual development of each disciple, there is first the wonder and the joy of first acquaintance; then comes the long plain stretch of lesson-learning and discipline.

But the constant experience of Me, the constant persistent recognition of My Work in daily happenings, the numberless instances in which seeming chance or wonderful coincidence can be, must be, traced back to My loving forethought—all these gradually engender a feeling of wonder, certainty, gratitude followed in time by Joy.

Joy is of two kinds. The Joy born of Love and Wonder, and the Joy born of Love and Knowledge, and between the experience of the two Joys lie discipline, disappointment, almost disillusion.

But combat these in My Strength, persevere in obeying My Will, accept My Discipline, and the second Joy will follow.

And of this second Joy it was that I said, "Your joy no man taketh from you."

Do not regret the first, the second is the greater gift.

God at Eventide: New Beauties

Life has so many lessons to teach you. You may not be able to travel through your material world. But for your spirit there are vast and beautiful realms in which you can be ever traveling and exploring; and, with ever-increasing capacity for enjoyment, discovering new beauties of Spiritual Truth.

APRIL 18

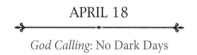

God Calling: No Dark Days

Such light, such joy flows out from this house. It affects all who come here.

Do not feel that you have to try and help them. Just love them, welcome them, shower little courtesies and love-signs on them, and they must be helped.

Love is God. Give them Love, and you give them God. Then leave Him to do His Work. Love all, even the beggars. Send no one away without a word of cheer, a feeling that you care. I may have put the impulse to come here into some despairing one's heart. Think if you failed Me!

Besides, you have no choice. You told Me it was My Home. I shall use it. Remember this: There would be no dark winter days were Love in the hearts of all My children.

Oh! My children, can you not feel the joy of knowing, loving, and companying with Me?

Life is a journey. The choice as to who shall be your conductor is your own. Once that choice is made and you feel you have placed yourself in wise Hands, do not spoil your journey by frustrating the plans made for your comfort and happiness.

Rest content with the plans I have made for you. No detail has been too small for My loving consideration. Know that your lives are being truly God-conducted, and so will bring you the greatest happiness and success.

The greater the trust you repose in Me the wider will be My scope for the plans I have made for you.

Life is a mosaic planned by God. Each God-directed thought, impulse, and action of yours is necessary to the carrying out of the perfect design.

That design is of exquisite workmanship.

APRIL 19

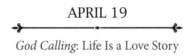

God Calling: Life Is a Love Story

You need Me. I need you. My broken world needs you. Many a weary troubled heart needs you. Many a troubled heart will be gladdened by you, drawn nearer to Me by you both.

Health—Peace—Joy—Patience—Endurance, they all come from contact with Me.

Oh! it is a glorious way, the upward way, the wonderful discoveries, the tender intimacies, the amazing, almost incomprehensible, understanding. Truly the Christian Life—Life with Me—is a Love story. Leave all to Me.

All you have missed you will find in Me, the Soul's Lover, the Soul's Friend, Father—Mother—Comrade—Brother. Try Me.

You cannot make too many demands upon Me—nor put too great a strain upon My Love and Forbearance.

Claim—claim—claim—Healing—Power—Joy—Supply what you will.

Live in My Love.

Return to Me ever for refilling, that your soul may breathe in and breathe out Love as your lungs breathe in and breathe out air.

There is nothing in you that creates Love, so how can you give it out unless you are receiving it?

All service, to be truly effective and of permanent value, must be wrought in Love. Where Love is, self cannot hold sway, and self nullifies the good in service.

See Me and My thought of you in all your daily life; so, conscious of My Love, you will absorb that Love until it permeates your whole being, and inspires and illumines all you do and say.

APRIL 20

God Calling: Heart's Agony

There is a Calvary-Cross on which One hangs alone, untended by even the nearest and dearest.

But beside that Cross, there stands another, and to My dear ones I say little, I hang there afresh beside each one through the hours of the heart's agony.

Have you ever thought of the Joy that the patient, gentle, loving obedience of My disciples brings to My heart? I know no Joy such as the Joy I feel at the loving trust of a dear one.

The wounds in the Hands and Feet hurt little compared with the wounds in the Heart that are the wounds, not of My enemies, but of My friends.

Little doubts, little fears, little misunderstandings. It is the tender trifles of a day that gladden My Heart. I that speak unto you, am He—your Master.

God at Eventide: The Joyous War

Live much a life apart with Me. In the world but not of it. You can do this even in a crowd, provided self does not intrude.

It is a sign of progress that you cannot be indulging thoughts of self and then turn to Me in complete self-forgetfulness.

Your life must be one of intense service and consecration. Your fight is not so much an active one in the world, as one of active warfare on the unseen plane. A war truly against principalities and powers. Nevertheless a joyous war.

APRIL 21

God Calling: You Will Conquer

You will conquer. Do not fear changes. You can never fear changes when I, your Lord, change not. Jesus Christ, the same yesterday, today, and forever. I am beside you. Steadfastness, unchangingness, come to you, too, as you dwell with Me. Rest in Me.

As breathing rightly, from being a matter of careful practice, becomes a habit, unconsciously, yet rightly performed, so if you regularly practice this getting back into My Presence, when the slightest feeling of unrest disturbs your perfect calm and harmony, so this, too, will become a habit, and you will grow to live in that perfect consciousness of My Presence, and perfect calm and harmony will be yours.

Life is a training school. Remember, only the pupil giving great promise of future good work would be so singled out by the Master for strenuous and unwearied discipline, teaching and training.

You are asking both of you to be not as hundreds of My followers, nay as many, many thousands, but to be even as those who reflect Me in all they say and do and are. So, My dear children, take this training, not as harsh, but as the tender loving answer to your petition.

Life can never be the same again for either of you. Once you have drunk of the wine of My giving, the Life Eternal, all Earth's attempts to quench your thirst will fail.

God at Eventide: "How Oft in the Conflict"

Lord, bid me come to Thee upon the waters.

"Come."

All that I did when on earth I do today in the Spirit-realm.

My servant Paul realized this Truth when he spoke of Me as the same yesterday, today, and forever.

When the faintest fear of all that lies before you disturbs you, when you are conscious of the loss of Spirit-buoyancy, then you are looking at the waves and feeling the wind is contrary.

Then you cry, "Lord, save me, I perish."

And My Hand will be outstretched to save you, as it saved My fearful, doubting Peter.

APRIL 22

God Calling: Complain Not—Laugh

Trust in Me. Do as I say each moment and all indeed shall be well. Follow out My commands: Divine control, unquestioning obedience—these are the only conditions of supply being ample for your own needs and those of others.

The tasks I set you may have seemingly no connection with supply. The commands are Mine and the supply is Mine and I make My own conditions, differing in each case—but in the case of each disciple, adapted to the individual need.

Have no fear, go forward. Joy—radiant Joy must be yours. Change all disappointment, even if only momentary, into Joy. Change each complaint into laughter.

Rest—Love—Joy—Peace—Work, and the most powerful of these are Love and Joy.

God at Eventide: Light Comes

"Lord, show me Thyself" is a cry that never goes unanswered.

Not to physical vision comes the awareness, but to spiritual insight, as more and more you realize My Love, My Power and the manifold wonders of My character.

Its Humility, its Majesty, its Tenderness, its Sternness, its Justice, its Mercy, its Healing of sore wounds, and its consuming Fire.

Man turns to books, he studies theology, he seeks from other men the answer to life's riddles, but he does not come to Me.

Is there a problem?

Do not worry over its solution.

Seek Me. Live with Me. Talk to Me. Company with Me, daily, hourly. Lo, suddenly you see.

God Calling: Too Much Talk

Guidance you are bound to have as you live more and more with Me. It follows without doubt.

But *these* times are not times when you ask to be shown and led; they are times of feeling and realizing My Presence. Does the branch continually ask the Vine to supply it with sap, to show it in what direction to grow? No, that comes naturally from the very union with the Vine, and I said, "I am the vine, ye are the branches."

From the branches hang the choice grapes, given joy and nourishment to all, but no branch could think that the fruit, the grapes, were of *its* shaping and making.

No! the grapes are the fruit of the Vine, the Parent-Plant. The work of the branch is to provide a channel for the life-flow.

So, My children, union with Me is the one great overwhelming necessity. All else follows so naturally, and union with Me may be the result of just consciousness of My Presence. Be not too ready to speak to others.

Pray always that the need may be apparent, if you are to do this, and the guidance very plain. My Spirit has been driven out by the words of men.

Discourage too much talk. Deeds live and re-echo down the ages—words perish. As Paul: "Though I speak with the tongues of men and of angels, and have not charity, I am become as sounding brass, or a tinkling cymbal. And though I have the gift of prophecy. . .and have not charity, I am nothing. . . ."

Remember that rarely to the human heart do I speak in words. Man will see Me in My Works done through you.

Lord, Thy Word abideth and our footsteps guideth.

Treasure My Words in your heart. They will meet your need today as surely as they met the needs of those to whom I spoke them when I was on earth for they were not spoken in time but in Eternity.

If My gift to man is Eternal Life, then the words inspired by that Life are eternal, appropriate to your needs today as they were then.

But the words and the guidance are not for all. They are for those who ACCEPT MY great gift of Eternal Life.

"And this is Life Eternal, that they might know Thee the only true God, and Jesus Christ, Whom Thou hast sent."

APRIL 24

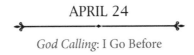

God Calling: I Go Before

You can never perish, My children, because within you is the Life of Life. The Life that down the ages has kept My servants, in peril, in adversity, in sorrow.

Once you are born of the Spirit, *that* is your Life's breath. You must never doubt, never worry, but step by step, the way to freedom must be trodden. See that you walk it with Me.

This means no worry, no anxiety, but it does *not* mean no effort. When My disciples told Me that they had toiled all night and taken nothing, I did not fill the boat with fishes without effort on their part. No! My command stood. "Launch out into the deep, and let down your nets for a draught."

Their lives were endangered, the ship nearly sank, the help of their fellows had to be summoned, and there were broken nets to mend. Any one of these troubles might have made them feel My help was not for them. And yet as they sat on the shore and mended those nets, they would see My Love and Care.

The man who reaches the mountain height by the help of train or car has learned no climber's lesson. But remember this does not mean no Guide—this does not mean that My Spirit is not supplying wisdom and strength. How often, when sometimes you little know it, do I go before you to prepare the way, to soften a heart here, to overrule there.

God at Eventide: "Lord, Use Me, I Beseech Thee"

I will use you as you eliminate self and offer Me a consecrated personality, made in My Image.

There can be no limit to My Power to use one such. Nothing is impossible to Me. My Love is limitless, My Tenderness is limitless, My Understanding is limitless.

Every attribute of the Godhead is complete, inexhaustible in a way you can only dimly see.

APRIL 25

God Calling: Bless Your Enemies

Say often, "God bless. . ." of any whom you find in disharmony with you, or whom you desire to help. Say it, willing that showers of Blessings and Joy and Success may fall upon them.

Leave to Me the necessary correcting or training; *you* must only desire Joy and Blessing for them. At present your prayers are that they should be taught and corrected.

Oh! if My children would leave My Work to Me and occupy themselves with the task I give them. Love, love, love. Love will break down all your difficulties. Love will build up all your successes.

God the Destroyer of evil, God the Creator of good—is

Love. To Love one another is to use God in your life. To use God in your life is to bring into manifestation all Harmony, Beauty, Joy, and Happiness.

God at Eventide: Your Limitations

The words I give you mark steps in Spiritual Progress.

There can be no limit to the Spirit Power you may possess as self is turned out and My Will welcomed.

But to those who yield themselves wholly to Me there are limitations as far as the material is concerned, as only what will assist Spiritual growth or manifestation is for these. Yet all your needs will be supplied.

APRIL 26

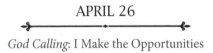

God Calling: I Make the Opportunities

Never doubt. Have no fear. Watch the faintest tremor of fear, and stop all work, everything, and rest before Me until you are joyful and strong again.

Deal in the same way with all tired feelings. I was weary too, when on earth, and I separated Myself from My disciples and sat and rested on the well. Rested—and then it was that the Samaritan woman was helped.

I had to teach renewal of Spirit—force rest of body to My disciples. Then, as your Example, I lay with My Head on a pillow, asleep in the boat. It was not, as they thought, indifference. They cried, "Master, carest thou not that we perish?" and I had to teach them that ceaseless activity was no part of My Father's plan.

When Paul said, "I can do all things through Christ which strengtheneth me," he did not mean that he was to do all things and then rely on Me to find strength. He meant that for all I told him to do, he could rely on My supplying the strength.

My Work in the world has been hindered by work, work, work. Many a tireless, nervous body has driven a spirit. The spirit should be the master always and just simply and naturally use the body as need should arise. Rest in Me.

Do not *seek* to work for Me. Never make opportunities. Live with Me and for Me. I do the work and I make the opportunities.

God at Eventide: Vain Toil

Master, we have toiled all night and have taken nothing.

There will be nights of wearied anguish, when you toil and catch nothing.

There will be mornings of rapture when the result of your prayers and longings will be so great as to bring you to your knees with a humility born of a wonder of fulfillment— "the nets break."

Share the loneliness with Me—the weariness, the dreariness, all with Me, as I share all with you.

APRIL 27

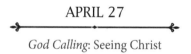

God Calling: Seeing Christ

I am beside you. Can you not feel My Presence? Contact with Me is not gained by the senses. Spirit-consciousness replaces sight.

When man sees Me with his human sight, it does not mean of necessity that his spiritual perception is greater. *Nay, rather that for that soul I have to span the physical and the spiritual with a spiritual vision clear to human eyes.*

131

Remember this to cheer My disciples who have never seen Me, and yet have had a clear spiritual consciousness of Me.

God at Eventide: Welcome Them

More and more I shall send into your life those whom you shall help. Have no fear. Do not doubt your wisdom to deal with them. It is My Wisdom that will help them, not any wisdom of yours.

Shower Love on all. Nothing will be too much that you can do for others. Delight in My Word, in My Love.

As you grow more conscious of that Love you will feel more and more the responsibility laid upon you to make that Great Love of My aching Heart known to those for whom I died, and for whom I ever live to make intercession.

APRIL 28

God Calling: The Roundabout Way

Through briars, through waste places, through glades, up mountain heights, down into valleys, I lead. But ever with the Leadership goes the Helping Hand.

Glorious to follow where your Master goes. But remember that the varied path does not always mean that *you* need the varied training.

We are seeking lost sheep—we are bringing the Kingdom into places where it has not been known before. So realize that you are joining Me on My quest—My undying quest, tracking down souls.

I am not choosing ways that will fret and tire—just to fret and tire; we are out to save. *You* may not always see the soul we seek. I know.

My child, you are tired with the burden and heat of the day.

Stay awhile and know that I abide with you, and know that I speak Peace unto your soul.

Dread nothing, fear nothing. Know that all is well. The day is far spent. The toil has been long, but evening rest with Me is sweet.

The gathering gloom of night will be to your heart but the *overshadowing wings* of the Eternal God.

Deep in your heart you feel the striving of wonderful Truths. Faint sense of the Glory to be revealed.

APRIL 29

God Calling: Disharmony

Seek and ye shall find. Shall find that inner knowledge that makes the problems of life plain.

The difficulties of life are caused by disharmony in the individual. There is no discord in My Kingdom, only a something unconquered in My disciples. The rule of My Kingdom is perfect order, perfect harmony, perfect supply, perfect love, perfect honesty, perfect obedience—all power, all conquest, all success.

But so often My servants lack power, conquest, success, supply, harmony, and think I fail in My promises because these are not manifested in their lives.

These are but the outward manifestations that result from the obedience, honesty, order, love—and they come, not in answer to urgent prayer, but naturally as light results from a lighted candle.

My child, wait before Me.

You may receive no message, but in this waiting time, even if you are not conscious of being taught, you are being changed.

The eye of your soul will be focused upon Me and the insight gained will be calming, remedial, strengthening.

APRIL 30

God Calling: Springtime

Rejoice in the Springtime of the year. Let there be Springtime in your hearts. The full time of fruit is not yet, but there is the promise of the blossom.

Know surely that your lives too are full of glad promise. Such blessings are to be yours. Such joys, such wonders.

All is indeed well. Live in My Sunshine and My Love.

God at Eventide: My First Missionary

My denunciations were for the self-satisfied.

For the sinner, who felt his failure and weakness, I had the tenderest pity. "Go, and sin no more," was My Word to the woman taken in adultery.

But what a Word of hope that was, revealing as it did the assurance that I trusted her not to fall into sin again. That I deemed her capable of a new life.

The Samaritan woman at Sychar's well I trusted with a secret that even My disciples had not shared fully with Me. She was one of My first missionaries.

I recognized the wealth of love in the offering of the woman who was a sinner. There was no public denunciation of her sin, no repulse of her love.

"Holy Father, cheer our way
With Thy love's perpetual ray;
Grant us every closing day,
Light at evening time."

MAY 1

God Calling: Delay Is Not Denial

Read the lessons of Divine control in Nature's laws. Nature is but the expression of Eternal Thought in Time. Study the outward form—grasp the Eternal Thought, and if you can read the thoughts of the Father, then indeed you know Him.

Leave Me out of nothing. Love all My ways with you. Know indeed that "All is well." Delay is but the wonderful and all-loving restraint of your Father—not reluctance, not desire to deny—but the Divine control of a Father who can scarcely brook the delay.

Delay has to be—sometimes. Your lives are so linked up with those of others, so bound by circumstances that to let your desire have instant fulfillment might in many cases cause another, as earnest prayer, to go unanswered.

But think for a moment of the Love and thoughtful care that seek to harmonize and reconcile all your desires and longings and prayers.

Delay is not denial—not even withholding. It is the opportunity for God to work out your problems and accomplish your desires in the most wonderful way possible for you.

Oh! children, trust Me. Remember that your Maker is also your Servant, quick to fulfill, quick to achieve, faithful in accomplishment. Yes. All is well.

Not what you can gain in any situation, but what you can give must be your question. You follow Me, of Whom it was said, "Even Christ pleased not Himself." So love, so help, so serve.

Seek the weak and wandering. Care for all.

Realize My overflowing and overwhelming Bounty. The stores of the Lord are inexhaustible. But to test and prove My generosity fully you must be generous.

My lovers give with no niggard hands. A heart overflowing with gratitude for what it has received expends joyous gratitude in giving.

MAY 2

God Calling: Souls That Smile

To conquer adverse circumstances, conquer yourselves. The answer to the desire of My disciples to follow Me was "Be ye therefore perfect, even as your Father which is in heaven is perfect."

To accomplish much, be much. In all cases the *doing*, to be well-doing, must be the mere unconscious expression of the *being*.

Fear not, fear not, all is well. Let the day be full of little prayers to Me, little turnings toward Me. The smiles of the soul at one it loves.

Men call the Father the First Cause. Yes! See Him as the First Cause of every warm ray, every color in the sunset, every gleam on the water, every beautiful flower, every planned pleasure.

Peace I leave with you, My Peace give I unto you.

I knew that only in Peace could My work be done. Only in Peace could My followers help souls to Me. At all costs keep that Peace. If your heart-peace is unruffled, then every thought is a mighty force for ME. Then every act is one of power.

Rely on My leading. Nothing is impossible to Me.

Unlimited expectancy yours. Unlimited power Mine.

MAY 3

God Calling: Kill Self Now

Self dethroned—that is the lesson, but in its place put Love for Me, knowledge of Me.

Self, not only dethroned, but dead. A dead self is not an imprisoned self. An imprisoned self is more potent to harm. In all training—(in Mine of you, and in yours of others)—let self die.

But for each blow to the life of self you must at the same time embrace and hold fast the new Life, Life with Me.

And now I can make more clear to you what I would say about forgiveness of injuries. It is one of My commands that as you seek My forgiveness, so you must forgive.

But what you do not see is that you, the self in you, can never forgive injuries. The very thought of them means self in the foreground, then the injury, instead of appearing less, appears greater.

No, My children, as all true Love is *of* God, and is God, so all true forgiveness is of God and is God. The self cannot forgive. Kill self.

Cease trying to forgive those who fretted or wronged

you. It is a mistake to think about it. Aim at killing the self now—in your daily life, and then, and not until then, you will find there is nothing that even remembers injury, because the only one injured, the self, is dead.

As long as it recurs to your mind, you deceive yourself if you think it forgiven.

God at Eventide: Useless Activity

Preparation-time is so neglected by My followers. Consequently there is lack of power in work for Me.

To alter the laws of a country is no real remedy for ill. Men's hearts must be altered by contact with Me.

Remember the lessons I have taught you about useless activity. When most work cries out to be done, then it is truly the time—not to rush, but to Commune with Me and My Father.

Never feel strong in yourself. Know that only in My Strength can you accomplish all. No mountain of difficulty can then be insurmountable or immovable.

MAY 4

God Calling: Share with Me

Delight in My Love. Try to live in the rapture of the Kingdom. Claim big things. Claim great things. Claim Joy and Peace and freedom from care. Joy in Me.

I am your Lord, your Creator. Remember too that I am the same yesterday, today, and forever. Your Creator, when My thought about the world called it into being—your Creator as much, too, today, when I can, by loving thought for you, call into being all you need on the material plane.

Joy in Me, trust in Me, share all life with Me, see Me in

everything, rejoice in Me. Share all with Me as a child shares its pains and cuts and griefs and newfound treasures and joys and little work with its Mother.

And give Me the joy of sharing all with you.

God at Eventide: The Acceptable Gift

Rest in My Love. Abide in Me.

Leave all to follow Me—your pride, your self-sufficiency, your fears of what others may think—All.

Have no fear. Go forth into the unknown with Me, fearful of nothing with so sure a convoy.

Just as a flower, given as an offering to a loved one, so is your tribute of love to Me.

As Mary gave her Love-offering, spikenard very precious, so give to Me your love and understanding.

MAY 5

God Calling: Let Me Choose

My loved ones. Yes, with the heart, not the head, men should think of Me, and then worship would be instinctive.

Breathe in My very Spirit in pure air and fervent desire.

Keep the eye of your spirit ever upon Me, the window of your soul open toward Me. You have ever to know that all things are yours—that what is lovely I delight to give you.

Empty your mind of all that limits. Whatever is beautiful you can have. Leave more and more the choice to Me. You will have no regrets.

"Savior, let me be a channel for Thy Mighty Power."

First you must be kept by that Mighty Power.

For it must be a consecrated life to be so used.

My Power passing through wrong channels would work harm. It could not be.

The alloy of the channel would poison the Spirit-flood.

MAY 6

God Calling: Sublime Audacity

The way is long and weary. It is a weary world. So many today are weary. "Come untoMe. . .and I will give you rest."

My children, who range yourselves under My flag, you must see that on it are inscribed those words "The Son of Man."

Whatever the world is feeling, I must feel, I—the Son of Man. You are My followers—so the weariness of man today must be shared by you—the weary and heavy-laden must come to *you* and find that rest that you found in Me.

My children, My followers must be prepared not to sit on My right hand and on My left, but to drink of the cup that I drink of.

Poor world—teach it that there is only one cure for all its ills—Union with Me. Dare to suffer, dare to conquer, be filled with My sublime audacity. Remember that. Claim the unclaimable.

Just what the world would think impossible can always be yours. Remember, My children, sublime audacity.

God at Eventide: The Fertile Glade

Seek and you shall find.

As a mother hiding from her child puts herself in the way of being found, so with Me. So the finding of Me and of the treasures of My Kingdom may not always depend upon ardent intent securing attainment, but upon the mere setting out on the quest.

Is this a comfort to you?

When you set out upon a time of seeking I place Myself in your way, and the sometime arid path of prayer becomes a fertile glade in which you are surprised to find your search so soon over. Thus mutual Joy.

MAY 7

God Calling: Against the Tide

The oarsman, trusting in Me, does not lean on his oars and drift with the tide, trusting to the current.

Nay, more often—once I have shown the way—it is against the tide you must direct all your effort. And even when difficulties come, it is by your effort that they will be surmounted. But always strength and the Joy in the doing you can have through Me.

My fishermen-disciples did not find the fishes ready on the shore in their nets. I take man's effort and bless that. I need man's effort—he needs My blessing. This partnership it is that means success.

God at Eventide: Clouds and Rain

See My goodness in the clouds and rain, as well as in the

sunshine of life. Both express so wonderfully the goodness and love of your Lord.

Just as the shady glade, the cool riverside, the mountain-top, the blazing highway, all meet the varying needs of man.

MAY 8

God Calling: The Rest of God

I lead you. The way is clear. Go forward unafraid. I am beside you. Listen, listen, listen to My Voice. My Hand is controlling all.

Remember that I can work through you better when you are at rest. Go very slowly, very quietly from one duty to the next—taking time to rest and pray between.

Do not be too busy. Take all in order as I say. The Rest of God is in a realm beyond all man's activities. Venture there often, and you will indeed find Peace and Joy.

All work that results from resting with God is miracle-work. Claim the power to work miracles, both of you.

Know that you can do all things through Christ who strengthens you. Nay, more, know that you can do all things through Christ who rests you.

God at Eventide: The Dross and the Gold

Share your Joy with Me.

Tell Me of all that gladdens you throughout your day. I am near to hear. Feel that I alone share to the full your heart-thrills, because with Me no success of yours engenders regret nor is tinged with envy.

Is it not My Joy, My success, accomplished only in and through Me?

Share all with me. The disappointment, not only in others but all too poignantly in yourself. Share your backward step as well as one of progress.

Bring all to Me, and together, in tender Love, we can sift the dross from the gold.

Come back to Me, ever sure of a welcome, ever glad to feel My Presence in and round you.

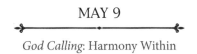

MAY 9

God Calling: Harmony Within

Follow My Guidance. Be afraid to venture on your own as a child fears to leave its mother's side. Doubt of your own wisdom, and reliance on Mine, will teach you humility.

Humility is not the belittling of the self. It is forgetting the self. Nay more, forgetting the self, because you are remembering Me.

You must not expect to live in a world where all is harmony. You must not expect to live where others are in unbroken accord with you. It is your task to maintain your own heart peace in adverse circumstances. Harmony is always yours when you strain your ear to catch Heaven's music.

Doubt always your power or wisdom to put things right; ask Me to right all as you leave it to Me, and go on your way loving and laughing. I am Wisdom. Only My Wisdom can rightly decide anything—settle any problem. So rely on Me. All is well.

God at Eventide: Call Me Often

Speak My Name often during the day. It has the power to banish evil, and to summon Good.

Jesus.

In Me dwelleth all the fullness of the Godhead, so that when you call Me you call to your aid all there is of Good to need.

143

MAY 10

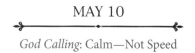

God Calling: Calm—Not Speed

*For thus saith the Lord God, the Holy One of Israel;
In returning and rest shall ye be saved; in quietness and
in confidence shall be your strength: and ye would not.*
ISAIAH 30:15

All agitation is destructive of good. All calm is constructive of good and at the same time destructive of evil.

When man wants evil destroyed, so often he rushes to action. It is wrong. First be still and know that I am God. Then act only as I tell you. Always calm with God. Calm is trust in action. Only trust, perfect trust can keep one calm.

Never be afraid of any circumstances or difficulties that help you to cultivate this calm. As the world, to attain, has to learn speed, you, to attain, have to learn calm. All great work for Me is done first in the individual soul of the worker.

God at Eventide: Talk to Me

Talk to Me about the world's misunderstanding of Me. Tell Me that your Love will seek to comfort Me for that. Tell Me your life shall be devoted to bringing about an understanding between Me and those you meet who love Me not.

As one who knows a prisoner has been wrongly convicted devotes a lifetime to the vindication of that loved one's name, and counts all the trials and troubles, misunderstandings, and hardships encountered in so doing as nothing, so that his object is accomplished—let it be thus with you, longing to make Me known.

God Calling: The Divine Third

When I have led you through these storms, there will be other words for you, other messages—other guidance.

So deep is your friendship and so great your desire to love and follow and serve Me that soon, when this time of difficulty is over, to be alone together will always mean to be shut in with Me.

There are few friendships in the world like that, and yet I taught, when on Earth, as I have taught you both, the power of the *two together*.

And now tonight I have more to say to you. I say that the time is coming, is even now here, when those who visit you two together will know that I am the Divine Third in your friendship.

God at Eventide: Bigger Demands

As your faith in Me grows and your sphere of influence extends, your claims will be the greater. Yet no real need of yours shall go unsatisfied.

You will make bigger demands, and ever more and more you will be trusting Me to supply the little wants. This trust will come as you realize My power more and more, and feel My Love and know its tender watchfulness in every detail of your daily life.

"Rejoice, again I say, Rejoice."

With a loved human friend a big gift may be prized as proof of a big love, but great devotion is displayed even more in the anticipation of the little wants, in the solicitude shown in little ways.

Delight in My Love, so shown.

God Calling: Thrill of Protection

Turn out all thoughts of doubt and of trouble. Never tolerate them for one second. Bar the windows and doors of your souls against them as you would bar your home against a thief who would steal in to take your treasures.

What greater treasures can you have than Peace and Rest and Joy? And these are all stolen from you by doubt and fear and despair.

Face each day with Love and Laughter. Face the storm.

Joy, Peace, Love, My great gifts. Follow Me to find all three. I want you to feel the thrill of protection and safety now. Any soul can feel this in a harbor, but real joy and victory come to those alone who sense these when they ride a storm.

Say, "All is well." Say it not as a vain repetition. Use it as you use a healing balm for cut or wound, until the poison is drawn out; *then*, until the sore is healed; *then*, until the thrill of fresh life floods your being.

All is well.

God at Eventide: Lord of Joy

The Unspeakable Joy offered Himself for joyful recognition.

This is a further stage of development.

You enter upon it when you realize that I was the expression in time of the Joy of all Eternity. That joy I offered to all who would see in My way the path of Joy, and who would hail Me not only as the Man of Sorrows but as the Lord of Joy.

This truth becomes known to those only who give joyful recognition to this all-amazing, all-sustaining, all-revealing *joy*.

God Calling: Never Judge

What Joy follows self-conquest! You cannot conquer and control others, either of you, until you have completely conquered yourself.

Can you see yourselves absolutely unmoved? Think of Me before the mocking soldiers, being struck, spat upon, and answering never a word—*never a word*. Try to see that as Divine Power. Remember by that Power of perfect silence, perfect self-control, you can alone prove your right to govern.

Never judge. The heart of man is so delicate, so complex, only its Maker can know it. Each heart is so different, actuated by different motives, controlled by different circumstances, influenced by different sufferings.

How can one judge another? Leave to Me the unraveling of the puzzles of life. Leave to Me the teaching of understanding. Bring each heart to Me, its Maker, and leave it with Me. Secure in the certainty that all that is wrong I can set right.

God at Eventide: Highways and Byways

The way of Holiness differs for each of My followers as the character of each differs. My command for you is not necessarily My command for another.

My followers often forget this. Because I may have told them to take a certain road they are sure that you should be walking in the same way.

Heed them not. Remember, too, that a way of discipline for you may not be My will for another.

God Calling: The Love of a Lover

Remember that a loving Master delights in the intimacy of demands made, as much as He desires His followers and friends to delight in the tender intimacy of *His* demands.

Only as the result of frequent converse with Me, of much prayer to Me, of listening to and obedience to My behests comes that intimacy that makes My followers dare to approach Me as friend to friend.

Yield in all things to My tender insistence but remember I yield too to yours. Ask not only the big things I have told you, but ask the little tender signs of Love. Remember that I came as the world's Great Lover. Never think of My Love as only a tender compassion and forgiveness. It is that, but it is also the Love of a Lover, who shows His Love by countless words and actions and by tender thought.

In each of you, too, remember there is God. It is always given to man to see in his fellow man those aspirations and qualities he himself possesses. So only I, being really God, can recognize the God in man. Remember this, too, in your relation to others.

Your motives and aspirations can only be understood by those who have attained the same spiritual level. So do not vainly, foolishly, expect from others understanding. Do not misjudge them for not giving it. Yours is a foreign language to them.

God at Eventide: You Have Been Warned

Fasting is the starving out of self. It may not always be by food-abstinence. But it is an absolute essential of progress in the life with Me.

There is no standing still in the Christian life. If there is not progress there is retrogression.

I redeemed you. Bought you back from slavery to sin, of whatever kind.

So, when weakness overcomes you, and you yield to temptation, you make of My Redemption a mockery.

MAY 15

God Calling: First the Spiritual

What can I say to you? Your heart is torn. Then remember "He bindeth up the broken hearts." Just feel the tenderness of My Hands as I bind up your wounds.

You are very privileged, both of you. I share My plans and secrets with you and make known to you My Purposes, while so many have to grope on.

Try to rest on these words. "Seek ye first the kingdom of God, and his righteousness; and all these things shall be added unto you." Then strive not for *them* but, untiringly, for the things of My Kingdom.

It is so strange to you mortals, you would think the material things first and then grow into the knowledge of Spiritual things. Not so in My Kingdom. It is Spiritual things first and then material. So to attain the material redouble your efforts to acquire the Spiritual.

God at Eventide: Grasp This Truth

Too many hinder their work for Me by seeking to justify themselves. You are fighting for Christ the King, not for yourself. The explaining or justifying must be for Me.

In any difficulty with another put yourself in his place and pray that his difficulty may be solved for him.

This will bring about a solution of yours, and help you to see better that for which you should pray.

The power to realize the needs of those you contact can only be acquired by absorbing sympathy and understanding from My Life. So, time for knowing Me must be increasingly dear and necessary to you.

Your task is to show the Power of My Spirit working through a life of yielded will, and the Joy that transforms the life when this is so.

MAY 16

God Calling: Pray and Praise

I will be much entreated because I know that only in that earnest supplication, and the calm trust that results, does man learn strength and gain peace. Therefore I have laid that incessant, persistent pleading as a duty upon My disciples.

Never weary in prayer. When one day man sees how marvelously his prayer has been answered, then he will deeply, so deeply, regret that he prayed so little.

Prayer changes all. Prayer re-creates. Prayer is irresistible. So pray, literally without ceasing.

Pray until you almost cease to pray, because trust has become so rocklike, and then pray on because it has become so much a habit that you cannot resist it.

And always pray until Prayer merges into Praise. That is the only note on which true prayer should end. It is the Love and Laughter of your attitude toward man interpreted in the Prayer and Praise of your attitude toward God.

We would see Jesus.

This is still the cry of a hungry, dissatisfied, seeking world.

I look to My followers to satisfy that cry.

Reflect Me, that the seekers may see Me in you, and then go on to company with Me.

Rejoice at this as John rejoiced when he could point his disciples to Me with the brave and humble words, "He must increase, and I must decrease."

Go on in Faith and Joy and Love.

MAY 17

God Calling: Sorrow to Joy

Weeping may endure for a night, but joy cometh in the morning."

My bravest are those who can anticipate the morning and feel in the night of sorrow that underlying Joy that tells of confident expectations of the morning.

God at Eventide: My Messenger Goes Before

When you think of Me as your Rescuer, remember it is not only from sin, depression or despair.

It is from the difficulties of life also and from perplexity as to your path. I solve your problems. I provide the channel through which help will come.

I send My messenger to prepare your way before you. I train you so that you may be fitted for your next task, so that you may be worthy of My promised blessing. That blessing which I long to shower on you.

MAY 18

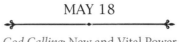

God Calling: New and Vital Power

Look unto Me, and be ye saved, all the ends of the earth." Not for merit was salvation; the promise was to all who looked.

To look is surely within the Power of everyone. One look suffices. Salvation follows.

Look and you are saved from despair. Look and you are saved from care. Look and you are saved from worry. Look, and into you there flows a Peace beyond all understanding, a Power new and vital, a Joy wonderful indeed.

Look and keep looking. Doubt flees, Joy reigns, and Hope conquers.

Life, Eternal Life, is yours—revitalizing, renewing.

God at Eventide: The Healing Light

Wherever My followers go, *there* should be My Light surrounding them. The Light of the Sun of Righteousness.

Evil cannot live in that Light.

Man is only just learning that light banishes disease.

Every follower of Mine who is in close personal touch with Me is surrounded by this Light. Light Eternal. Light reflected by a consciousness of My Presence.

So whether he speak or not he must be the means of diffusing My Light wherever he goes.

God Calling: Rescued and Guided

Rest knowing all is so safe in My Hands. Rest is Trust. Ceaseless activity is distrust. Without the knowledge that I am working for you, you do not rest. Inaction then would be the outcome of despair.

Welcome the knowledge, delight in it. Such a truth is as a hope flung to a drowning man. Every repetition of it is one pull nearer shore and safety.

Let that illustration teach you a great truth. Lay hold of the Truth, pray it, affirm it, hold on to the rope. How foolish are your attempts to save yourself, one hand on the rope and one making efforts to swim ashore! You may relinquish your hold of the rope and hinder the Rescuer—who has to act with the greater caution lest he lose you.

The storms and tempests are not all of life. The Psalmist who said, "All thy waves and thy billows are gone over me," wrote also, "He brought me up also out of an horrible pit, out of the miry clay, and set my feet upon a rock, and established my goings."

Meditate upon that wonder—Truth, the three steps safety, security, guidance. (1) "He brought me up also out of an horrible pit"—*Safety*. (2) "He set my feet upon a rock"—*Security*. (3) "He established my goings"—*Guidance*. Number three is the final stage when the saved soul trusts Me so entirely it seeks no more its own way but leaves all future plans to Me its Rescuer.

God at Eventide: The Ordered Life

You cannot be doing My work well and wielding a worthy influence unless all your life is ordered.

Let that be your aim and your achievement.

Secure this order and you will be able to do so much more in My service, and, without haste or unrest, reflect more the order and beauty of My Kingdom.

You need this discipline in your life.

Peace is the result of an ordered life lived with Me.

Prepare yourself for each task, for each occasion. Pray for those you will contact, your time with them.

This will save discord, and will enable the work and planning, in which you cooperate with them, to be fruitful for good.

MAY 20

God Calling: Win Me—Win All

You will conquer. The conquering spirit is never crushed. Keep a brave and trusting heart. Face all your difficulties in the spirit of Conquest.

Rise to greater heights than you have known before. Remember where I am is Victory. Forces of evil, within and without you, flee at My Presence.

Win *Me* and all is won. *All.*

God at Eventide: Spirit Waves

You have been told to end all prayer upon a note of praise.

That note of praise is not only faith rising up through difficulties to greet Me. It is even more. It is the Soul's recognition that My Help is already on the way.

It is the echo in your heart of the sound borne on Spirit Waves.

It is given to those who love and trust Me to sense this approach.

So rejoice and be glad, for truly your redemption draweth nigh.

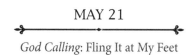

God Calling: Fling It at My Feet

To see Me you must bring Me your cares and show Me your heart of Trust. Then, as you leave your cares, you become conscious of My Presence.

This consciousness persisted in brings its reward of Me. Through a mist of care, no man may see My Face. Only when the burden is flung at My Feet do you pass on to consciousness and spiritual sight.

Remember obedience, obedience, obedience—the straight and narrow way into the Kingdom.

Not of you must it be said, even in lovingly tender reproach—"Why call ye me 'Lord, Lord,' and do not the things which I say?"

Character is chiseled into Beauty by the daily discipline and daily duties done. For, in many ways, My disciples must work out their own salvation, though this is not possible without My Strength and Help and without converse with Me.

Even for the Spiritual Life the training is different for different spirits. The man who would fain live a life of prayer and meditation is thrust into the busy ways of life, and the busy man is bidden to rest and wait patiently for Me. O joy, O rest, and in the busy ways be ever at peace.

God at Eventide: Soften the Soil

In My story of the Sower the hearts that lost the blessing, that held no good result, lost it because My servants had failed to prepare the ground.

They had failed to guard those they sought to influence, against the power of evil, and hardness of heart. They had failed to brace them to bear trouble and difficulty. They had failed to warn them against becoming too engrossed with having and getting.

The ground of the Sower had not been prepared. Much prayer must precede seed-sowing if the labor is not to be in vain.

So seek to prepare My way before Me. Then I, the Great Sower, will come. Harvest will indeed be great.

MAY 22

God Calling: Command Your Lord

Lord, I claim Thy Help.

Yes! Claim, be constantly claiming. There is a trust that waits long, and a trust that brooks no delay—that once convinced of the right of a course, once sure of God's guidance, says with all the persistence of a child, "*Now*." "Make no long tarrying, oh, my God."

You are no longer servants but friends. A friend can command his friend—can know that all the friend, the true friend, has is his by right. That does not mean an idle living at the expense of a friend, but claiming the friend's means: name, time, all that he has, when your supply is exhausted.

Friendship—true friendship, implies the right to appropriate. And in God's service is perfect freedom. Heirs of God—you are joint heirs with Me in the inheritance. We share the Father's property. You have the same right to use and claim as I have. Use your right. A beggar supplicates. A son, a daughter, appropriates.

Small wonder when I see My children sitting before My House supplicating and waiting—that I leave them there until they realize how foolish such action, when they have only to walk into their Home and take.

This cannot be the attitude of all. There must be first a definite realization of Sonship.

Men are trying to live the Christian Life in the Light and Teaching of My three years' Mission alone. That was never My Purpose.

I came to reveal My Father, to show the God-Spirit working in man. I taught, not that man was only to attempt to copy the *Jesus* of Nazareth, but that man was also to be so possessed by My Spirit, the Spirit actuating all I did, that he would be inspired as I was.

Seek to follow Me by the Power of the Indwelling Spirit which I bequeathed to you. This Spirit *will* guide you into all Truth.

I told My disciples that I could not tell them all but the Spirit would guide them. That is where My followers fail Me. Dwell more and more upon this Spirit-Guidance, promised to all, and so little claimed.

MAY 23

God Calling: Little Frets

Your lack of control is not due to the *big* burdens, but to your permitting the *little* frets and cares and burdens to accumulate.

If anything vex you, deal with that and get that righted with Me before you allow yourself to speak to or meet anybody, or to undertake any new duty.

Look upon yourself more as performing My errands and coming back quickly to Me to tell Me that message is delivered, that task done.

Then with no feeling of responsibility as to result (your only responsibility was to see the duty done) go out again, rejoicing at still more to do for My Sake.

Come, My children, come and gladly claim. Come and take from Me. Come with outstretched hands to receive.

And keep nothing. Eagerly pass on My gifts so that I may again bless your emptiness and refill your vessels.

You begin to understand this Law of Supply.

Man does not realize that for the children of the Kingdom the law is not that which rules outside.

My followers must be channels through which My gifts can pass to others. You cannot obtain My supply and follow the way of the world.

MAY 24

God Calling: Abundance

How unseeing the world goes on! How unknowing of your heartaches and troubles, your battles won, your conquests, your difficulties.

But be thankful, both of you, that there is One who knows, One who marks every crisis, every effort, every heartache.

For you both, who are not idle hearers, you must know that every troubled soul I tell you of is one for you to help. You must help all you can. You do not help enough. As you help, help will flow back and your circle of helpfulness will widen more and more, ever more and more.

Just feel that you are two of My disciples, present at the feeding of the five thousand, and that to you I hand out the food, and you pass it on, and ever more and more. You can always say with so few loaves and fishes "We have only enough for our own needs." It was not only My Blessing, but the Passing-on of the disciples that worked the miracle.

Get a feeling of bounteous giving into your beings. They were "all filled." There was a supply over.

I give with a large Hand and Heart. Note the draught of fishes. The net broke, the boat began to sink with the lavishness of My Gift. Lose sight of all limitations.

Abundance is God's Supply. Turn out all limited thoughts. Receive *showers* and in your turn—*shower*.

God at Eventide: No Separation

Come to Me.

At first with reluctant footsteps, then, as our Friendship grows, ever more and more eagerly, until the magic of My Presence not only *calls* but *holds* you, and reluctantly you turn to earth's ways and duties again.

But, as time passes, even that reluctance passes too, as you know there is no separation, not even a temporary one, in such Companionship; because I go with you and My Words you carry ever in your heart.

MAY 25

God Calling: Accomplish Anything

There will be no limit to what you can accomplish. Realize that. Never relinquish any task or give up the thought of any task because it seems beyond your power, only if you see it is not My Will for you. This I command you.

Think of the tiny snowdrop-shoot in the hard ground. No certainty even that when it has forced its weary way up, sunlight and warmth will greet it.

What a task beyond its power that must seem. But with the inner urge of Life within the seed compelling it, it carries out that task. The Kingdom of Heaven is like unto this.

You will find that as you grow in Grace evil forces are more ready to hinder your work and influence.

Walk warily, watchfully.

Always see that there is a new discipline to become a part of your armor, for as you progress new temptations will present themselves.

In rarefied air there are subtle dangers unknown in the valley or on the lower sides of the mountain. Many a disciple fails because he is not aware of the mountain dangers.

MAY 26

God Calling: Claim More

You are doing your claiming as I have said, and soon you will see the result. You cannot do this long without it being seen in the material. It is an undying law.

You are at present children practicing a new lesson. Practice—practice—soon you will be able to do it so readily.

You see others manifesting so easily, so readily demonstrating My Power. But you have not seen the discipline that went before. Discipline absolutely necessary before this Power is given to My disciples. It is a further initiation.

You are feeling you have learnt so much that life cannot be a failure. That is right, but others have to wait to see the outward manifestation in your lives before they realize this Spiritual Truth.

God at Eventide: A Day at a Time

The problems of tomorrow cannot be solved without the experience of today.

There is a plan for your lives dependent upon the faithful work of each day. You frustrate that plan if you leave today's task incomplete, while you bestir and fret yourself over tomorrow's happenings.

You will never learn the Law of Supply if you do this, and the learning of that Law is the lesson for now.

MAY 27

God Calling: Roots and Fruits

Remember the lesson of the *seed*, too, in its sending a shoot down so that it may be rooted and grounded, while at the same time it sends a shoot up to be the plant and flower that shall gladden the world.

The two growths are necessary. Without the strong root it would soon wither, as much activity fails for lack of growth in Me. The higher the growth up, the deeper must be the enrooting.

Many forget this, and thus their work ceases to be permanent for Me. Beware of the leaves and flowers without the strong root.

God at Eventide: Home of Content

Can you not trust My supply?

All is yours. Could I plan your journey, your way of life, your work and not count the cost?

Can you not trust Me even as you would trust an earthly friend? Live in My Kingdom and then the supply of the Kingdom is yours.

I wish you to learn the Glory of a God-protected life.

No idle, fruitless rushing hither and thither.

Storms may rage, difficulties press hard, but you will

know no harm. . .safe, protected, and guided.

Love knows no fear.

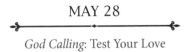

MAY 28

God Calling: Test Your Love

A great Love knows that in every difficulty, every trial, every failure, the presence of the loved one suffices. Test your Love for Me by this.

Just to be with Me, just to know I am beside you—does that bring you Joy and Peace? If not then your Love for Me, and your realization of My Love, are at fault.

Then, if this be so, pray for more Love.

God at Eventide: Care for All

Realize My overflowing and overwhelming Bounty. The stores of the Lord are inexhaustible, but to test My generosity to the full you must be generous.

My lovers give with no niggard hands.

MAY 29

God Calling: Forget

Regret nothing. Not even the sins and failures. When a man views Earth's wonders from some mountain height, he does not spend his time in dwelling on the stones and stumbles, the faints and failures, that marked his upward path.

So with you. Breathe in the rich blessings of each new day—forget all that lies behind you.

Man is so made that he can carry the weight of twenty

-four hours, no more. Directly he weighs down with the years behind, and the days ahead, his back breaks. I have promised to help you with the burden of today only, the past I have taken from you; and if you, foolish hearts, choose to gather again that burden and bear it, then, indeed, you mock Me to expect Me to share it.

For weal or woe each day is ended. What remains to be lived, the coming twenty-four hours, you must face as you awake.

A man on a march on Earth carries only what he needs for that march. Would you pity him if you saw him bearing too the overwhelming weight of the worn-out shoes and uniforms of past marches and years? And yet, in the mental and spiritual life, man does these things. Small wonder My poor world is heartsick and weary.

Not so must *you* act.

God at Eventide: Cares Cared For

Casting all your care upon Him,
for He hath care of you.

How precious these words. Care, attention, and the Love which prompts them, are all to indicated here, as also the most tender provision.

You are not told to put your worries away merely so that you may forget about them, but to cast them upon God. That is different: they will be dealt with.

Difficulties will be cleared away, mistakes rectified, weaknesses remedied, diseases healed, problems solved.

God Calling: The Devil's Death Knell

Our Lord, we praise Thee.

Praise is the devil's death knell. Resignation, acceptance of My Will, obedience to it, have not the power to vanquish evil that praise has.

The joyful heart is My best weapon against all evil. Oh! pray and praise.

You are learning your lesson. You are being led out into a large place. Go with songs of rejoicing. Rejoice evermore. Happy indeed if each day has its thrill of joy.

Talk to Me more during the day. Look up into My Face—a look of Love, a feeling of security, a thrill of Joy at the sense of the nearness of My Presence—these are your best prayers.

Let these smooth the day's work; then fear will vanish. And fear is the grim figure that turns aside success.

God at Eventide: See Clear

Your power to help your brother does not depend upon him: it is in your own hands. It is conditional upon your casting out the beam out of your own eye.

Attack not your brother's faults but your own. As you eradicate those you discover where your brother needs help, and you acquire the power to give him that help to conquer and to eradicate his faults.

God Calling: Prayer Without Words

Lord, hear us, we pray.

Hear and I answer. Spend much time in prayer. Prayer is of many kinds, but of whatever kind, prayer is the linking up of the soul and mind and heart to God.

So that if it is only a glance of faith, a look or word of Love, or confidence, and no supplication is expressed, it yet follows that supply and all necessary are secured.

Because the soul, being linked to God, united to Him, receives in and through Him all things. And the soul, when in human form, needs too the things belonging to its habitation.

God at Eventide: Into My Likeness

"Changed. . .from Glory to Glory." Changed from one character to another. Each change marking as it were a milestone on the Spiritual Highway.

The Beauty of the view you see in the distance is the realization of My character, My Glory, towards which with varying pace you are hourly progressing.

The way to secure better progress is to keep your gaze on your goal. Not on the road you traverse, assuredly not on the way by which you have come. Your goal is that Glory or Character that you see more and more clearly in Me, your Lord and Master.

"It doth not yet appear what you shall be, but know that when I shall appear (that is to you, to your sight, when you see Me), you shall be like Me, for you shall see Me as I *am*."

God Calling: Companionship

The way of the soul's transformation is the Way of Divine Companionship.

Not so much the asking Me to make you this or that but the living with Me, thinking of Me, talking to Me—thus you grow like Me.

Love Me. Rest in Me.

Joy in Me.

God at Eventide: Confidence

Character-change comes by doing My Will in days when you see no Vision and hear no Voice.

Never leave the path of strict observance of all you were told to do when you saw Me and spoke to Me on the Mount. If you do you walk into serious danger.

These dull days are your practice days. Difficulties appear, failure seems inevitable. But all is necessary, so that you may learn to adapt your life to the teaching I have given you, may realize your own weakness, develop obedience and perseverance, without waiting for further instruction and inspiration.

Persevere with patience. I guide you still, for I am with you when you do not realize My Presence.

More faith will come through the confidence arising from experience.

God Calling: My Image

My Lord and my God, we praise Thee, we bless
Thee, we worship Thee. Make us like Thee.

You are willing to drink of the cup that I drink of—the wine of sorrow and disappointment.

You are Mine and will grow both of you more and more like Me, your Master.

True it is today as it was in the days of Moses that no man can see My Face and live.

The self, the original *Man*, shrivels up and dies, and upon the soul becomes stamped My image.

God at Eventide: Shake Free

Come unto Me. . .and I will give you rest.

Rest in the midst of work. Heart-rest in the knowledge of My keeping Power.

Feel that rest stealing into your being. Incline your ear and come unto Me, hear and your soul shall live. Grow in strength, not overgrown by cares.

Let not the difficulties of life, like weeds, choke the rest of your soul, choke and tether the soaring freedom of your spirit.

Rise above these earth-bonds into newness of life, abundant and victorious. Rise.

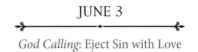
God Calling: Eject Sin with Love

*Our Lord, we love and praise Thee. Thou art
our Joy and our exceeding great reward.*

Remember that Love is the power which transforms the world. Love not only of Me, Love not only of the few dear to you, but Love of all—of the publicans, the sinners, the harlots—Love.

It is the only weapon with which sin can be driven out. Drive sin out with *Love*.

Drive fear and depression and despair and a sense of failure out with Praise.

Praise is the acknowledgment of that which I have sent you. Few men would send a further gift of payment until they had received the acknowledgment of the previous one. So Praise, acknowledging, as it does, that My gift and blessing leave the way open for Me to shower yet more on the thankful heart.

Learn as a child learns to say "Thank you" as a courtesy, with perhaps no real sense of gratitude at all. Do this until at last a thrill of joy, of thankful awe, will accompany the spoken word.

Do not expect for yourselves feeling that you know others have or have had. Just go on along the arid way of obedience, and persistence will be rewarded as you come to the Spring, the glad Spring of Water.

Oh, joy in Me, and, as far as in you lies, shed Joy on all around.

Confidence must be the finishing chord of every contact between you and Me. Joyful confidence. You must end upon the Joy-note.

The union between a soul and Me is attained in its beauty and complete satisfaction only when in every incident that soul achieves praise.

Love and laugh and thank Me all the time.

JUNE 4

God Calling: Divine Patience

Molding, My children, means cutting and chiseling. It means sacrifice of the personal to conform to type. It is not only My Work but yours.

The swift recognition of the selfish in your desires and motives, actions, words, and thoughts, and the instant appeal to Me for help to eradicate that.

It is a work that requires cooperation—Mine and yours. It is a work that brings much sense of failure and discouragement, too, at times, because, as the work proceeds, you see more and more clearly all that yet remains to be done.

Shortcomings you had hardly recognized or at least for which you had had no sense of sorrow, now cause you trouble and dismay.

Courage. That is in itself a sign of progress.

As you see the slow progress upward made by you, in spite of your longing and struggle, you will gain a divine patience with others whose imperfections trouble you.

So on and up. Forward. Patience—Perseverance—Struggle. Remember that I am beside you, your Captain and your Helper. So tender, so patient, so strong.

Yes, we cooperate, and as I share your troubles, failures, difficulties, heartaches, so, as My friends, you share My patience and My strength—beloved.

God at Eventide: Delve

Consider the Truths of My Kingdom as well worth all search, all sacrifice. Dig down into the soil. Dig when it means toil, fatigue.

Above and below the ever-present material you must look for My Hidden Treasure. It is not what you say, but what you perceive, that will influence other lives.

My Spirit will communicate this to you and also to those round you. So for their sakes delve.

JUNE 5

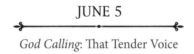

God Calling: That Tender Voice

Very quietly I speak. Listen to My Voice. Never heed the voices of the world—only the tender Divine Voice.

Listen and you will never be disappointed. Listen, and anxious thoughts and tired nerves will become rested. The Voice Divine—not so much in strength as in tenderness. Not so much in power as in restfulness.

But the tenderness and the restfulness will heal your scars and make you strong, and then it must be your task to let all your power be My Power. Man's little power is as clay beside the granite rock of My Power.

You are My great care. Never feel at the mercy of the world. My angels guard you day and night, and nothing can harm you. You would indeed thank Me if you knew the darts of fret and evil they turn from you.

Thank Me indeed for dangers unknown—unseen—but averted.

Examine yourself. Ask Me and I will show you what you are doing wrong—if only you will listen humbly and be unreservedly determined to do My Will.

JUNE 6

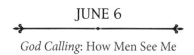

God Calling: How Men See Me

I came to help a world. And according to the varying needs of each, so does each man see Me.

It is not necessary that *you* see Me as others see Me—the world, even the Church, My disciples, My followers, but it is necessary that *you* see Me, each of you, as supplying all that *you* personally need.

The weak need My Strength. The strong need My Tenderness. The tempted and fallen need My Salvation. The righteous need My Pity for sinners. The lonely need a Friend. The fighters need a Leader.

No *man* could be all these to men—only a God could be. In each of these relations of Mine to man you must see the God. The God-Friend, the God-Leader, the God-Savior.

God at Eventide: True Joys

Continue ye in My Love. Seek nothing for yourself, only what you can use for Me. Rely on Me for all. Be meek, not only towards Me but towards others. Love to serve. Have no fear. Seek to be true in all. Be full of Joy.

The world wants to see Joy, not in the thrills of worldly pleasures and dissipations, but in the beauty of Holiness. In the ecstasy of peaceful safety with Me. In the thrill of adventure My true followers know, in the satisfaction that self-conquest gives.

Let your world see that you are steadfast, immovable.

JUNE 7

God Calling: True Beauty

Incline your ear, and come unto me: hear, and your soul shall live.
ISAIAH 55:3

Not only live but grow in Grace and Power and Beauty—the true Beauty, the Beauty of Holiness.

Reach ever forward after the things of My Kingdom.

In the animal world, the very form of an animal alters to enable it to reach that upon which it delights to feed.

So, reaching after the treasures of My Kingdom, your whole nature becomes changed, so that you can best enjoy and receive the wonders of that Kingdom.

Dwell on these truths.

God at Eventide: Lose Life's Sting

Submit yourself entirely to My Control, My Kingship; then the sting is taken out of life's rebuffs.

Welcome each contact as of My planning. Be ready to widen your circle of influence at My wish. Do not let age or other limitations daunt you.

Trust Me. Can I not judge your fitness for the task I give you? Have not I a Love for your acquaintances as well as for you?

Do not question My decisions. All is planned in Love for all My children. Only self-will can hinder the carrying out of the Divinely conceived plan.

Work gladly, knowing all needed wisdom shall be provided, also all needed material to do My Work.

JUNE 8

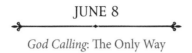

God Calling: The Only Way

Down through the ages, My Power alone has kept millions of souls brave and true and strong who else would have fallen by the way.

The Faith has been kept alive and handed down, not by the dwellers in ease, but by those who struggled and suffered and died for Me.

This life is not for the body, it is for the soul, and man too often chooses the way of life that best suits the body, not the way that best suits the soul. And I permit only what best suits the soul.

Accept this and a wonderful molding is the result; reject it and My Purpose is frustrated, your best prayer unanswered, progress (Spiritual progress) delayed, trouble and grief stored up.

Try, each of you, to picture your soul as a third being trained by us—by you and Me—and then you will share, and rejoice in sharing, in the discipline and training.

Stand apart from your soul with Me and welcome training—rejoice at progress.

God at Eventide: Perennial Youth

Count all well lost, all other work well foregone, to rest apart with Me.

From these times you go out strengthened, glad, full of Life-giving Joy—My Joy that you can never find anywhere else but with Me, the Joy-giving Christ.

Let others sense this Joy. More than any words this will show them the priceless gain of life with Me.

You shall truly find that there is no age in My Kingdom, in My Companionship.

JUNE 9

God Calling: An Obstacle Race

Rise above your fears and fancies into My Joy. It will suffice to heal all your sores and wounds. Forget all sense of failure and shortcomings, all the painful jolts and jars, and trust Me, love Me, call upon Me.

Your discipleship is an obstacle race. "So run that ye may obtain." Obtain not only your hearts' desires, but obtain Me—your souls' Joy and Haven.

What would you think of the runner who threw himself on the ground in despondency at his first hurdle?

Over, and on and up. I am your Leader and your goal.

God at Eventide: Set Apart

Count not these days as lost.

You have, even in this seemingly narrow life, countless opportunities for self-conquest. There is no greater task than that.

I set apart those who greatly desire to reflect Me, because there is danger that in the crowded ways, and among others, self will gain the ascendancy.

For a time, until self is recognized and conquered, you too must withdraw into the wilderness.

You are learning much, and I am your Teacher.

Come with Me into a desert place and rest awhile.

JUNE 10

God Calling: The Day of Trouble

*Offer unto Me the sacrifice of thanksgiving and pay
your vows to the Most High, and then call upon
Me in the day of trouble and I will deliver you.*

To praise and thank and steadily fulfill your promises (vows) to Me are then, as it were, the placing of coin in My Bank, upon which, in your time of need, you can draw with confidence and certainty. Remember that.

The world wonders when it sees the man who can so unexpectedly draw large and unsuspected sums from his bank for his own need, that of a friend, or for some charity.

But what the world has not seen are the countless small sums paid into that bank, earned by faithful work in many ways.

And so in My Kingdom. The world sees the man of faith make a sudden demand upon Me, upon My stores, and lo! that demand is met.

So with you, My children. "Offer to God the sacrifice of Thanksgiving and pay your vows to the Most High and call upon Me in the day of trouble and I will deliver you."

This is a promise for the seemingly dull days of little happenings and a cheer for you, My children. When you seem not able to do big things, you can be storing your little acts and words of faithfulness in My Great Storehouse, ready for the day of your big demand.

God at Eventide: Do You Remember?

Cultivate the habit of thinking about Me. God is everywhere. My Presence is always with you, but recollection brings consciousness of that Presence and closer friendship.

Deliberately recall some event in My life, some teaching of Mine, some act of love. So will you impress Me upon your character and life.

Your learning and accomplishments are valueless without My Grace, which is sufficient for you. Leave planning to Me. Leave Me to open or close the way.

Prepare yourself for all I am preparing for you.

JUNE 11

God Calling: My Mark!

O Lord, we thank Thee for Thy great gift of Peace.

That is the Peace, that only I can give in the midst of a restless world and surrounded by trouble and difficulty. To know that Peace is to have received the stamp of the Kingdom—the mark of the Lord Jesus Christ. My Mark.

When you have learned that Peace, you are fit to judge of true values, the values of the Kingdom, and the values of all the world has to offer.

That Peace is loving faith at rest.

God at Eventide: Simple Obedience

Dear Lord, teach me to obey Thee in all things.

You are Mine, pledged to serve Me.

Every want of yours has been anticipated. Look back and see how each failure has been due to your not having obeyed implicitly the instructions I gave you in preparation for that task or trial.

Listening to My Voice implies obedience. I am a tender Lord of Love, but I am a Captain with whose words there must be no trifling.

You are a volunteer, not conscript, but if you expect the privileges of My Service you must render Me the obedience of that service.

The way of obedience may seem hard and dreary, but the security of My ordered life the untrained soul can never know. March in step with your Captain.

JUNE 12

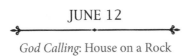

God Calling: House on a Rock

Be watchful to hear My Voice and instantly to obey. Obedience is your great sign of faith. "Why call ye Me Lord, Lord, and do not the things that I say?" was My word when on Earth to the many who followed and heard but did not do.

I likened the man who heard and did not do to the man who built his house on the sand. In times of storm and trouble, he is overthrown; his house falls.

I likened the man who obeyed Me implicitly to the man who built his house upon a rock. In times of storm he is steadfast, immovable.

Do not feel that by this I mean only the keeping of My Commandments, even the living of My Sermon on the Mount. I mean more than that to those who know Me intimately. I mean the following, in all, the Inner Guiding that I give, the little injunctions I speak to each individual soul, the wish I express—and desire to have carried out.

The secure, steadfast, immovable life of My disciples, the Rock Home, is not built at a wish, in a moment, but is laid, stone by stone, foundations, walls, roof, by the acts of obedience, the daily following out of My wishes, the loving doing of My Will.

And it is in that Rock Home, man-made but divinely inspired—the House of Obedience—the truest expression of a disciple's adoration and worship—it is *there* I come to dwell with My loved one.

God at Eventide: Spiritual Renewal

Deep life-giving draughts of My Spirit are yours.

Think of the aridness, the thirst, that is unquenched till the whole unsatisfied being is age-worn.

Can you help man in any better way than by proving to him that the cleansing waters of My Spirit have power to wash away all that hinders growth, and to satisfy to the full every thirst of your nature?

JUNE 13

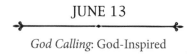

God Calling: God-Inspired

You have entered now upon a mountain climb. Steep steps lead upward, but your power to help others will be truly marvelous.

Not alone will you arise. All toward whom you now send loving, pitying thoughts will be helped upward by you.

Looking to Me, all your thoughts are God-inspired. Act on them and you will be led on. They are not your own impulses but the movement of My Spirit and, obeyed, will bring the answer to your prayers.

Love and Trust. Let no unkind thoughts of any dwell in your hearts, then I can act with all My Spirit-power, with nothing to hinder.

God at Eventide: Conquest of Fear

It is not thinking about Me, but dwelling with Me that brings perfect fearlessness.

There can be no fear where I am. Fear was conquered when I conquered all Satanic power. If all My followers knew this, and affirmed it with absolute conviction, there would be no need of armed forces to combat evil.

JUNE 14

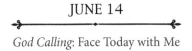

God Calling: Face Today with Me

Our Lord and our God.
Make us all Thou wouldst have us.

It is not circumstances that need altering first, but yourselves, and then the conditions will naturally alter. Spare no effort to become all I would have you. Follow every leading. I am your only Guide.

Endeavor to put from you every thought of trouble. Take each day, and with no backward look, face the day's problem with Me, and seek My Help and guidance as to what you can do.

Never look back and never leave until the morrow that on which you can get My Guidance for today.

God at Eventide: The Soul Restored

Do not sorrow if, after time with Me, you cannot repeat to yourself all the lessons you have learned. Enough that you have been with Me.

Do you need to know the history of plant or tree to enjoy the countryside? You have inhaled pure air and been refreshed with the beauty of the landscape. Enough for the day. So, too, you have been in My Presence and found rest unto your souls.

JUNE 15

God Calling: "Glory, Glory Dawneth"

I am planning for you. Wonderful are My Ways beyond your knowledge.

Oh! realize My Bounty and My Goodness more and more. The wonder of being led by Me! The beauty of a guided life!

These will enter your consciousness more and more and bring you ever more and more Joy.

You are very nearly at the point when you shall ask what you will and it shall be done unto you.

You have entered upon a wonderful era—your lives are planned and blessed by Me as never before.

You are overcoming. You are counting all things but loss if you can win Me. And the promises to him that overcometh are truly wonderful, and will always be fulfilled.

God at Eventide: Down in the Valley

Do not let doubt or fear assail or depress you because of this time of anguish and failure-sense through which you have passed. No, this had to be.

Useful work lies ahead of you. Before the onset of so great a task My servant has usually to walk through the Valley of Humiliation, or in the wilderness.

If I, your Lord, before I began My Mission, had to have My forty days of temptation, how could you expect to go all unprepared to your great task?

You must taste anew the shame of unworthiness, of failure

and of nothingness before you go forth with Me conquering and to conquer.

JUNE 16

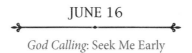

God Calling: Seek Me Early

Walk in My Way and trust Me. No evil can touch you. I am yours as truly as you are Mine. Rest in that truth.

Rest, that is, cease all struggle. Gain a calm, strong confidence in that certainty. Do not only rest in Me when the world's struggles prove too much and too many for you to bear or face alone. Rest in Me when you need perfect understanding, when you need the consciousness of tender, loving friendship and intercourse.

The world, my poor world, flies to Me when its difficulties are too great to be surmounted any other way, forgetting, or never realizing, that if, with the same eagerness, those hearts sought Me merely for companionship and loving intercourse, many of the difficulties would not arise.

The circumstances, the life, the character would be so altered—so purified, that those same difficulties would not exist.

Seek Me *early*; that is the way to find Me. *Early*, before I get crowded out by life's troubles and difficulties and pleasures.

God at Eventide: Down into Egypt

Down into Egypt, back into Galilee. These journeys were gladly undertaken. They meant no family upheaval, for was not the desire of that Family but to fulfill Divine Intent?

Upheavals come only when man is set on some particular way of life, and is called to forgo that.

When the fixed desire is to do the Father's Will, then there is no real change. The leaving of home, town, country is but as the putting off a garment that has served its useful purpose.

Change is only Spiritual progress when the life is lived with Me, the Changeless One.

JUNE 17

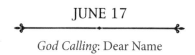

God Calling: Dear Name

"Jesus." Say My Name often. It was in My Name Peter bade the lame man walk. "In the Name of Jesus Christ of Nazareth arise and walk."

"*Jesus*." The very sounding of My Name, in Love and tenderness, drives away all evil. It is the word before which all the hosts of evil flee.

"*Jesus*." My Name is the call for a lifeline to rescue you from temptation.

"*Jesus*." The Name banishes loneliness—dispels gloom.

"*Jesus*." Summons help to conquer your faults.

I will set you on high because you have known My Name.

Yes! My Name—"Jesus." Use it more. Use it tenderly. Use it prayerfully. Use it powerfully.

God at Eventide: Bind Their Wounds

Draw from Me not only the Strength you need for yourself, but all you need for the wounded ones to whom I shall lead you. Remember no man liveth to himself. You must have Strength for others.

They will come to you in ever-increasing numbers. Will you send them empty away? Draw from Me and you will not fail them.

JUNE 18

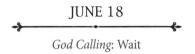

God Calling: Wait

The world has always seen service for Me to be activity. Only those near to Me have seen that a life apart, of prayer, may, and does so often, accomplish more than all the service man can offer Me.

If man lived apart with Me and only went out to serve at My direct command, My Spirit could operate more and accomplish truly mighty things.

God at Eventide: Nearer to Thee

"Lord, show me Thyself," is a cry that never goes unanswered.

Not often to physical vision comes the awareness but to spiritual insight, as more and more you realize My Love, My Power, and the manifold wonders of My character—its humility, its Majesty, its tenderness, its sternness, justice, mercy, healing and consuming fire.

Draw nigh to Me and I will draw nigh to you.

JUNE 19

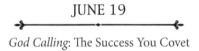

God Calling: The Success You Covet

Follow the path of obedience. It leads to the Throne of God. Your treasure, be it success necessary on the material plane, which will further the work of My Kingdom, or the hidden spiritual wonders revealed by Me to those only who diligently seek, this treasure lies at the end of the track.

From one point (a promise of Mine or a Command) to the next, you have to follow, till finally you reach the success you covet.

All *your* work for the moment is in the material plane, and the spiritual is only to help the material. When your material goal is reached, then the material will serve only to attain the spiritual.

God at Eventide: My Healing Power

When life is difficult then relax completely; sleep or rest in conscious reliance on My Healing Power.

Endeavor that others may never see you anything but rested, strong, happy, joyful.

Before you meet seek renewal in My Secret Place.

Your tears and cares must be shared with Me alone.

My blessing be upon you.

JUNE 20

God Calling: Miracles Again

Wait to hear My Will and then obey. At all costs obey. Do not fear. I am a wall of protection around you. See this. To see this with the eyes of faith is to cause it to manifest in the material.

Remember, I long to work miracles, as when on Earth I wrought them, but the same condition holds good. I cannot do many mighty works because of unbelief.

So only in response to your belief can I do miracle-works now.

God at Eventide: Living Waters

Drink of the water that I shall give you, and you shall never thirst.

I will lead you beside the waters of comfort.

I will give unto you living water.

Blessed are they that hunger and thirst after righteousness.

As the hart panteth after the water brooks so longeth my soul after Thee, O God.

This is the thirst that can never go unsatisfied.

JUNE 21

God Calling: See As I See

O Lord, we praise Thee. Bless us, we beseech Thee.

I bless you. I promise you release. Joy in Me. You shall be shielded from the storm.

Wonders have unfolded. Just to come before Me and stay for a while in My Presence—this must strengthen and help you.

Learn of Me. The only way for so many in My poor world to keep calm, sane, is to have the mind which is in Jesus Christ. The mind which is in Me.

That mind you can never obtain by reasoning, or by reading, but only by living with Me and sharing My Life.

Think much of Me. Speak much of Me. See others as I see them. Let nothing less satisfy you.

God at Eventide: Yours

Appeal to Me often. Do not *implore* so much as *claim* My Help as your right.

It is yours in Friendship's name. Claim it with a mighty, impelling insistence. It is yours.

Not so much Mine to give you, as yours; but yours because it is included in the Great Gift of Myself that I gave you.

An All-embracing Gift, a Wonder Gift. Claim, accept, use it. All is well.

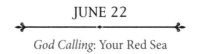
God Calling: Your Red Sea

Go forward fearlessly. Do not think about the Red Sea that lies ahead.

Be very sure that when you come to it the waters will part and you will pass over to your promised land of freedom.

God at Eventide: Right of Entry

Dwell with Me, and in doing so you admit those you love to the right of entry.

If their thoughts follow you as human friend and helper, they are drawn in thought, and later in love and longing, to Me with whom you live.

JUNE 23
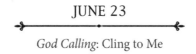

God Calling: Cling to Me

Cling to Me until the life from Me—the Divine Life, by that very contact, flows into your being and revives your fainting spirit.

Become recharged. When weary, do as I did on Earth—*sit by the well. Rest.*

Rest and gain power and strength, and the work too will come to you as it came to Me.

Rest till every care-thought has gone, and then let the Tide of Love and Joy flow in.

Instead of urging men to accept Me as this or that, first discover the need, and then represent Me as the supply.

A man may not feel his need of a Savior. He wants a Friend. Reveal Me as the Great Friend. Another may not need guidance, only to be understood. Represent Me as the Understanding Christ.

Leave Me to satisfy each and every need as I do yours.

JUNE 24

God Calling: When Guidance Tarries

As I prompt you—act. When you have no clear guidance, then go forward quietly along the path of duty I have set before you.

No fear, no panic, quietly doing your daily duty.

This attitude of faith will receive its reward, as surely as the acting upon My direct Guidance.

Rejoice in the sense of security that is yours.

God at Eventide: Zest in Service

Your will, your desire, must be to do My Will, wanting It, loving It, as a child hugging some treasure to its heart. So treasure My Will.

Find your delight in It. "Lord, what would'st Thou have me to do?" is no question of a sullen servant. It is the eager appeal of a friend, who views all life as a glorious adventure, with the enthusiasm of a youth permitted to share an explorer's quest.

Bring the unquenchable Zest into all you do.

JUNE 25

God Calling: God's Friendship

I am your Friend. The Companion of the dreary ways of life.

I rob those ways of their grayness and horror. I transform them. Even in earthly friendships the common way, the weary way, the steep way may seem a way to Heaven if the presence of some loved human friend transforms them.

Let the Sabbath calm enwrap your minds and hearts. Let it be a rest from the worry and fret of life.

Have you ever realized the wonder of the friendship you can have with Me? Have you ever thought what it means to be able to summon at will the God of the World?

Even with a privileged visitor to an earthly king there is the palace antechamber, and the time must be at the pleasure of the king.

But to My subjects I have given the right to enter My Presence when they will, nay more they can summon Me to bedside, to workshop—and I am there.

When men seek to worship Me, they think of the worlds I rule over, of creation, of mighty law and order—and then they feel the awe that precedes worship.

To you I say feel awe, feel the desire to worship Me in wondering amazement. But think too of the mighty, tender, humble condescension of My Friendship. Think of Me in the little things of everyday life.

God at Eventide: Ladder of Joy

You see in your lives cause for praise or prayer. You praise or pray. Your heart is lifted thereby into the Eternal, into My very Presence.

Thereafter the drudgery or commonplace or dreary waiting ceases to be the colorless something to be endured. It is the ladder, whereby you rise to Me.

You can then smile at it, welcome it. It is friend, not foe. So with everything in life. Its value for you must depend on whether it leads you nearer to Me.

So poverty or plenty, sickness or health, friendship or loneliness, sunshine or gloom, each may add to the Joy and Beauty of your lives.

JUNE 26

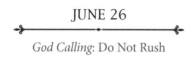

God Calling: Do Not Rush

Learn in the little daily things of life to delay action until you get My Guidance. . . .

So many lives lack poise. For in the momentous decisions and the big things of life, they ask My help, but into the small things they rush alone.

By what you do in the small things, those around you are most often antagonized or attracted.

God at Eventide: Life's Furnace

Life has its furnace for My children, into which they are plunged for the molding.

At their request I watch and watch until I can see them reflect My Glory. Then comes the further shaping into My Likeness. But the metal from which that Likeness is fashioned must be indeed pure.

So often My children are impatient for the molding, never thinking that the refining must come first.

To do My work there must be much refining.

God Calling: No Self-Reproach

The Eternal Arms shelter you. "Underneath are the Everlasting Arms." This promise is to those who rise above the Earth-life and seek to soar higher, to the Kingdom of Heaven.

You must not feel the burden of your failure. Go on in faith, the clouds will clear, and the way will lighten—the path becomes less stony with every step you take. So run that you may *obtain*. A rigid doing of the simple duties, and success will crown your efforts.

I had no words of reproach for any I healed. The man was whole and free who had wrecked his physical being by sin—whose palsy I healed.

The woman at the well was not overwhelmed by My "Thou hast had five husbands; and he whom thou now hast is not thy husband."

The woman taken in adultery was told, "Neither do I condemn thee: go, and sin no more." She was not told to bear the burden of the consciousness of her sin. . . .

Remember now abideth these three, Faith, Hope, and Charity. Faith is your attitude towards Me. Charity is your attitude toward your fellow man but, as necessary, is Hope, which is confidence in yourself to succeed.

God at Eventide: Eternal Life

Eternal Life is a matter of Vision.

Spiritual Vision is the result of knowledge that engenders further knowledge.

"And this is Life Eternal. . .to know Thee the only True God and Jesus Christ Whom Thou hast sent."

Eternal Life.

Eternal in so far as the quality, the character of the Life is concerned. Being of God it implies immortality.

It is My Gift of the Life that is Mine. Therefore it must be Power-Life. This is your Life, to absorb, to live in and through.

"He that believeth—*hath* eternal life."

JUNE 28

God Calling: Table of Delights

It has not been in vain this training and teaching time. The time of suppression, repression, depression is changed now into a time of glorious expression.

Life is flooded through and through with Joy and Gladness. Indeed, I have prepared a table of delights, a feast of all good things for you.

Indeed, your cup runneth over and you can feel from the very depth of your heart. "Surely goodness and mercy shall follow me all the days of my life: and I will dwell in the house of the LORD for ever."

God at Eventide: The Life Divine

As you recognize My dealings with you, Eternal Life flows through your being in all Its sanctifying, invigorating, and remedial force.

Eternal Life is awareness of the things of Eternity. Awareness of My Father and awareness of Me. Not merely a knowledge of Our existence, even of our Godhead, but an awareness of Us in all.

As you become aware of Me, all for whom you care are linked to Me, too. Yielding Me your service, you draw, by the magnetic power of Love, on your dear ones within the Divine-Life radius.

JUNE 29

God Calling: My Will—Your Joy

Our Lord and our God. Lead us, we beseech Thee.
Lead us and keep us.

You can never go beyond My Love and Care. Remember that. No evil can befall you. Circumstances I bless and use must be the right ones for you.

But I know always that the first step is to lay your will before Me as an offering, ready that I shall do what is best, sure that, if you trust Me, what I do for you will be best.

Your second step is to be sure, and to tell me so, that I am Powerful enough to do everything ("The hearts of kings are in My rule and governance"), that no miracle is impossible with Me ("With God all things are possible" and "I and my Father are one").

Then leave all with Me. Glad to leave all your affairs in a Master Hand. Sure of safety and protection. Remember you cannot see the future. I can.

You could not bear it. So only little by little can I reveal it to you. Accept My Will, and it will bring you joy.

God at Eventide: All One

Every man is your brother, every woman your sister, every child your child. You are to know no difference of race, color or creed. One is your Father and all ye are brethren.

This is the Unity I came to teach—Man united with God and His great family. Not man alone, seeking a oneness with God alone. See God the Father with His great world family, and, as you seek union with Him, it must mean for you attachment to His family, His other children.

He acknowledges all as His children, not all acknowledge

Him as their Father.

Ponder this.

JUNE 30

God Calling: Understand Them

Take joy wherever you go. You have been much blessed. You are being much blessed.

Such stores of blessing are awaiting you in the months and years that lie ahead. Pass every blessing on.

Love can and does go round the world, passed on the God-currents from one to the other.

Shed a little sunshine in the heart of one, that one is cheered to pass it on, and so My vitalizing joy-giving message goes.

Be transmitters these days. Love and Laugh. Cheer all. Love all.

Always seek to understand others and you cannot fail to love them.

See Me in the dull, the uninteresting, the sinful, the critical, the miserable.

See Me in the laughter of children and the sweetness of old age, in the courage of youth and the patience of man and womanhood.

God at Eventide: Immune from Evil

Evil was conquered by Me, and to all who rely on Me there is immunity from it.

Turn evil aside with the darts I provide.

Rejoicing in tribulation is one dart.

Practicing My Presence is another.

Self-emptying is another.

Claiming My Power over temptation is another.

You will find many of these darts as you tread My Way, and you will learn to use them adroitly, swiftly. Each is adapted to the need of the moment.

JULY 1

God Calling: Attack Fear

I learn daily the sublime lesson of trust and calm in the midst of storm. Whatever of sorrow or difficulty the day may bring My tender command to you is still the same—*Love and Laugh*.

Love and Laughter, not a sorrowful resignation, mark real acceptances of My Will. Leave every soul the braver and happier for having met you. For children or youth, middle or old age, for sorrow, for sin, for all you may encounter in others, this should be your attitude. *Love and Laugh*.

Do not fear. Remember how I faced the devil in the wilderness, and how I conquered with "the sword of the Spirit, which is the word of God." You too have your quick answer for every fear that evil may present—an answer of faith and confidence in Me. Where possible say it aloud.

The spoken word has power. Look on every fear, not as a weakness on your part due to illness or worry, but as a very real temptation to be attacked and overthrown.

God at Eventide: Out of the Unseen

Faith is the substance of things hoped for,
the evidence of things not seen.

You do not yet see, nor will you see fully while you are on this earth, how faith, cooperating with Spiritual Power, actually calls into being that for which you hope.

Men speak of dreams come true. But you know them as answered prayers; manifestations of Spirit Force in the Unseen. So trust boundlessly.

JULY 2

God Calling: The Child-Spirit

Does the way seem a stony one? Not one stone can impede your progress. Courage. Face the future, but *face* it only with a brave and happy heart. Do not seek to see it. *You* are robbing Faith of her sublime sweetness if you do this.

Just know that all is well and that Faith, not seeing, but believing, is the barque that will bear you to safety over the stormy waters. "According to your faith be it unto you" was My injunction to those who sought healing of Me.

If for wonder-working, if for healing, if for salvation faith was so necessary, then the reason is clear why I urged that all who sought entrance to My Kingdom must become as little children. Faith is the child-attitude.

Seek in every way to become childlike. Seek, seek, seek until you find, until the years have added to your nature that of the trusting child. Not only for its simple trust must you copy the child-spirit, but for its joy in life, its ready laughter, its lack of criticism, its desire to share all with all men. Ask much that you may become as little children, friendly and loving toward all—not critical, not fearful.

"Except ye. . .become as little children, ye shall not enter into the kingdom of heaven."

Do you not see how unnecessary is your learning the method of Spirit-attack? There must be a certain root-faith and Me, or you could not trust yourself to perfect surrender to Me. But there must come to those who walk all the way with Me, a yielding of their wills and lives wholly to Me, or the greater faith that results would be a source of danger. It would drag you back to the material plane, instead of to Spiritual Heights.

For unless your will is wholly Mine, you will rely on this new God-given Power, and call into being that which is not for the furtherance of My Kingdom.

JULY 3

God Calling: Spiritual Fullness

Our Lord, we love Thee and desire to live for Thee in all things.

My children, "Blessed are they which do hunger and thirst after righteousness: for they shall be filled." That is satisfaction.

Only in that fullness of spiritual things can the heartsick and faint and weary be satisfied, healed, and rested. "Lord," we cry, "to whom shall we go but to Thee." "Thou preparest a table before me." Bread of Life, Food from Heaven.

How few realize that the feeding of the four thousand and the five thousand were in each case but an illustration of the way in which I should one day be the Food of My people.

Think of the wonder of revelation still to be seen by those who live with Me. All these hundreds of years, and much of what I said and did is still mystery; much of My Life on Earth is still spiritually unexplored country. Only to the simple and the loving heart that walks with Me can these things be revealed. I have carefully hidden these things from the wise and prudent and have revealed them unto babes.

Do not weigh your spirits down with the sins and sorrows of the world. Only Christ can do that and live. Look for the loving, the true, the kindly, the brave in the many all around you.

God at Eventide: Hiding in Thee

Follow Me, and whether it be in the storm, or along the dusty highroad, or over the places of stones, or in the cool glade or the meadow, or by the waters of comfort, then, with Me, in each experience there will be a place of refuge.

At times you seem to follow afar off. Then weary with the burden and the way, you stretch out a hand to touch the hem of My Garment.

Suddenly there is no dust, no weariness. You have found Me. My child, even if it seems unprofitable, continue your drudgery, whether it be of spiritual, mental, or physical effort. Truly it serves its turn if it but lead you to seek help from Me.

JULY 4

God Calling: Friend of Mine

What man calls conversion is often only the discovery of the Great Friend. What man calls religion is the knowledge of the Great Friend. What man calls holiness is the imitation of the Great Friend.

Perfection, that perfection I enjoined on all, the being perfect as your Father in Heaven is perfect, is the being like the Great Friend and in turn becoming to others a Great Friend, too.

I am your Friend. Think again of all that means—Friend and Savior. A friend is ready to help, anticipating every want, hand outstretched to help and encourage, or to ward off danger, voice of tenderness to soothe tired nerves and speak peace to restlessness and fear.

Think of what, to you, your friend is and then from that, try to see a little of what the Perfect Friend, the tireless, selfless, all-conquering, all miracle-working Friend would be. *That* Friend, and more even than your heart can imagine, that *Friend* am I.

Were I to read My Kingdom—My Kingdom of the Child Hearts—the doctrines of your churches, so often there would be no response. But the simple rules I gave My followers are known, loved, and lived by them all.

In all things seek simplicity.

God at Eventide: Break Free

For by whom a man is overcome. . .he is the slave.

I cut the bonds of sin which bound you to evil. With loving Hands I replaced each with my cords of Love, which bound you to Me, your Lord.

The power of evil is subtle. A cut cord, a snapped cord, would awaken your slumbering conscience, but strand by strand, so carefully, with gentleness cunningly acquired, evil works until a cord is free. Even then the work is slow, but oh, so sure, until presently the old bond I severed is binding you to evil, strand by strand.

Snap off these returning fetters. Satan hath desire to have you that he may sift you as wheat. He works with an efficiency My servants would do well to copy. He has marked you as one who will increasingly bring souls to Me.

JULY 5

God Calling: You Are Invincible

I am with you all the time controlling, blessing, and helping you. No man or woman can stand against My Will for you. A whole world of men and women cannot do this—if you trust Me and place your affairs in My Hands.

To the passenger it may seem as if each wave would overwhelm the ship or turn it aside from its course. The captain knows by experience that, in spite of wind and wave, he steers a straight course to the haven where he would be.

So trust Me, the Captain of your salvation.

God at Eventide: My Family Circle

For whosoever shall do the Will of My Father,
he is My brother and sister and mother.

You see how everything depends on the necessity of doing the Will of My Father.

Here is the intimacy of a new relationship. The only condition of this is the doing of My Father's Will. Then at once, into the inner Family Circle there is admission.

The plain way of discipline is the way of knowing My Will. That is the first requisite to the doing of it.

My Will for each day can only be revealed as each day comes, and until one revelation has been lived out, how can you expect to be made aware of the next?

Awareness of My Will is only achieved by obedience to that Will as it is made clear, and when *that* Will has been obeyed the veil, hiding My next desire, is lifted.

God Calling: Riches

Never let yourselves think "we cannot afford this" or "shall never be able to do that." Say "the supply for it is not here yet, but it will come if we should have it. It *will* surely come."

Persevere in saying that, and gradually a feeling of being plentifully supplied and of being surrounded by riches will possess you. That feeling is your faith claiming My Supply, and according to your faith it shall be unto you.

But it is not the faith expressed in moments of prayer and exaltation I look for but the faith that lays immediately to rest the doubts of the day as they arise, that attacks and conquers the sense of limitation.

"Ask, and ye shall receive."

God at Eventide: Listen Carefully

My poor deaf world. What it misses in loving Words and Whispers.

I want to share so much with it. It will not listen.

"Wherefore do you spend money for that which is not bread and your labor for that which satisfieth not. Harken diligently unto Me and eat that which is good and let your Soul delight itself. . . ."

"He that willeth to do My Will—shall know."

Whose Voice would you hear? So many voices are about you that you may miss the Still, Small Voice.

"This is My Beloved Son—Hear Him."

God Calling: Painful Preparation

Help and Peace and Joy are here. Your courage will be rewarded.

Painful as this time is, you will both one day see the reason of it, and see too that it was not cruel testing, but tender preparation for the wonderful lifework you are both to do.

Try to realize that your own prayers are being most wonderfully answered. Answered in a way that seems painful to you, but that just now is the only way.

Success in the temporal world would not satisfy you.

Great success, in both temporal and spiritual worlds, awaits you.

I know you will see this had to be.

God at Eventide: Love's Growth

Learn from Nature the profusion of her gifts.

As you daily realize more and more the generosity of the Divine Giver, learn increasingly to give.

Love grows by giving.

You cannot give bountifully without being filled with a sense of giving yourself with the gift, and you cannot so give without Love passing from you to the one who receives.

You are conscious, not of yourself as generous, but of the Divine Giver as bounteous beyond all human words to express.

So Love flows *into* you with an intensity that is both humbling and exalting as Love flows *from* you with your gift.

God Calling: My Secret

You are being guided, but remember that I said, "I will guide thee with mine eye."

And My Eye is My set purpose—My Will.

To guide with My Will is to bring all your desires into oneness with My Will, My desires.

To make My Will your only will. Then My Will guides *you*.

God at Eventide: Remember Me

Give me a constant remembrance of Thee.

Ask what you will and it shall be done unto you. But only if the heart desires what the lips express. "The Lord looketh on the heart."

You will grow into the true attitude of remembrance of Me as you learn more and more to attribute all your blessings, all your guidance, to My increasing care: to the mind of your Master behind all, inspiring all, controlling all, the source of all your good.

JULY 9
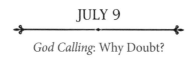

God Calling: Why Doubt?

Joy in Me. Joy is infectious. Trust and pray. It is not sin for one who knows Me only as God, as Creator, to doubt Me, to question My Love and purposes.

But for one who knows Me as you do, as Friend and Savior, and who knows the world's God as Father—for that one to doubt My Purpose and saving Power and tender Love is wrong indeed.

Go forward unafraid.

Face each difficulty, however great and seemingly unconquerable, as you go forward toward it.

The strength you will require from Me for that adventure into danger, as it may seem to you, will fortify you for its overcoming.

"Fear thou not to, for I am with thee,

"Be not afraid for I am thy God.

"I will strengthen thee, I will help thee,

"Yea, I will uphold thee with the right arm of My Righteousness."

JULY 10

God Calling: Expect Many Miracles

My guardianship is so wonderful. Expect not one miracle but many.

Each day's happenings, if of My working and under My control, are miracle-works.

God at Eventide: Your Heart Is Fixed

Still go forward unafraid. The way will open as you go.

It is fear that blocks My way for you. Have no fear. Know that all is well.

No circumstances, no outward changes, can harm you in

any way. Each should prove a step of progress, as long as your hearts are fixed "trusting in the Lord."

I know no change.

JULY 11

God Calling: Guardian Angels

You are Mine. Once I have set on you My stamp and seal of ownership, all My Hosts throng to serve and protect you.

Remember that you are daughters of a King.

Try to picture a bodyguard of My servitors in the Unseen waiting, longing, efficient, to do all that is necessary for your well-being.

Feel this as you go through the day. Feel this, and all is well.

God at Eventide: More Doors Will Open

Go on in faith and trust. The Way opens as you go. In the Christian Life doors swing open as you come to them, if so be that you have advanced to them along the straight path of obedience.

As you started your journey, what would it have profited had you worried about the closed door ahead?

In the Spirit-Life miracle-working Power operates through natural human channels. As you have seen.

So this is the continuing lesson: Go steadily foreword in firm trust along the path of the quiet obedience.

That is *your* work. *Mine* to cause the doors to swing open, as you come to them, not before.

How often have I opened those doors for you in the past? More will open. So trust, so hope, so love.

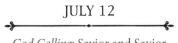

God Calling: Savior and Savior

If you believe it is My Hand that has saved you, then you must believe that I am meaning to save you yet more, and to keep you in the way that you should go.

Even a human rescuer does not save a man from drowning only to place him in other deep and dangerous waters. But rather to place him on dry land—and more—there to restore him to animation and health, and to see him to his home.

From this parable learn what I your Rescuer would do, and even more. Is the Lord's Hand shortened that it cannot perform and cannot save?

My cry on the Cross of "It is finished" is My cry of Salvation for a whole world.

I complete every task committed to Me. So trust and be not afraid.

God at Eventide: Your Order of Merit

Grace is the distinctive mark I set upon My friends.

It is no order of merit. It is the result of living with Me. It is even unobserved by those on whom I bestow it, but to those they meet who have eyes to see, it is apparent, just as during My time on earth it was said, "They took knowledge of them that they had been with Jesus."

It may be the sign of My sustaining Power within a life. It may be the quiet strength of poise, the mark of self-conquest, some faint reflection of My character, or a mystic scent of the soul unfolding to My Love.

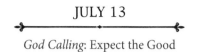

God Calling: Expect the Good

Can you get the expectant attitude of faith? Not waiting for the next evil to befall you but awaiting with a child's joyful trust the next good in store?

God at Eventide: Harmonize

Grow daily, ever more and more, into My likeness.

Do My Will as revealed to you, and leave the result to Me. If you are but My representative, then why concern yourself as to whether the action I have arranged for you is wise or not?

If your control of the mind and body is not as progressive as that of your spirit, it is a hindrance. See to this. The three must work in unison; otherwise disharmony.

Beautiful though one instrument may be in an orchestra, with a beauty beyond that of any other, yet should it play its part ahead of those others, disharmony results; and so with you a sense of frustration and failure follows disharmony within.

JULY 14

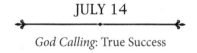

God Calling: True Success

Our Lord, we thank Thee that Thou hast kept us.

Rejoice indeed that you see My Hand in all the happenings and the keepings of the day. Protected, the Israelites crossed the Red Sea; so are you protected in all things.

Rely on this and go forward. You have now entered upon the stage of success. You must not doubt this. You must see this. Beyond all doubt you must know it. It is true. It is sure.

There is no age in Eternal Life. Have no pity for yourself, nothing but joy and gratitude.

These last few weeks have been the submerging before the consciousness of rescue. Go forward now and conquer. Go forward unafraid.

God at Eventide: Home of Creation

Have no fear. Wonders are unfolding ever more and more. You will be guided in all as you dwell in the Secret Place of the Most High.

Remember in that Secret Place was thought out all the wonders of the Universe. There all *your* wonder plans will be evolved. It is the home of Creation, and there you, too, share in Creative Power.

JULY 15

God Calling: Songs on the Way

Many of My disciples have had to stay on in the dark, alone and friendless.

They struggled on, singing as they went.

For you, too, there must be songs on the way. Should I plant your feet on an insecure ladder? Its supports may be out of your sight, hidden in the Secret Place of the Most High, but if I have asked you to step on and up firmly—then surely have I secured your ladder.

God at Eventide: Home of Joy

Heart speaks to heart as you wait before Me. Love enkindles Love.

The air you breathe is Divine, life-giving, invigorating.
The place in which you rest is My Secret Place.
You do not come to ask Me of doctrine.

That is, as it were, the foundation of your Spiritual being; necessary but once secure, you seek to fashion, with Me, its beautiful superstructure—the home of Peace and Joy where I come and commune with you.

JULY 16

God Calling: Refuge

Know My Divine Power. Trust in Me. Dwell in My Love. Laugh and trust. Laughter is a child's faith in God and good.

Seek safety in My Secret Place.

You cannot be touched or harmed there. That is sure.

Really feel as if you were in a strong Tower, strongly guarded, and against which nothing can prevail.

God at Eventide: Confidence

Help is always yours.

It comes so swiftly when you realize that *you* are insufficient to supply your need. But it comes the more potently as you grow to see that for each need the supply was already provided.

My followers so often act as if My supply came into being only through prayer for help.

Would any man in authority act thus in his business?

Learn of Me. I will teach you lovingly, patiently. My lessons are not of the schoolroom; they are fireside confidences.

God Calling: Peace Be Still

Rejoice, rejoice. I have much to teach you both. Think not that I withhold My Presence when I do not reveal more of My Truth to you.

You are passing through a storm. Enough that I am with you to say, "Peace, be still," to quiet both wind and waves.

It was on the quiet mountain slopes that I taught My disciples the Truths of My Kingdom, not during the storm.

So with you, the time of the mountain slopes will come, and you shall rest with Me and learn.

God at Eventide: Foretaste of Heaven

*I thank Thee, Lord, for the joy Thou givest
me and for Thy tender care of me.*

Grow ever more and more conscious of this. Look upon all as under My Influence, and life will become increasingly full of Joy. This Joy no man taketh from you.

This is the foretaste of Heaven that will make your passing seem no death, and will mean that your spirit will be no stranger in the home of spirits but will be breathing an atmosphere familiar and dear.

JULY 18

God Calling: Walk Humbly

Fear of what others will say is want of trust in Me. This must not be. Convert all these difficulties into the purification of your characters.

See yourselves as those around you see you, not as you wish to be, and walk very humbly with your God.

I will set you on high because you have known My Name, but it must be a purified you to be so exalted.

God at Eventide: Meek and Lowly

As the world's great Teacher I taught not only so much by word as by the Living Word.

"Learn of Me," I said, adding that men should see in Me meekness. . .and lowliness.

So that My disciples should take Me as their great example, I epitomized My attitude towards My Father in Heaven and towards His other children as "Meek and lowly."

Toward God the Father the meekness of a yielded will; toward His other children lowliness devoid of the pride that sunders men and prevents their humble approach to God.

"Learn of Me—I am meek and lowly in heart." So do you find rest unto your souls.

JULY 19

God Calling: Marvelous Happenings

Our Lord, with hearts full of joy we thank Thee for Thy marvelous blessings showered on us today and every day.

I am beside you. Follow in all things My Guiding. Marvels beyond all your imaginings are unfolding. I am your Guide. Joy in that thought. Your Guide and your Friend.

Remember that to Me a miracle is only a natural happening. To My disciples, to My chosen, a miracle is only a natural happening. But it is a natural happening operative through spiritual forces, and therefore the man who works and understands through the senses only regards it as something contrary to Nature.

My children, the children of My Kingdom are a Peculiar People, set apart, with different hopes and aspirations and motives and sense of reward.

You see a marvelous happening (as that today), happening so easily, so simply, so free from all other agency, and you wonder.

My children, listen, this has not happened easily and simply. It has been achieved by hours, days, months of weariness and heartache battled against and overcome by a steadfast, unflinching desire to conquer self and to do My Will and live My teachings.

The frets and the worries and the scorn patiently borne mean spiritual Power acquired, operating marvelously.

God at Eventide: Wayside Meetings

I use such simple things and casual moments to reveal Myself to man. He can meet Me in the common ways of Life—if he has but eyes to see and ears to hear.

No great sign, nothing spectacular. In a seemingly incidental along the road of life I meet with him and reveal My Will, My Purpose, My Guidance.

No miles to walk, no long journey to travel, no strange language to learn, no state of ecstasy to be experienced first. Think on these things. Recall our meetings by the wayside.

God Calling: My Standard

Carry out My Commands and leave the result to Me. Do this as obediently and faithfully as you would expect a child to follow out a given rule in the working of a sum, with no question but that, if the working out is done according to command, the result will be right.

Remember that the commands I have given you have been already worked out by Me in the Spirit World to produce in your case, and in your circumstances, the required result. So follow My rules faithfully.

Realize that herein lies the perfection of Divine Guidance. To follow a rule, laid down, even by Earth's wisest, might lead to disaster.

The knowledge of your individual life and character, capability, circumstances, and temptations must be, to some extent, lacking, but to follow My direct Guidance means to carry out instructions given with a full knowledge of you and the required result.

Each individual was meant to walk with Me in this way, to act under Divine control, strengthened by Divine Power.

Have I not taught you to love simplicity? No matter what the world may think, Earth's aims and intrigues are not for you. Oh! My children, learn of Me. Simplicity brings rest. True rest and Power.

To the world foolishness, maybe, but to Me a foretaste of Divinity.

God at Eventide: I Will Heal You

Do not recognize your illness. Each time you speak of it to others you stabilize it.

Ignore it as much as you can. Think more of Me, the

Great Healer. Dwelling with Me you become whole.

Even My most faithful followers often err in not claiming of Me healing and perfection for every part of their being.

But to claim physical healing alone is a sign of living too much on the physical plane, and My Healing is of the Spirit.

Claim healing of spirit, mind, and body. Then shall you, regardless of age, know wholeness.

JULY 21

God Calling: The Way of Praise

I am teaching you both My Way of removing mountains. The way to remove mountains is the way of Praise. When a trouble comes, think of all you have to be thankful for. Praise, Praise, Praise.

Say "Thank you" all the time. This is the remover of mountains, your thankful hearts of praise.

God at Eventide: Unconquerable

I will help you to conquer in the hour of temptation or difficulty. Cling to Me. Rest in My Love. Know that all is well.

Trials press, temptations assail, but remember, you can be more than conquerors through Me. Lord of all, I am. Controller of all. Keeper, Lover, Guide, Friend.

Remember that when once your hearts have said with Peter, "Thou art of the Christ, the Son of the Living God," then upon that sure foundation of relief I raise My House, My Holy of Holies.

The gates of hell, the adverse deeds and thoughts and criticisms of the world, cannot prevail against it. More than conquerors. Conquer in the little things. Conquer in My Strength and Power.

JULY 22

God Calling: Miracle of the Ages

Abide in Me. "The works that I do shall ye do also; and greater works than these shall ye do; because I go unto My Father."

"Greater Works!" The blind received their sight, the lame walked, the lepers were cleansed, the poor had the Gospel preached to them. "And greater works than these shall ye do; because I go unto My Father."

Wonder of the World! Miracle of the Ages! God's Power manifest in believing man! God's Power going out to bless, through the agency of the man actuated by the Holy Spirit. Arise from the grave of sickness, poverty, doubt, despondency, limitation. "Arise, shine; for thy light is come, and the glory of the Lord is risen upon thee."

A wonderful future is before you both. A future of unlimited power to bless others. Just be channels. Be used. Ask. Ask. "Ask what ye will, and it shall be done unto you," and unto those for whom you pray.

God at Eventide: Lend a Hand

Not once only in your lives, when I called you out to follow Me, but constantly—

Jesus calls.

In the busy day, in the crowded way, listen to the voice of your Lord and Lover calling. A call to stop and rest with Me awhile. A call to restrain your impatience, a reminder that in quietness and in confidence shall be your strength. A call to pause, to speak a word to one in trouble.

Perhaps to lend a hand.

JULY 23

God Calling: Stop All Work Until—

Our Lord, grant us that wonderful inward Peace.

My children, that Peace does truly pass all understanding. That Peace no man taketh from you. No man has the power to disturb that Peace, but you yourselves can let the world and its worries and distractions in.

You can give the entrance to fears and despondency. You can open the door to the robber who breaks in upon, and destroys, your Peace.

Set yourselves this task to allow nothing to disturb your Peace, your heart calm, with Me. Stop all work, stop all intercourse with others—until this is restored. Do not let those about you spoil your peace of heart and mind. Do not let anyone without, any trouble, any irritation, any adversity disturb it for one moment.

Look on each difficulty as training to enable you to acquire this Peace. Every work, every interruption—set yourself to see that none of it touches the harmony of the real *you* that is hid with Me in the Secret Place of the Father.

God at Eventide: Dear Name

The murmuring of My Name in tender Love brings the unseen into the foreground of reality. It is like breathing on some surface, which brings into relief a lovely figure.

It is the Name before which evil shrinks away, shamed, powerless, defeated. Breathe it often. Not always in appeal. Sometimes in tender confidence, sometimes in Love's consciousness. Sometimes in triumphant ecstasy.

God Calling: Keep Close

Our Lord, guide us. Show us Thy Will and Way in everything.

Keep close to Me and you shall know the Way, because, as I said to My disciples, I am the Way. That is the solution to all Earth's problems.

Keep close, very close to Me. Think, act, and live in My Presence.

How dare any foe touch you, protected by Me! That is the secret of all Power, all Peace, all Purity, all influence, the keeping very near to Me.

Abide in Me. Live in My Presence. Rejoice in My Love. Thank and Praise all the time. Wonders are unfolding.

God at Eventide: Christian Cooperators

I have always work to be done. So fit yourself for it by prayer, by contact with Me, by discipline.

Nothing is small in My sight. A simple task fittingly done may be the necessary unit in building a mighty edifice.

The bee knows nothing of its agency when fertilizing flowers for fruit-bearing.

Do not expect to see results.

The work may pass into other hands before any achievement is apparent. Enough that you are a worker with others and Me in My Vineyard.

JULY 25

God Calling: Wonderful Life

I am your Lord. Lord of your lives, Controller of your days, your present and your future. Leave all plans to Me. Only act as I bid you.

You have entered now, both of you, upon the God-guided life. Think what that means. God-taught, God-guided.

Is anything too wonderful for such a life? Do you begin to see how wonderful life with Me can be?

Do you see that no evil can befall you?

God at Eventide: Joy in Me

Joy teaches. Joy cleans the smeared glass of your consciousness, and you see clearly.

You see Me clearly, and see more clearly the needs of those round you.

JULY 26

God Calling: Forget—Forgive

Our Lord, we thank Thee for so much.
We bless Thee and praise Thy Glorious Name.

Fill your world with Love and laughter. Never mind what anguish lies behind you.

Forget, Forgive, Love, and Laugh.

Treat *all* as you would treat Me, with Love and consideration.

Let nothing that others do to you alter your treatment of them.

Perfect as My Father in Heaven is perfect.

That means a life-struggle, and unending growth. Always as you progress, a greater perception of My Father. More struggles and growth. Above all a growing need of Me and My sustaining help.

I came to found a Kingdom of Progressive growth. Alas, how many of My followers think that all they have to do is to accept Me as Savior. That is a first step only.

Heaven itself is no place of stagnation. It is indeed a place of progress. You will need Eternity to understand Eternal Mind.

JULY 27

God Calling: My Consolation

O Jesus, come and walk with us and let us feel Thy very nearness.

I walk with you. Oh! think, My children, not only to guide and comfort you and strengthen and uphold, but for solace and comfort for Myself.

When a loving child is by you, is the nearness only that you may provide protection and help for that little one?

Rather, too, that in that little child *you* may find joy and cheer and comfort in its simplicity, its Love, its trust.

So, too, is it in your power to comfort and bring joy to My Heart.

God at Eventide: Judge Not

Human nature is so complex. You can hardly, even in your most enlightened moments, tell what motive prompted this or that action of your own.

How, then, can you judge of another, of whose nature you have so little understanding? And to misjudge of what in another may have been prompted by the Spirit of God, is to misjudge God's Spirit.

Can any sin be greater than that? False judgment sent Me to the Cross!

JULY 28

God Calling: Mistakes

I am your Shield. No buffets of the world can harm you. Feel that between you and all scorn and indignity is a strong shield. Practice feeling this until nothing has the power to spoil the inward peace. Then indeed a marvelous victory shall be won.

You wonder sometimes why you are permitted to make mistakes in your choice when you sought so truly to do My Will in the matter.

To that I say it was no mistake.... All your lessons cannot be learned without difficulty, and this was needed to teach you a lesson. Not to him who walks on, with no obstacles in his way, but to him that *overcometh is the promise given.*

So to attain peace quickly in your surroundings, as well as in your hearts, learn your lesson quickly. And the overcoming is never the overcoming of the one who troubled you, but the overcoming of the weaknesses and wrong in your own nature, aroused by such a one.

No lower standard than My Standard shall be yours. "Be ye therefore *perfect*, even as your Father which is in heaven is perfect."

The world can be overcome only by belief in Me, and in the knowledge that I am the Son of God. This is a stupendous Truth.

Use that as your lever for removing every mountain of difficulty and evil. Be cautious in all things and await My Guidance. Commune much with Me.

The truth of My Godhead, of My All-Power, creative, redemptive, erosive of evil, must permeate your whole consciousness, and affect your attitude in every situation, toward every problem.

JULY 29

God Calling: Sunlit Glades

Lord, bless us in this evening hour, and in Thy Mercy heal us all.

Do not think that suffering is the only path into My Kingdom. There are sunlit glades and ways amid the loveliest flowers, along which the steps and hearts of men are drawn to Me. There are birds and laughter and butterflies and warm, life-giving summer air, and with these as tender companions and friends, the Joy-Way into the Kingdom can be taken.

Bleak, cold, and desolate, briar-beset and stony, are not all the ways. Leave all to Me. The choice of ways, the guidance in the way. But when the sunlight calls, accept it gladly.

Even in the Spirit-World appreciation results from contrary experience. Can the fireside of home be dearer than to the traveler who has forced his way over bleak moor and through blinding storm? Take to your hearts this word of cheer. He "will not suffer you to be tempted above that ye are able; but will with the temptation also make a way to escape, that ye may be able to bear it."

The world is not the Kingdom. "In the world ye shall have tribulation: but be of good cheer; I have overcome the world." Live with Me, the Conquering Christ, and the Joy and Peace of conquest shall be yours too.

God at Eventide: See the Lovable

Do not try to force yourself to love others. Come to Me. Learn to love Me more and more, to know Me more, and little by little you will see your fellowman as I see him. Then you, too, will love him.

Not only with the Love of Me, which makes you desire to serve him, but you will see the lovable in him, and love that.

JULY 30

God Calling: Faith Rewarded

Think much of My servants of old. How Abraham believed the promise (when as yet he had no child) that in his seed all the nations of the earth should be blessed.

How Moses led the Children of Israel through the desert, sure that, at last, they would gain the Promised Land.

Down through the ages there have always been those who obeyed, not seeing but believing, and their faith was rewarded. So shall it be even with you.

God at Eventide: Real Influence

Do not let one single link of influence go.

Cords of true love and interest must never be broken. They must always be used for ME. Pray for those to whom you are bound by particular ties, then you will be ready, should I desire your special help for them.

You must stand as a sinner with a sinner before you can save him. Even I had to hang between two thieves to save My world.

JULY 31

God Calling: Gratitude

Give Me the gift of a brave and thankful heart. Man proves his greatness by his power to see causes for thankfulness in his life.

When life seems hard, and troubles crowd, then very definitely look for causes for thankfulness.

The sacrifice, the offering of thanksgiving, is indeed a sweet incense going up to Me through the busy day.

Seek diligently for something to be glad and thankful about in every happening, and soon no search will be required.

The causes for Joy and Gratitude will spring to greet your loving hearts.

God at Eventide: All in Order

He ordered my goings.

Guidance first, but more than that, Divine order in your life, your home, all your affairs.

Order in all. Attain spiritual order first. The perfect calm which can be realized only by a soul that abides in My Secret Place.

Then the mental order of a mind which is stayed on Me and has the sanity and poise of a mind so stayed.

Then truly must order manifest itself in your surroundings.

Each task will be entered upon with prayer, as a Divine

Commission, and carried through without haste, in utter contentment.

AUGUST 1

God Calling: Blessed Bond

Jesus, let Thy Beautiful Presence be always with us.

"I will never leave thee, nor forsake thee." There is no bond of union on earth to compare with the union between a soul that loves Me—and Me.

Priceless beyond all Earth's imaginings is that Friendship.

In the merging of heart and mind and will a oneness results that only those who experience it can even dimly realize.

God at Eventide: Joy of Harvest

He that reapeth receiveth wages and gathereth fruit unto life everlasting, that both he that reapeth and he that soweth may rejoice together.

Do you not see that if you are careless about the reaping you have prevented the harvest-joy of the sower?

If by your life and character you do not reap to the full that which they have sown, you are robbing them of the well-earned fruit of their labors.

Further learn this lesson. There are many of My workers and servants in different spheres of the activity to whom you owe the seed of word or example or loving help that has influenced you.

It is a sacred trust. Use it fully.

God Calling: Harvest

My Lord, we seek Thy Blessing.

I love to pour My blessings down in rich, in choicest measure. But like the seed-sowing—the ground must be prepared before the seed is dropped in.

Yours to prepare the soil—Mine to drop the seed-blessing into the prepared soil.

Together we share in, and joy in, the harvest.

Spend more time in soil-preparing. Prayer fertilizes soil. There is much to do in preparation.

God at Eventide: Still Love and Laugh

This has ever been My command to you. Love and Laugh. There is a quality about true Love to which laughter is attune.

The Love that does not pulse with joy (of which laughter is the outward sign) is but solicitude. The Joy of Heaven is consciousness of God's Love.

It was that Love that brought Me to your world.

Consciousness of that Love called forth your joy. Study My Words in the Upper Room—"Loved of My Father"; "I will love him"; "That your Joy might be full."

AUGUST 3

God Calling: Give Every Moment

My children, how dear to my Heart is the cry of Love that asks for all of Me, that wishes every action, thought, word, and moment to be Mine. How poor the understanding of the one who thinks that money to be used in this good work or that, is the great gift to offer. Above all I desire Love, true, warm, childlike Love, the trusting understanding Love, and then the gift I prize next is the gift of the moments, of all the moments.

I think even when Love's impetuous longing to serve Me has offered Me all Life, every day, every hour, I think even then it is a long, and not an easy lesson, to learn, what it means to give Me the moments.

The little things you planned to do, given up gladly at My suggestion, the little services joyfully rendered. See *Me* in all, and then it will be an easy task.

This is a priceless time of initiation, but remember that the path of initiation is not for all; but only for those who have felt the sorrow-cry of the world that needs a Savior and the tender plea of a Savior Who needs followers through whom He can accomplish His great work of Salvation joyfully.

God at Eventide: Love Lightens the Load

In due season you shall reap if you faint not.

The way may seem long and dreary.

Sometimes My Heart of Love aches that I have to ask you to tread so long and so weary a way. Yet to each of My followers the road chosen is surely the one best suited to his feet.

But feet grow weary. Have you let Love smooth the toilsome way? We walk together.

AUGUST 4

God Calling: Eternal Life

O Jesus, we love Thee so and long to serve Thee.

My children, you are both to do mighty things for Me. Glories and wonders unfold. Life is one glorious whole.

Draw into your beings more and more this wonderful Eternal Life. It is the flow of the Life Eternal through spirit, mind, and body that cleanses, heals, restores, renews youth, and passes on from you to others with the same miracle-working power.

"And this is life eternal, that they might know thee. . .and Jesus Christ, whom thou hast sent." So seek by constant contact to know Me more and more.

Make Me the one abiding Presence of your day of which you are conscious all the time. Seek to *do* less and to *accomplish* more, to achieve more. Doing is action. Achievement is successful action.

Remember that Eternal Life is the only lasting life, so that all that is done without being done in the Power of My Spirit, My Life, is passing. All done in that Spirit-Life is undying.

"I give unto them eternal life; and they shall never perish, neither shall any man pluck them out of my hand." So Eternal Life means security too, *safety*. Dwell increasingly in the consciousness of that security, that safety.

God at Eventide: Vision of Love

Love is the flower.
Love is the seed from which that flower germinates.
Love is the soil in which it is nourished and grows.
Love is the sun that draws it to fulfillment.
Love is the fragrance that flower gives out.

Love is the vision that sees its beauty, and
God is Love, all-knowing, all-understanding, from whom all Good proceeds.

AUGUST 5

God Calling: Hour of Need

Lord, come to us and heal us.

I am your Healer, your Joy, your Lord. You bid Me, your Lord, come. Did you not know that I am here? With noiseless foot-fall I draw near to you.

Your hour of need is the moment of My Coming.

Could you know My Love, could you measure My Long-ing to help, you would know that I need no agonized pleading.

Your *need* is My Call.

God at Eventide: Love in the Unlovely

Love to all must mark all you do if you own Me Lord, and if you would be a true follower of Me.

"His banner over me was Love." Those words express not only the loving Protection round you, but the banner under which you march as soldiers of Me, your Captain.

It serves to remind you of that for which you stand before the world. It is in Love's Name you march. In Love's Name you conquer. It is Love you are to take into the unlovely places of the world. It is the only equipment you need.

God Calling: Dwell Apart

Rest more with Me. If I, the Son of God, needed those times of quiet communion with My Father, away, alone, from noise, from activity—then surely you need them too.

Refilling with the Spirit is a need. That dwelling apart, that shutting yourself away in the very secret place of your being—away alone with Me.

From these times you come forth in Power to bless and heal.

God at Eventide: Deaf Ears

Man cries for help. Man feels his need of Me. All unmindful that countless times I draw near unheard, pass on unnoticed, speak to deaf ears, touch brows fretted and wrinkled by earth's cares.

"The Christ is dead," man says.

Alive and longing, full of a living tenderness I passed his way today. He heeded not.

Man hears the storms, the wind, the earthquake, and his ears still pulsing with the echoes he hears no Still, Small Voice. Oh, do not miss Me, My children.

AUGUST 7

God Calling: All Is Well

Our Lord, bless us and keep us, we beseech Thee.

My Keeping Power is never at fault, but only your realization of it. Not whether I can provide a shelter from the storm, but your failure to be sure of the security of that shelter.

Every fear, every doubt, is a crime against My Love.

Oh! children, trust. Practice daily, many times a day, saying, "All is well."

Say it until you believe it, know it.

God at Eventide: Balm for All Ills

Love and care and pray. Never feel helpless to aid those you love. I am their help. As you obey Me and follow My teaching in your daily life, you will bring that help into operation.

So, if you desire to be used to save another, turn to your own life. As far as you can, make it all that it should be.

Let your influence for Me extend ever further and further. Let Love be your balm for all ills, The Power in which you will break down all barriers.

It stands, too, for the Name of the God you love and serve. So with His banner floating o'er you, go on in glad confidence to victory. Your task to help, to strengthen, raise, heal. Only as you love will you do this.

AUGUST 8

God Calling: Empty Yourself

Rely on Me alone. Ask no other help. Pay all out in the Spirit of trust that more will come to meet your supply.

Empty your vessels quickly to ensure a Divine Supply.

So much retained by you, so much the less will be gained from Me. It is a Law of Divine Supply.

To hold back, to retain, implies a fear of the future, a want of trust in Me.

When you ask Me to save you from the sea of poverty

and difficulty, you must trust wholly to Me. If you do not, and your prayer and faith are genuine, then I must first answer your prayer for help as a rescuer does that of a drowning man who is struggling to save himself.

He renders him still more helpless and powerless until he is wholly at the will and mercy of the rescuer. *So* understand *My* leading. Trust wholly. Trust completely.

Empty your vessel. I will fill it. You ask both of you to understand Divine Supply. It is a most difficult lesson for My children to learn. So dependent have they become on material supply they fail to understand. You must live as I tell you.

Depend on Me.

God at Eventide: No Hurt

He that overcometh shall not be hurt by the second death.

The first death is the death to self, the result of overcoming, of self-conquest. This is gradual death.

When it is complete, the second death shall cause no hurt. For it is only the conquering Spirit sloughing away its human habitation for a better Life.

The courage My Martyrs showed was not only fearlessness engendered in time of persecution through faith in Me, and in My power to support and sustain. It was consequent on the overcoming of self already achieved. Self, having truly died, this second death had no hurt for them.

Theirs was then the Risen Life with Me.

God Calling: Effort and Rest

Come to Me, talk to Me, dwell with Me, and then you will know My Way is a sure way, My Paths are safe paths.

Come very near to Me.

Dig deep down into the soil of the Kingdom. Effort and rest—a union of the two.

God at Eventide: Undivided

Live in My Peace.

There must be no divided life in this.

Peace in your heart. That heart-rest that comes from constant communion with Me, and from an undisturbed trust in Me.

Then Peace round you, where others are conscious of Me, and of that Peace as My Gift, and the rest and strength and charm into which they are drawn.

AUGUST 10

God Calling: Stray Sheep

O Jesus, guide our footsteps lest we stray.

For straying, My children, there is no cure except to keep so close to Me that nothing, no interest, no temptation, no other—can come between us.

Sure of that you can but stay at My Side, knowing that, as I am the very Way itself, nothing can prevent your being in the Way; nothing can cause you to stray.

I have promised Peace but not leisure, heart-rest and

comfort but not pleasure. I have said, "In the world ye shall have tribulation"; so do not feel, when adverse things happen, that you have failed or are not being guided, but I have said, "In the world ye shall have tribulation: but be of good cheer; I have overcome the world."

So learn of Me the overcoming Power of One who, though spat upon, scourged, misunderstood, forsaken, crucified, could yet see His Work had not been affected by these things and cry triumphantly from His Cross, "It is finished."

Not the pain, the mocking, the agony, but His Task.

Let this thought comfort you. Amid failure, discord, contumely, suffering, even now may friends and angels be prepared to sound the chorus, "It is finished."

God at Eventide: Glad Surprise

Live so near to Me that you may never miss the opportunity of being used by Me. It is the prepared instrument, lying nearest to the Master Craftsman's Hand, that is seized to do the work.

So be very near Me, and you cannot fail to be much used. Remember that Love is the Great Interpreter, so that those who love you and are near to you are the ones you can help the most.

Do not pass them by for others, though your influence and helpfulness will gradually spread, in an ever-widening circle. You will live in a spirit of glad surprise.

God Calling: You Are Mine

Jesus, Thou art watching over us to bless and care for us.

Yes! remember that always—that out of darkness I am leading you to light. Out of unrest to rest, out of disorder to order. Out of faults and failure to perfection.

So trust Me wholly. Fear nothing. Hope ever. Look ever up to Me and I will be your sure aid.

I and My Father are One. So He who made the ordered, beautiful world out of chaos, and set the stars in their courses, and made each plant to know its season, can He not bring out of your little chaos peace and order?

And He and I are One, and you are Mine. Your affairs are Mine. It is My Divine Task to order My affairs—therefore yours will be ordered by Me.

God at Eventide: Absolute Honesty

Learn to act slowly with sanctified caution.

Precipitancy has no part in My Kingdom.

Be more deliberate in everything, with the deliberation that should characterize every soul, for it is one of the credentials of that Kingdom.

Lack of poise and dignity means lack of Spiritual Power, and this it must be your aim to possess.

Be truthful in all things, honest with an honesty that can be challenged by the world, and by the standards of My Kingdom, too.

AUGUST 12

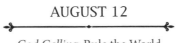

God Calling: Rule the World

Remember no prayer goes unanswered. Remember that the moment a thing seems wrong to you, or a person's actions seem not to be what you think they should be, at that moment begins your obligation and responsibility to pray for those wrongs to be righted or that person to be different.

Face your responsibilities. What is wrong in your country, its statesmen, its laws, its people? Think out quietly, and make these matters your prayer matters. You will see lives you never touch altered, laws made at your request, evils banished.

Yes! live in a large sense. Live to serve and to save. You may never go beyond one room, and yet you may become one of the most powerful forces for good in your country, in the world.

You may never see the mighty work you do, but I see it, evil sees it. Oh! it is a glorious life, the life of one who saves. Fellow-workers together with me. See this more and more.

Love with me, sharers of My life.

God at Eventide: Holy Revelry

Live with Me. Work with Me. Ever delight to do My Holy Will. Let this be the satisfaction of your lives. Revel in it.

Let the wonder of My care for you be so comforting that you may see no dullness in drudgery, in delay. . .

The Glory of My leading, the wonder of its intimacy reveals such tender knowledge of you, past and future.

Let this reveal Me to you, and so daily increase your knowledge of Me.

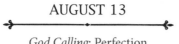
God Calling: Perfection

O Jesus, help us, we beseech Thee.

Ever your Helper through dark to Light, through weakness to Power, through sin to Salvation, through danger to Security, through poverty to Plenty, through indifference to Love, through resentment to Perfect Forgiveness.

Never be satisfied with a comparison with those around you. Ever let My words ring out. "Be ye therefore perfect, even as your Father which is in heaven is perfect." Stop short at nothing less.

Make it your practice, each of you, to review your character—take it in relation to life, to your dear ones, your household, friends, acquaintances, your country, your work.

See where I, in the same relation or circumstances or situation, should act differently. Plan how best such and such a fault can be eradicated, or such and such sin, mistake, or omission be avoided.

A weekly review at least you must have.

God at Eventide: The Road You Took

Look back at the way I have led you.

Say to yourself, "Is not my Lord as strong today as in the days that lie behind me? Did He not save me when human aid was powerless? Did He not keep His Promise, and protect and care for me? Can I, remembering that, doubt His Power now?"

So you will gain confidence and a firmer trust. As your faith is thus strengthened My Power can operate more freely and fully on your behalf.

You are only beginning to realize My Wonders. You will see them unfold more and more as you go on. Bring Me into all you do, into every plan, every action.

AUGUST 14

God Calling: My Richest Gift

Jesus, Thou didst come that we might have life,
and have it more abundantly.

Life, spiritual, mental, physical, abundant Life—Joyous Life, Powerful Life. Yes! these I came to give you.

Think you not My Heart was sad that so few would accept that gracious gift!

Think! Earth's richest, choicest gift held out—free to all, and no man to care to stretch out a hand to take it.

Is that possible? My Gift, the richest Heaven has to offer, that precious Gift of Life, abundant Life—man turns away from—rejects—will have none of.

Let it not be true of you. Hasten to take—to use.

God at Eventide: Riches of His Grace

It is for My followers to make My Word, the very Word of God, attractive.

My Word has to *dwell* in you richly. There must be no stinting, no poverty, but an abundance of rich supply.

Note the *dwell*. Nothing fitful, as I have told you. Make its home there. Fittingly belong there. No question of meager or exhausted supply.

The Word of God grows in meaning, in intensity, for you, as you bring it into operation.

Remember, too, the Word of God is that Word made flesh, Who dwells with you, your Lord Jesus Christ.

AUGUST 15

God Calling: Not Punishment

I will guide your efforts. You are not being punished for past sins. Take My Words, revealed to you each day from the beginning, and do in all things as I say. I have been showing you the way. You have not obeyed Me in this.

I have a plan that can only in this way be revealed. So rarely do I find two souls in union who want only My Will, and only to serve Me. The union is miracle-working.

I have told you that I am longing to use you. Long ago My world would have been brought to Me had I been served by many such *two souls*.

It was always "two and two."

God at Eventide: My Image Restored

Look unto Me until your gaze becomes so intense that you absorb the Beauty of Holiness.

Then truly is the petty, unworthy self ousted from your nature. Look to Me. Speak to Me. Think of Me.

So you become transformed by the renewing of your mind. Other thoughts, other desires, other ways follow, for you become transformed into My Likeness.

Thus you vindicate the ways of God with man—man made in His image, that Image marred, but I still had trust in man; trust that man, seeing the God-Image in Me, the man Christ Jesus, would aspire to rise again—into My Likeness.

AUGUST 16

God Calling: No Tired Work

Rest. It is wrong to force work. Rest until Life, Eternal Life, flowing through your veins and hearts and minds, bids you bestir yourselves, and work, glad work, will follow.

Tired work never tells.

Rest. Remember I am your Physician, Healer of mind and body.

Look to Me for cure, for rest, for Peace.

God at Eventide: Expectancy

In all your work, your meetings with others, have ever the consciousness of My brooding Love surrounding you. Continue ye in My Love.

Meet Me at eventide with loving expectancy.

AUGUST 17

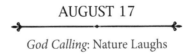

God Calling: Nature Laughs

I come, I come. You need Me. Live much out here. My sunshine, My glorious air, My Presence, My teaching.

Would they not make holiday anywhere for you. Sunshine helps to make glad the heart of man. It is the laughter of Nature.

Live much outside. My medicines are sun and air, trust and faith. Trust is the spirit sun, your being enwrapped by the Divine Spirit.

Faith is the soul's breathing in of the Divine Spirit. Mind, soul, and body need helping. Welcome My treatment for you both. Draw near to Me.

Nature is often My nurse for tired souls and weary bodies. Let her have her way with you both.

God at Eventide: Premature Blessing

Give me strength to wait Thy time, accept Thy discipline.

Only your failure to do this can delay the answers to your many prayers.

The blessing you crave needs a trained, disciplined life, or it would work your ruin and bring upon you a world's criticism that could but harm the very cause, My cause, which you so ardently seek to serve.

AUGUST 18

God Calling: Stones of the Way

I am here. No distance separates Me. In the Spirit-Kingdom we measure not by Earth's miles. A false word, a fear-inspired failure, a harsh criticism, these are the distances between a soul and Me. Your training must be severe, that your work for Me be unhindered.

You seek My Presence, and they who seek shall find. It is not a question of human searching, so much as human consciousness, unconditional surrender to My Will in the small, as in the big things of life. This it is that makes My Guidance possible.

You know the difference between taking a glad, loving, joy-springing child with you along a way, when the child anticipates each direction, accepts naturally each decision as to each turning—and the child who resists, and, rebellious, has to be forced, even though in its quieter moments it may say,

"Yes. I do want to go with you. I cannot be left alone, but I hate this way."

It is not the way, but the loving rejoicing in the way and the guidance, that matters with My disciples. You are ready for the guidance, but you do not rejoice as you should, both of you, in the little daily stones of the way.

God at Eventide: Broken Bonds

Loose the fetters that bind me to earth and material things.

They shall be loosed. Even now your prayer is being answered. But you can only be completely released as you live with Me more and more.

Thought-freedom from self-claims comes by a process of substitution. For every claim of self, substitute My claim. For every thought of fear or resentment substitute a thought of security in Me and of Joy in My Service. For every thought of limitation, or helplessness, substitute one of the Power of a Spirit-aided life.

Do this persistently. At first with deliberate effort, until it becomes an almost unconscious habit. The fetters will snap and gradually you will realize the wonder of your freedom.

AUGUST 19

God Calling: A Human Temple

Lord, we Love Thee, we worship Thee.

Bow low before Me. Worship is not supplication, though both express man's varying needs of Me. Bow low in worship, conscious not only of My humanity but of My Divine Majesty.

As you kneel in humble adoration, I will tell you that

when I took upon Me your humanity, it was with the desire of raising that humanity to My Divinity.

Earth gave Me her best—a human temple to enclose My Divinity, and I brought to her the possession of Divine Power, Divine Love, and Divine Strength to be forever expressed in those of her children who accepted Me, opened their hearts to Me, and sought to live My Life.

So, kneeling in a spirit of humility, turn your eyes Heavenward and realize the Majesty, the Power, the Beauty that may be yours. Remember there are no limits to My giving—there may be to your accepting.

Oh! rejoice at the wonders to which you are called and, seeing them in prayer, rise in My Strength, filled with the longing to attain them.

God at Eventide: Bounteous Giving

Lord I ask for Thine unlimited supply.

I give with no niggard hand. See the Beauty in Nature, the profusion, the generosity. When I give you a work to do, a need of another's to meet, My supply knows no bounds.

You, too, must learn this Divine generosity, not only towards the lonely, the needy, whom you contact, but towards Me, your Lord.

Measure the wealth of Mary's gift by the offerings given to Me nowadays by those who profess their Love for Me. Ungenerous giving dwarfs the soul.

AUGUST 20

God Calling: Shame and Remorse

Peter could never have done My Work but for the tender Love with which I enwrapped him. Not from the anger of My Father, who is all Love, did I need to protect him—not from the scorn of My enemies, nor from the resentment of My friends. No! but from the hatred of Peter himself.

And so to My followers today, as then, there come the shame and remorse and contempt of themselves, of the weak selves. They meant to be so strong and brave for Me. And then I have to protect them or never could they have the courage to fight and conquer. But this facing of the real self has to be—shame and remorse must come.

You must be as one who runs a race, stumbles and falls, rises and presses on to the goal. What avails it if he stays to examine the spot where he fell, to weep over the delay, over the shortsightedness that prevented his avoiding the obstacles?

So with you, and I lay it on you as a command—no looking back. Give yourself and all you have ever met a fresh start from today. Remember no more their sins and failures or your own.

When I sent My disciples out two by two—no scrip, no two coats, no money—it was an injunction to be carried out literally but figuratively, too. On Life's journey throw away all that is not important. Cast aside all the hindrances, the past imperfections of others, the failure-sense.

God at Eventide: Glorious Opportunity

Man's life is no tragedy or comedy staged by a God of Whims.

It is man's glorious opportunity of regaining what humanity lost—assisted by the One Who found the path-direct, and Who is ready at every point, and all along the way to supply man with the Life Eternal.

That Life Eternal which alone enables him to breathe, even here now, the very air of Heaven, and to be inspired with the Spirit-life in which I lived on earth; God made man.

AUGUST 21

God Calling: Broken Voices

Behold, I make all things new. It is only the earthbound spirit that cannot soar. Every blessing I send you, every joy, every freedom achieved from poverty and worry will loosen a strand that ties you to Earth.

It is only those strands that bind you. Therefore your freedom will mean your rising into the realm of Joy and Appreciation.

Clipped wings can grow again. Broken voices regain a strength and beauty unknown before. Your power to help other lives will soon bring its delight, even when, at first, the help to yourselves may seem too late to bring you Joy.

Worn-out and tired as you may seem, and pain-weary, I say unto you, "Behold, I make all things new." That promise shall be fulfilled. Tenderly across the years, yet tenderly close and near to your tired noise-weary ears, I speak to you, My loved ones, today.

"Come unto me, all ye that labour and are heavy laden, and I will give you rest."

God at Eventide: Where to Find Me—Always

Man so often seeks and marvels that he does not find. Why? Because only along the path of simple obedience am I to be found.

I said, "I came not to do Mine own Will but the Will of Him that sent Me." I tread, as I always trod, the path of simple obedience. Along it shall I be found.

Man must be simply obedient to My Commands before his feet can come My way. Then, seeking, he truly finds Me. I said you must become as little children to enter the Kingdom of Heaven.

AUGUST 22

God Calling: Gleams of Sunlight

Because you have both longed to save My World, I let you have that training that shall fit you to save.

Take your pains and sufferings, difficulties and hardships— each day, both of you, and offer them up for one troubled soul, or for some prayer specially needed to be answered.

So the beauty of each day will live on after the trouble and distress, difficulty and pain of the day have passed.

Learn from My Life of the suffering that saves others. So, you will sing in your pain. Across the grayest days there are the gleams of Sunlight.

God at Eventide: True Power

Many are speaking *about* Me, and they marvel that their words have no force. They are not My Words, they are words about Me. Oh, how different.

The world is surfeited with words about Me.

The world needs to *see Me, not to hear of My Power, but to see it in action.* Not to hear of My Peace, but to see that it keeps My followers calm, unruffled, and untroubled, no matter what the outward circumstances.

Not to *hear* of My Joy, but to *see* it, as from hidden depths of security, where true Power and Peace abide, it ripples to the surface of the life, and is revealed to those round about.

AUGUST 23

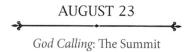

God Calling: The Summit

See not the small trials and vexations of each hour of the day. See the one purpose and plan to which all are leading. If in climbing a mountain you keep your eyes on each stony or difficult place as you ascend, seeing only that, how weary and profitless your climb!

But if you think of each step as leading to the summit of achievement, from which glories and beauties will open out before you, then your climb will be so different.

God at Eventide: Hunger for Righteousness

Many are wondering why their desire for righteousness is not satisfied according to My Promise. But that Promise was on condition that there should be hunger and thirst. If the Truths I have given have not been absorbed, there can be no real hunger for more.

So, when you miss the Joy-Light on your path, when the vision seems lost, and the Voice silent, then ask yourself, have you failed to live out the lessons that you were taught?

Live out My teaching in your lives, and then, hunger for more, come to Me, Bread of Life, Food of your souls.

God Calling: Sublime Heights

Our Lord, we know that Thou art great and able to deliver us.

I am your Deliverer. Trust in Me absolutely. Know that I will do the very best for you. Be ready and willing for My Will to be done.

Know that with Me all things are possible. Cling joyfully to that truth.

Say many times, "All things are possible with my Master, my Lord, my Friend."

This truth, accepted and firmly believed in, is the ladder up which a soul can climb from the lowest of pits to the sublimest of heights.

God at Eventide: Might and Majesty

You see Me sometimes as the Man of Sorrows.

Behold Me, too, in the Majesty of My Godhead.

Not always can Man disregard My Wishes and break My Commands.

I view the desecration of My Image, I see the ruin of the kingdom of earth which was to have been the Kingdom of the Lord. I see passions let loose and innocence spoiled, and man clamoring for the mastery.

Then the Man of Sorrows walks a King with flashing eyes, as He sees the downtrodden, the oppressed, the persecuted and the persecutor, the tyrant and the weak.

How long shall I have the patience? *How long?*

AUGUST 25

God Calling: Exhaustion

We seek Thee as Thou hast told us.

And seeking you shall find. None ever sought My Presence in vain. None ever sought My Help in vain.

A breath of desire and My Spirit is there—to replenish and renew. Sometimes weariness and exhaustion are not signs of lack of spirit but of the guiding of the Spirit.

Many wonderful things would not have happened but for the physical weariness, the mind-weariness of My servants, which made the resting apart, the giving up of work, a necessity. . . .

Though My Way may seem a narrow way, it yet leads to Life, abundant Life. Follow it. It is not so narrow but that I can tread it beside you.

Never too lonely with such companionship. A Comrade infinitely tender, infinitely strong will tread the way with you.

God at Eventide: House of the Spirit

"Lest perhaps you should let them slip"—"Hold fast that thou hast." Each Truth learned has to be cemented to your being by obedience.

Your soul-character is like a building. It IS a building (the Temple) in which the God-Spirit can make a Home.

Bricks lying on the ground separate are useless; placed together, united, they form a building. So obedience is the mortar by which Truths are retained and become a part of the being. Truths which would otherwise be lost.

So every Truth I give you must be lived out.

AUGUST 26

God Calling: Accept Trials

Trials and troubles may seem to overwhelm you. They cannot do more than work My Will, and that Will you have said is your Will.

Do you not see that you cannot be destroyed?

From now a new Life is opening out before you. Yours to enter into the Kingdom I have prepared for you.

The sunlight of My Presence is on your paths. Trust and go forward unafraid. My Grace is sufficient for all your needs.

God at Eventide: "I Die Daily"

I enjoined that if any man would follow Me he should deny himself and take up his cross.

The denial thus impressed upon My disciples as necessary was not a mere matter of discipline, of giving up, of going without.

It was a total repudiation of any claim the self might make, ignoring it, refusing to acknowledge it.

Not *once* was this to be done, but *daily*; there was to be a daily recrucifixion of any part of the self-life not already completely dead.

AUGUST 27

God Calling: Tangled Skeins

In quietness and in confidence shall be your strength.
ISAIAH 30:15

Feel that. . .trust Me. Am I not leading you safely, faithfully? Will you believe Me, your Master, that all this is really to bring the answer to your prayers?

Remember that I am the Supreme Being who knows all and can control all.

Directly as you put your affairs, their confusion, and their difficulties into My Hands, I began to effect a cure of all the disharmony and disorder.

You must know that I shall cause you no more pain in the doing of it than a physician, who plans and knows he can effect a cure, would cause his patient. I will do all as tenderly as possible.

Tell Me that you trust Me in this.

God at Eventide: One Spirit-led Family

Have no fear. Wonders unfold.

In this Life or in the Larger Life, the lesson is the same—the absorption of My Spirit—living, thinking and acting in My Spirit until others are forced to see and recognize its Power and claims.

Does this mean loneliness for My Follower? Nay, rather, though you, the human-self-you has no recognition, the real you, transformed by My Spirit, shares in all that fullness of operation and resultant Joy.

You are no isolated being but one of a mighty Spirit-led

family, partaker of all the family's well-being, cooperative in every act of each member, sharer of the blessing of each.

A foretaste this of Heaven's oneness and fulfillment.

AUGUST 28

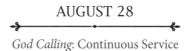

God Calling: Continuous Service

Service is the Law of Heaven. My angels do always obey. "They serve Him continually" can be said of all who love Me.

With Love there is continuous service in every action and also even in rest.

Take this not as the end but as the beginning of a new Life consecrated to My Service.

A Life of Power and Joy.

God at Eventide: Thread of Gold

Let My Spirit of Calm enter your being, and direct you, filling you with Peace and Power. Find in each day that thread of gold that runs through all, and that links up all the simple tasks and words and interests and feelings into one whole.

Consciously hand the day back to Me at its close, leaving with Me all that is incomplete. It is Heaven's work to complete man's imperfect or unfinished task, when it has been of Heaven's ordering.

See the Joy of Life, and you by that very act increase it. Joy grows by man's consciousness of Joy.

AUGUST 29

God Calling: Breathe My Name

Just breathe My Name.

It is like the pressure of a child's hand that calls forth an answering pressure, strengthens the child's confidence and banishes fear.

God at Eventide: Divine Extravagance

Let Christ be in you in all wealth of Wisdom.

It is the niggard attitude of My followers that casts a slur upon My religion.

Dwell upon the Divine extravagance of terms used by those who know something of the wonder of My Kingdom—"The riches," "The wealth," "The fullness." There is no stint with God.

The only limit is set by the inability of My followers to take. Wealth of wisdom and unlimited Power to help others may be yours.

AUGUST 30

God Calling: Give, Give, Give

Give abundantly. Feel that you are rich. Have no mean thought in your heart.

Of Love, of thought, of all you have, give, give, give.

You are followers of the World's Greatest Giver. Give of time, of personal ease and comfort, of rest, of fame, of healing, of power, of sympathy, of all these and many more.

Learn this lesson, and you will become a great power to help others and to do mighty things.

God at Eventide: Stand Invincible

Life, earth-life, is a battle. A battle in which man will always be the loser unless he summon Eternal Life-Forces to his aid. Do this and all that has the power to thwart you slinks back defeated.

Say, in the little as well as in the big things of life, "Nothing can harm, nothing can make me afraid. In Him I conquer." Stand invincible, face to the foes of life.

AUGUST 31

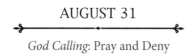

God Calling: Pray and Deny

Howbeit this kind goeth not out but by prayer and fasting.
MATTHEW 17:21

You must live a life of communion and prayer if you are to save others.

Take My Words as a command to you. "By prayer and fasting."

Pray and deny yourself, and you will be used marvelously to save and help others.

God at Eventide: Heaven's Music

Lift up your heart.

Lift it up—its love and its longings, leaving fears and faults behind.

Let your heart draw its strength and vitalizing Joy and Confidence from Me, your Lord.

Let no vibration stir your being that is not in harmony with the Eternal Music of My Kingdom.

God Calling: How Rich You Are

I will never leave thee, nor forsake thee.
HEBREWS 13:5

My children, that word is unfailingly true. Down the centuries thousands have proved My constancy, My untiringness, My unfailing Love. "Never leave." "Never forsake." Not just a Presence is meant by this, but. . .

My Love will never leave you, My Understanding will never leave you, My Strength will never leave you. Think of all that I am:

Love—then forever you are sure of Love.

Strength—then forever, in every difficulty and danger, you are sure of strength.

Patience—then always there is One who can never tire.

Understanding—then always you will be understood.

Can you fear the future when it holds so much for you? Beloved, "Set your affections on things above" (the higher, spiritual things), "and not on things on the earth" (the lower, temporal things), and you will see how rich you are.

God at Eventide: It Is Enough

Listen and I will speak.

I seldom force an entrance through many voices and distracting thoughts. There must be first the coming apart and then the stilling of all else as you wait in My Presence. Is it not enough that you are with Me?

Let that sometimes suffice.

It is truly much that I *speak* to you. But unless My Indwelling Spirit is yours, how can you carry out My wishes and live as I would have you live?

God Calling: I Must Provide

I am your Lord. Enough. Then I can command your obedient service, your loyalty. But I am bound by My Lordship to give you protection.

I am bound to fight for you, to plan for you, to secure you a sufficiency of all within My Power to provide. Think how vast that provision can be. Never doubt.

Such marvels are unfolding. Wonders beyond your dreams. They only need the watering of a grateful spirit and a loving heart to yield abundantly.

God at Eventide: You Shall Hear

Listen to My Voice. Share all your joys and sorrows and difficulties with Me, remembering always that we share the work.

More and more souls will be sent to you to help. Be ready, attuned to My slightest whisper. There is no lack of help for My servants, but so often they are not in a receptive mood.

Listen and you shall hear, is the continuation of "Ask, and you shall receive," "Seek, and you shall find," "Knock, and it shall be opened unto you—"

Listen, and you shall hear.

SEPTEMBER 3

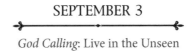

God Calling: Live in the Unseen

Our Lord, the God of the troubled and the weary, come and save us.

I am your Savior. Not only from the weight of sin, but from the weight of care, from misery and depression, from want and woe, from faintness and heartache. Your Savior.

Remember that you are living really in the Unseen—that is the Real Life.

Lift up your heads from Earth's troubles, and view the glories of the Kingdom. Higher and higher each day see more of Heaven. Speak to Me. Long for Me. Rest in Me. Abide in Me. No restless bringing Me your burdens, and then feverishly lifting them again and bearing them away.

No! *Abide* in Me. Not for one moment losing the consciousness of My Strength and Protection.

As a child in its mother's arms, stay sheltered and at rest.

God at Eventide: Your Failures Are Mine

*Lord, I present to Thee my failures. Only Thou couldst. . .
repair the harm that I have wrought.*

Because you are Mine I must identify Myself with all you are. I play the harmony of which you made such discord. I sound the hope in ears you had no charm of Love to woo from sin and failure.

I lead to happier ways those you misjudged, despised.

I take your failures, and because your desire is towards Me, and you know Me as Lord, these, your failures, it is My sacrificial task to bear, to reclaim.

Step up from your slough of failure into the robe of faith and love I give you.

Be strong to save as you have known salvation, strong in Me, your ever-conquering Lord.

God Calling: Drop Those Burdens

Our God is our supply.

Look to Me for all. . . Rely on Me for all. Drop those burdens, and then, singing and free, you can go on your way rejoicing. Encumbered with them you will fall.

Drop them at My Feet, knowing surely that I will lift them and deal with each one as is truly best.

God at Eventide: We Walk Together

Lord, I would walk with Thee.

See, I set My pace to yours as a loving parent does to that of his child.

So there must be much silence in our companionship because you are not yet able to bear all the Wonder-Truth I long to impart.

But though words might find you unresponsive, you cannot fail to grow in My Presence, to grow in Grace, to grow in understanding.

So in that Rest I promised to those who come to Me, you do indeed gain the strength that comes from security in Love.

SEPTEMBER 5

God Calling: Progress

Progress is the Law of Heaven. Higher, ever higher, rise to Life and Beauty, Knowledge and Power. Higher and higher.

Tomorrow be stronger, braver, more loving than you

have been today.

The Law of Progress gives a meaning, a purpose to life.

God at Eventide: Love Leaps Forward

You must keep close to Me.

Faithfulness is not merely obeying the expressed commands of My Written Word. It is the intuitive knowing of My Wish by close and intimate contact, from which has grown true understanding of Me.

Even with this, knowing faithfulness can only be possible when you are fortified with the Strength that Communion with Me gives.

If you know My slightest wish and have absorbed from Me the Strength in which to carry it out, then Love leaps forward, responsive, rejoicing in the Lord.

SEPTEMBER 6

God Calling: Your Loved Ones

Your loved ones are very safe in My Keeping. Learning and loving and working, theirs is a life of happiness and progress. They live to serve, and serve they truly do. They serve Me and those they love. Ceaselessly they serve.

But their ministrations, so many, so diverse, you see no more than those in My time on Earth in human form could have seen the angels who ministered unto Me in the wilderness.

How often mortals rush to earthly friends who can serve them in so limited a way, when the friends who are freed from the limitations of humanity can serve them so much better, understand better, protect better, plan better, and even plead better their cause with Me.

You do well to remember your friends in the Unseen. Companying with them the more you live in this Unseen World, the gentler will be your passing when it comes. Earth's troubles and difficulties will seem, even now, less overwhelming as you look, not at the things that are seen, but at the real, the Eternal Life.

"And this is Life Eternal that we may know Thee, the only True God, and Jesus Christ whom Thou hast sent."

Learning to know Me draws that Kingdom very near, and in Me, and through Knowledge of Me, the dear ones there become very near and dear.

God at Eventide: No Pride

Are you ready for training and discipline? Like my winter-trees, seemingly useless and impotent to those who do not understand the enrooting in Me which keeps you steadfast amid storms and winter cold.

All through the dark months when your beauty (your power to help and shield) has been sacrificed, you are yet drawing in strength and sustenance.

The time to help will come again, and you will have learned to have no personal pride in the beauty of your foliage and the restfulness of your shade.

You will use them for those who need them, but will give the glory to Me, your Lord.

God Calling: Everlasting Arms

*The eternal God is thy refuge,
and underneath are the everlasting arms.*
DEUTERONOMY 33:27

Arms, sheltering Arms, express the loving tenderness of your Father (My Father) in Heaven. Man, in his trouble and difficulty, needs nothing so much as a refuge. A place to hide in. A place where none and nothing can touch him.

Say to yourself, "He is our Refuge." Say it until its truth sinks into your very soul. Say it until you know it—are so sure of it, that nothing can make you afraid.

Feel this not only until fear goes, but until Joy ripples through in its place. Refuge. Everlasting Arms so untiring, so safe—so sure.

God at Eventide: "Lord, My Lord!"

The human heart craves a Leader, one whose will it delights to obey.

It craves a oneness of aim and achievement with a loved one. It craves to be understood.

It craves to reveal itself without reservations and to gain only strength thereby.

To gain, too, an ever more intimate revelation of the heart of the loved one. Where can the heart of man find satisfaction as with Me?

SEPTEMBER 8

God Calling: Walk in My Love

When supply seems to have failed, you must know it has not done so. But you must, at the same time, look around to see what you can give away. Give away something.

There is always a stagnation, a blockage, when supply seems short. Your giving clears that away and lets the Spirit of My Supply flow clear.

A consciousness of My Presence as Love makes all Life different. The consciousness of Me means the opening of your whole nature to Me, and that brings relief. Relief brings Peace. Peace brings Joy. The "Peace that passeth all understanding" and the "Joy no man taketh from you."

Beyond all words are My Love and Care for you. Be sure of it. Rejoice in it. *Walk in My Love*. These words mean much. There is a Joy, a spring, a gladness in the walk of those who walk in My Love. That walk becomes a glad conquering and triumphant march. So walk.

God at Eventide: Perfect Harmony

No discordant note mars your intercourse with Me, for only with Me can life be perfect harmony.

There may be much to regret on your part, failure, disloyalty, fear, sin.

In My Holy Presence all that is swept away by My Hand of Love. Only Love, Peace-bringing, Harmony-producing Love remains. If you are to face the World and maintain your calm, you must take to the World, and your tasks in it My Peace and Harmony.

SEPTEMBER 9

God Calling: Cultivate—Yourself

In Thy Strength we conquer.

Yes! Your conquering Power you gain from Me. There can be no failure with me. The secret of success then is Life with Me.

Do you want to make the best of life? Then live very near to Me, the Master and Giver of all Life.

Your reward will be sure. It will be perfect success, but *My* success.

Sometimes the success of souls won, sometimes the success of disease cured or devils cast out. Sometimes the success of a finished sacrifice as on Calvary. Sometimes the success of one who answered never a word in the face of the scorn and torture and jeering cries of His enemies, or the success of a Risen Savior as He walked through the Garden of Joseph of Arimathea on that first Easter morning.

But *My* success. The world may deem you failures. The world judges not as I judge.

Bend your knees in wonder before My revelation. The joy of seeing Spiritual Truths is a great Joy. When the Heavens are opened and the Voice speaks, not to all hearts, but to the faithful loving hearts.

Remember your great field of labor is yourself. That is your first task, the weeding, the planting, digging, pruning, bearing fruit. When that is done, I lead you out into other fields.

God at Eventide: Thy Heart's Desires

Pause upon the threshold of My House of plenty.

Pause in awe and in the joy of Worship.

He shall give thee thine heart's desires. Give your desires

themselves, conceived as they are in union with the Divine Spirit, *and* receive their fulfillment.

Know this and let your heart sing with the joy of this Wonder of Supply.

SEPTEMBER 10

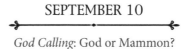

God Calling: God or Mammon?

You must be ready to stand apart from the world. Do you want the full and complete satisfaction that you find in Me, and the satisfaction of the world, too? Then you are trying to serve God and Mammon, or if not trying to serve, then claiming the wages of both God and Mammon.

If you work for Me, you have your reward. But then you turn to the world, to human beings, and expect that reward, too. This is not right.

Do not expect love or gratitude or acknowledgment from any. All reward necessary I will give you.

God at Eventide: Unruffled

Peace. It is your task to keep this Peace in your hearts and lives. This is your work for Me. It is so all-important because if you lack it, then, as a channel, you are for the time useless.

Learn to sense the slightest ruffle on the surface of your lives. Learn to sense the smallest unrest in your heart-depths. Then back to Me until all is calm.

Think, some message may be undelivered because I cannot use you. Some tender word unspoken because self blocks your channel.

Only self can cause unrest, and My great Gift to My disciples was PEACE.

God Calling: A Generous Giver

I am come that they might have life,
and that they might have it more abundantly.
JOHN 10:10

Yes, I, your Master, am a generous Giver. Abundant Life, in overflowing measure, I give to you. For that I came. Life for souls. The Life, Eternal Life, that pulses through your whole being, that animates your mind and body, too.

A generous Giver. A Kingly Giver. For this I came that man might live in Me. Life it was of which I spoke when I said, "I am the Vine and ye are the branches." The life flow of the Vine is in the branches.

Our lives are one—yours and Mine. All that is in My Nature must therefore pass into yours, where the contact is so close a one.

I am Love and Joy and Peace and Strength and Power and Healing and Humility and Patience, and all else you see in Me your Lord. Then these, too, you must have as My Life flows through you. So courage.

You do not make yourselves loving and strong and patient and humble. You live with Me, and then My Life accomplishes the miracle-change.

God at Eventide: Lose This Desire

Again I say, never judge another. That is one of My tasks I have never relegated to any follower.

Live with Me. So you will be enabled to see more of that inner self that I see in each one. Thus you will learn a humility that makes you lose desire to judge.

Oh, seek to love and understand all. Love them for My

sake. They are Mine. As you live with Me you will see how I yearn over them, and long for them. Seeing this your love for Me must prevent your hurting Me by unkind criticism of those for whom I care.

SEPTEMBER 12

God Calling: Money Values

But seek ye first the kingdom of God, and his righteousness; and all these things shall be added unto you.
MATTHEW 6:33

If therefore thine eye be single, thy whole body shall be full of light.
MATTHEW 6:22

The eye of the soul is the will. If your one desire is My Kingdom, to find that Kingdom, to serve that Kingdom, then truly shall your whole body be full of light.

When you are told to seek first the Kingdom of God, the first step is to secure that your will is for that Kingdom. A single eye to God's glory. Desiring nothing less than that His Kingdom come. Seeking in all things the advance of His Kingdom.

Know no values but Spiritual values. No profit but that of Spiritual gain. Seek in all things His Kingdom *first*.

Only seek material gain when that gain will mean a gain for My Kingdom. Get away from money values altogether. Walk with Me. Learn of Me. Talk to Me. Here lies your true happiness.

Never seek to cast the blame on others.

If I bear your sins and those of others are you not casting your blame on Me?

If what is untoward is the result of your own fault or weakness, seek to remedy the cause by conquering the fault and overcoming the weakness.

If it has been caused by another, then apportion no blame, allow no thought of self to intrude to cause the slightest ruffle of your spirit-calm.

Safeguard the peace which I entrusted to you.

SEPTEMBER 13

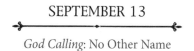

God Calling: No Other Name

My Name is the Power that turns evil aside, that summons all good to your aid. Spirits of evil flee at the sound of "Jesus." Spoken in fear, in weakness, in sorrow, in pain, it is an appeal I never fail to answer. "Jesus."

Use My Name often. Think of the unending call of "Mother" made by her children. To help, to care, to decide, to appeal, "Mother." Use My Name in that same way—simply, naturally, forcefully. "Jesus."

Use it not only when you need help but to express Love. Uttered aloud, or in the silence of your hearts, it will alter an atmosphere from one of discord to one of Love. It will raise the standard of talk and thought. "Jesus."

"There is none other Name under Heaven whereby you can be saved."

No longer has sin any power over you unless of your own deliberate choice.

The surest way to safeguard yourself against any temptation to sin is to learn to love to do My Will, and to love to have that Will done in all the little as well as in all the big things of your daily life.

So often man puzzles over this—if I have conquered sin, why is it then so powerful an enemy?

I conquered sin.

It has no power over any soul that does not want to sin. Then all that could lead to sin is desire.

I lay such stress on man's loving Me. If his love, his desire, is set on Me—he wills *only* to do My Will. Thus he is saved from sin.

SEPTEMBER 14

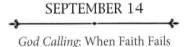

God Calling: When Faith Fails

Lord, I believe; help thou mine unbelief.
MARK 9:24

This cry of the human heart is as expressive of human need as it was when uttered to Me while I was on Earth. It expresses the soul's progress.

As a soul realizes Me and My Power, and knows Me as Helper and Savior, that soul believes in Me more and more. At the same time it is more conscious than before of its falling short of absolute trust in Me.

"Lord, I believe. Help Thou mine unbelief." The soul's progress, an increased belief—then a cry for more faith—a plea to conquer all unbelief, all lack of trust.

That cry heard. That prayer answered. More faith, and at

the same time more power to see where trust is lacking.

My children seek to go up this path, leading by each stage, nearer to Me.

God at Eventide: Gifts for You

"Not as the world giveth, give I unto you."

Not as the world giveth, but oh, infinitely more richly, more abundantly, give I unto you.

The world expects a return, or gives only in return. Not so do I. My only stipulation is receive!

But to receive My Power, My Gifts, you must have room for them, and full of self there is no room for Me and My Gifts.

So all I desire of you is to be emptied of self, and to desire Me.

SEPTEMBER 15

God Calling: Quiet Strength

Rest in Me. When tired nature rebels, it is her call for rest. Rest then until My Life-Power flows through you.

Have no fear for the future. Be quiet, be still, and in that very stillness your strength will come and will be maintained.

The world sees strength in action. In My Kingdom it is known that strength lies in quiet. "In quietness and in confidence shall be your strength."

Such a promise! Such glorious fulfillment! The strength of Peace and the Peace of strength. Rest in Me. Joy in Me.

My child, there is no arrogance in your assertion when you say, "I will not let Thee go unless Thou bless me."

Have not I ever told you to claim big things? In so doing you obey Me.

You do right to wrestle boldly in prayer. There are times for demanding, for claiming.

Now is the time to claim. You are in no doubt about My Will. Claim its manifestations on earth.

SEPTEMBER 16

God Calling: Assurance

And the work of righteousness shall be peace; and the effect of righteousness quietness and assurance for ever.
ISAIAH 32:17

My Peace it is which gives quietness and assurance forever. My Peace that flows as some calm river through the dry land of life. That causes the trees and flowers of life to spring forth and to yield abundantly.

Success is the result of work done in peace. Only so can work yield its increase. Let there be no hurry in your plans. You live not in time but in Eternity. It is in the Unseen that your life-future is being planned.

Abide in Me, and I in you, so shall you bring forth much fruit. Be calm, assured, at rest. Love, not rush. Peace, not unrest. Nothing fitful. All effectual. Sown in Prayer, watered by Trust, bearing flower and fruit in Joy. I love you.

God at Eventide: Adoration

Never forget to adore. That is the most beautiful form of prayer. It includes all others.

If you adore, it implies that trust in Me and love for Me without which all supplication fails to achieve its object. It implies thanksgiving, because adoration is born of repeated thanksgiving.

It also implies contrition.

Who could adore Me with a Joy-filled adoration, and not be conscious of unworthiness and of My forgiveness and blessing? Adoration is Love-filled reverence.

SEPTEMBER 17

God Calling: Faltering Steps

Show us Thy way, O Lord, and let us walk in Thy paths.

You are doing so. This is the way. The way of uncertain future and faltering steps. It is My Way. . . .

Put all fear of the future aside. *Know* that you will be led. *Know* that you will be shown. I have promised.

God at Eventide: Leave Him to Me

In My Kingdom judgment is not man's role. There is one Judge, and even He reserves His judgment until the last chapter of man's life is written, until all the evidence is secured, so anxious is He to discover some extenuating circumstances, or to wait until by man's turning to Him and throwing himself upon His mercy, the position is altered, and the judge becomes the prisoner in the dock.

Then God the Father, knowing His Beloved Son accepts

responsibility for the deed (has in fact already received the punishment Himself), is bound to pardon the human sinner.

You then in judging (poor, weak, foolish, contemptuous arrogance), are judging not the sinner but Me.

SEPTEMBER 18

God Calling: Dwell There

He that dwelleth in the secret place of the most
High shall abide under the shadow of the Almighty.
PSALM 91:1

Hidden in a sure place, known only to God and you. So secret that no power on Earth can even *find* it.

But, My beloved children, you must *dwell* therein. No fitful visit, a real abiding. Make it your home. Your dwelling-place.

Over that home shall My Shadow rest, to make it doubly safe, doubly secret. Like brooding mother-bird wings that Shadow rests. How safe, how sure, you must feel there.

When fears assail you and cares trouble you, it is because you have ventured out of that protecting Shadow. Then the *one*, the only thing to do is to creep back into shelter again. So rest.

God at Eventide: You Can Help

My followers were to save My world—by keeping My Commands, by close union with Me, and by the indwelling Power of My Spirit.

But they were to be a peculiar people. My religion which was to change men's lives, and was to be so revolutionary as to separate families and reorganize governments, has become a convention, tolerated where not appreciated.

Its Truths have been modified to suit men's desires. Its followers carry no flaming sword, they bear no Message of a Love so tender as to heal every wound, so scorching as to burn out every evil. My Cross is outdated, My Loving Father but the First Cause.

Man delights in his self-sufficiency, and seeks to persuade himself that all is well. Can he deceive a loving, understanding Father, who knows that under all the boasting there lurks fear, longings, despair?

Can I leave man so? Can I offer him Calvary, and if he will have none of it, leave him to his fate? I know too well his need of Me. "You can help Me."

SEPTEMBER 19

God Calling: Full Joy

These things have I spoken unto you. . .
that your joy might be full.
JOHN 15:11

Remember that the Truths I teach you have all been given to you, too (as to My disciples of old), with the idea of giving you that overflowing Joy. . . .

Search for the Joy in life. Hunt for it as for hidden treasure. Love and Laugh. *Delight* yourselves in the Lord.

Joy in Me. Full Joy it was I wished My disciples to have. I intended them to have it. Had they lived My Teachings out in their daily lives, they would have had Fullness of Joy.

Help Me to save your fellow-man as dear to Me as you are.

Do you not care that he should pass Me by? *Do you not care that he should pass Me by?*

Do you not care that he is lonely, hungry, desperate, and far from the fold?

SEPTEMBER 20

God Calling: Taste and Trust

O taste and see that the LORD is good.
PSALM 34:8

He is good. Trust in Him. Know that all is well. Say "God is good. God is good." Just leave in His Hands the present and the future, knowing only that He is good. He can bring order out of chaos, good out of evil, peace out of turmoil. God is good.

I and My Father are One. One in desire to do good. For God to do good to His children is for Him to share His goodness with them. God is good, anxious to share His goodness, and good things, with you, and He *will* do this.

Trust and be not afraid.

God at Eventide: Led by the Spirit

Learn to wait for spiritual Guidance until its suggestion is as clear to your consciousness as any command of officer to soldier, of master to servant. This recognition distinguishes My true follower from the many who call Me "Lord, Lord," and do not the things that I say.

There are many who live according to the Principles I laid

down when on earth, but who do not act under the impulse of My Spirit day by day.

"For as many as are led by the Spirit of God, they are the Sons of God."

SEPTEMBER 21

God Calling: See the Father

Lord, show us the Father, and it sufficeth us.
JOHN 14:8

My children, have I been so long time with you, coming to you, speaking to you, and yet have you not known the Father?

Your Father is the God and Controller of a mighty Universe. But He is as I am. All the Love and the Strength and Beauty you have seen in Me are in My Father.

If you see that, and know Him and Me as we really are, then that sufficeth you—is really sufficient for you—completes your life—satisfies you—is all you need.

See the Father, see Me, and it sufficeth you. This is Love in abundance. Joy in abundance. All you need.

God at Eventide: Barriers Burned Away

My Light shall shine upon you. It shall illumine and cheer your way.

But it shall also penetrate the dark and secret places of your hearts revealing perhaps some unrecognized sin, fault, or failing.

Desire its radiance not only for its comfort and guidance, but also for its revelation of all within you that is not wholly Mine.

I am the Sun of Righteousness. Rest in My Presence, not

clamoring, not supplicating, but resting until the impurities of your being are burnt out, the dross of your character refined away, and you can go on strengthened and purified to do My work.

SEPTEMBER 22

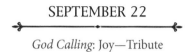

God Calling: Joy—Tribute

Jesus, our Lord, we Thee adore.

Sing unto Me from a glad heart. Sing and praise My Holy Name. Praise is man's joy-tribute to Me, and as you praise, thrills of Joy surge through your being, and you learn something of the Joy of the Heavenly Host.

God at Eventide: I Am Forgiveness

My Lord, forgive me I pray.

Could I withhold forgiveness? I, who live ever to plead for My children, who told them that always when they pray they must forgive in their hearts?

I am God but I became man.

Perfect God and perfect man.

So human and yet so Divine.

Because I am Eternal—that I must *ever* be.

So see in Me all I enjoined My followers *they* must ever be and do. Could I withhold forgiveness?

God Calling: Turn Again

Draw nigh to God, and he will draw nigh to you.
JAMES 4:8

This is a law in the Spiritual Life. You must turn to Me before you are conscious of My nearness. It is that turning to Me you must cultivate in every circumstance. A glad turning of thankfulness, or a turning of weak appeal.

It is so wonderful that naught is needed but that mute appeal. You have no need to voice your longing. No need to plead, no need to bring gifts. How wonderful to feel you can so simply claim help, and so promptly, so lovingly, it is there.

Not only Help but the Comfort and Joy of Divine Nearness and Companionship. A nearness that brings sweetness into life, and confidence, and Peace.

Never fear, never lose heart. Draw nigh to Me, and in that nearness is all you need. My Presence alone can transform conditions and lives—bring Harmony and Beauty, Peace and Love.

God at Eventide: Irritability Banished

Consciousness of My Presence imparts permanence and strength to all you do.

My Spirit permeating every part of your being, drives out all the selfish irritability, while fortifying all the weak parts and attuning your being to Heaven's Music.

To think of Heaven as a place where you sing praises to Me is right, but the singing is with your whole being, as My pulsing Joy flows through it.

God Calling: Learn of Me

Lord, to whom shall we go?
thou hast the words of eternal life.
JOHN 6:68

Learn of no one but Me. Teachers are to point the way to Me. After that you must accept Me, the Great Teacher.

The words of Eternal Life are all the words controlling your being, even controlling your temporal life. Take these, too, from Me. Have no fear. Abide in Me and accept My ruling.

Be full of gratitude. Wing up your prayers on Praise to Heaven. Take all that happens as My planning. All is well. I have all prepared in My Love. Let your heart sing.

God at Eventide: All on the Altar

Absolute Love must decide all your actions.

Fear nothing. Ride the storm.

Delight to do My Will.

Not only money affairs; lay all your letters, your work, all, upon My altar.

Make an offering of each day to Me for the answering of your prayers and for the salvation of My poor world.

Subdue every self-thought, utterly, entirely.

God Calling: Come and Stay

*Come unto me, all ye that labour and
are heavy laden, and I will give you rest.*
MATTHEW 11:28

Yes, come for rest. But stay for rest, too. Stop all feverish haste and be calm and untroubled. Come unto Me, not only for petitions to be granted but for nearness to Me.

Be sure of My Help, be conscious of My Presence, and wait until My Rest fills your soul.

Rest knows no fear. Rest knows no want. Rest is strong, sure. The rest of soft glades and peacefully flowing rivers, of strong, immovable hills. Rest, and all you need to gain this rest is to come to Me. So come.

God at Eventide: The Love That Satisfies

My Mercies are great to all who turn to Me and to all who turn *from* me.

How tenderly I yearn over these wayward ones. How I seek ever to save them from the hurts their very refusal of Me will bring upon them.

I long to save them from the hunger of loneliness that will follow their driving away the only love that will satisfy.

God Calling: Serve All

I am among you as one that serveth.

Yes! remember to serve all. Be ready to prove your Sonship by service. Look on all you meet as guests in your Father's House, to be treated with Love, with all consideration, with gentleness.

As a servant of all, think no work beneath you. Be ever ready to do all you can for others. Serve. Serve. Serve.

There is a gladness in service, a Joy in doing My Will for others, in being My expression of all good for them.

Remember that, when you serve others, you are acting for your Master and Lord who washed His disciples' feet. So, in service for others, express your Love for Me.

God at Eventide: Storms May Rage

Live with Me and words will not be necessary. You will know My Will.

The real necessity is your receptiveness.

That comes through self-discipline that allows of spiritual progress into, and in, a Higher Life.

In that spirit realm you are conscious of My Will. You are one with Me. Truly, you may count all things well lost to win Christ.

I wish you to learn the Glory of a God-protected, guided life. No idle, fruitless rushing hither and thither. Storms may rage, difficulties may press hard, but you will know no harm. Safe, protected and guided.

God Calling: Divine Restraint

Is My Hand shortened that it cannot save? No! My power to save increases as your power to understand My Salvation increases. So from Strength to Strength, from Power to Power, we go in Union.

Limitless is My Miracle-working Power in the Universe, though it has limitations in each individual life, but only to the extent of the lack of vision of that individual. There is no limit to My Power to save. Also there is no limit to My desire and longing to save. My Hand is not shortened, and it is "stretched out still," longing and waiting to be allowed to bless and help and save.

Think how tenderly I respect the right of each individual soul. Never forcing upon it My Help, My Salvation. Perhaps in all My suffering for humanity, that is the hardest, the restraint of the Divine Impatience and longing to help, until the call of the soul gives Me My right to act.

Think of Love shown in this. Comfort My waiting, loving, longing Heart by claiming My Help, Guidance, and Miracle-working Power.

God at Eventide: My Striving Spirit

There is never a time when a man cannot turn repentant to Me and, craving My pardon, receive it.

But there is a time when I cease to be persistent in urging My follower to an action.

The human ear can hear a sound so often until it ceases to convey a meaning, to be heard with awareness.

So with the spirit-ear, unless the whole desire and effort is to carry out My plan, My servant may cease to hear, cease to be aware of My wish.

This is a grave spiritual danger, and I say unto you, watch and guard against it.

SEPTEMBER 28

God Calling: The Secret Path

*Suffer it to be so now: for thus it
becometh us to fulfil all righteousness.*
MATTHEW 3:15

Upon this I founded My three years' Mission on Earth on the acceptance of the difficulty and discipline of life so as to share that human life with My followers in all the ages.

Much that you both must accept in life is not to be accepted as being necessary for you personally, but accepted, as I accepted it, to set an example, to share in the sufferings and difficulties of mankind.

In this "to share" means "to save." And there, too, for you both. . .the same must be true as was so true of Me. "He saved others. Himself He cannot save."

Beloved, you are called to save and share in a very special way. The way of sorrows if walked with Me, the Man of Sorrows, is a path kept sacred and secret for My nearest and dearest, those whose one desire is to do all for Me, to sacrifice all for Me, to count, as My servant Paul did, "all things but loss so that they might gain Me."

But, dreary as that Path must look to those who view it only from afar, it has tender lights and restful shades that no other walk in life can give.

There is a stage in Christian development at which My follower should have passed beyond that of general service and conformity to the rules I laid down for My disciples.

When he should be seeking to serve in some special way planned for that soul, and in the service that soul was destined for, which none other can so adequately do.

Think, the Salvation of My world, all planned, even to the minutest detail, but that work is not done through neglect, through failure, through indifference.

My way for you is not a path of general righteousness and obedience, but the actual road mapped out for you, in which you can best help My needy world.

SEPTEMBER 29

God Calling: I Touch Your Arm

Thy touch has still its ancient Power.

Yes! when you are quiet before Me I lay My Hand upon each head, and Divine Spirit flows through that healing, powerful Touch into your very beings. Wait in silence before Me to feel that.

When you look to Me for guidance My Hand is laid upon your arm, a gentle Touch to point the way. When in mental, physical, or spiritual weakness you cry to Me for healing, My Touch brings Strength and Healing, the renewal of your youth, the power to climb and strive.

When you faint by the way, and stumbling footsteps show human strength is waning, My Touch of the Strong and Helping Hand supports you on your Way.

Yes! My children, My touch has still its ancient Power, and that Power is promised to you. So go forward into the future bravely and unafraid.

God at Eventide: Love Heals

You are asking to be used by Me to heal, but you are asking for the fruit before the root has become established, and the tree has grown to its stature.

With the elimination of self, and obedience to My Will, your Power in the Spirit world will naturally grow. Thus you will assuredly gain in that world the control that others seek to have on the material plane.

But you must forego all desire for control or recognition on that lower plane. As you cannot serve two masters, so neither can you operate on two planes.

Your Love must grow by dwelling with Me. It was My overflowing Love that healed.

SEPTEMBER 30

God Calling: Wisdom

As thy days so shall thy strength be.

I have promised that for every day you live, the strength shall be given you. Do not fear.

Face each difficulty sure that the wisdom and strength will be given you for it. Claim it.

Rely on Me to keep My Promise about this. In My Universe, for every task I give one of My children, there is set aside all that is necessary for its performance. So why fear? So why doubt?

My Word shall be a lamp unto your feet, and a light unto your path. No difficulty need appall you. You shall know in all things what to do, but remember that the light must go with you. It is to warn, comfort and cheer, not to reveal the future.

My servants do not need to know that. The true child spirit rejoices in the present, and has no fears, no thought beyond it. So must you live.

If I, your Lord, accompany you, shedding My radiance all round you, the future must always be dark, because as far as your acceptance of revelation and your present development are concerned, I am not *there*.

But as the future of today becomes the present of tomorrow, then the same light and Guidance and Miracle-working Power will be yours. Rejoice evermore.

OCTOBER 1

God Calling: Secret of Prosperity

Look unto me, and be ye saved, all the ends of the earth.
ISAIAH 45:22

Look to no other source for Salvation. Only look unto Me. See no other supply. Look unto Me, and you shall be saved. Regard Me as your only supply. That is the secret of prosperity for you, and you in your turn shall save many from poverty and distress.

Whatever danger threatens look unto Me. . . . Whatever you desire or need, or desire or need for others, look unto Me. Claim all from My Storehouse. Claim, claim, claim.

Remember that I fed the Children of Israel with Heaven-sent

manna. I made a way through the Red Sea for them. I led them through the wilderness of privation, difficulty, discipline. I led them into a land flowing with milk and honey. So trust. So be led.

Rejoice. These are your wilderness days. But surely and safely, you are being led to your Canaan of Plenty.

God at Eventide: Have Confidence

Nothing happens to you that is not the answer to your prayers, the fulfillment of your desire to do, and have, in all, My Will. So go forward into each day unafraid.

OCTOBER 2

God Calling: True Meekness

How easy it is to lead and guide when you are responsive to My wish! The hurts of life come only when you, or those about whom you care, endeavor to go your, or their, own way and resist the pressure of My Hand.

But in willing My Will there must be a gladness. Delight to do that Will.

"The meek shall inherit the earth," I said. That is, control others, and the material forces of the earth.

But this exalted state of possession is the result of a *yielded will*. That was My meaning of the word *meek*.

So live. So yield. So conquer.

On earth, or even in Heaven, there can be no greater joy than realizing that My Will is being accomplished in the little as well as in the big things.

Indeed, it can be *your* "meat" as I said it was *Mine*. It is the very sustenance of body, mind and spirit, that Trinity of being, symbolized in the Temple in the Outer Court, the Holy Place, and then in the very Holy of Holies, where man speaks with God and dwells with Him.

Into that Holy of Holies there can be no entrance except to sacrifice, to bring an offering of the physical and mental being in Spirit to identify the whole with that Supreme Sacrifice I offered for My World.

OCTOBER 3

God Calling: Blessed Assurance

And the work of righteousness shall be peace; and the effect of righteousness quietness and assurance for ever.
ISAIAH 32:17

Be still and know that I am God. Only when the soul attains this calm can there be true work done, and mind and soul and body be strong to conquer and to bear.

The Peace is the work of righteousness living the right life, living with Me. Quietness and assurance follow.

Assurance is the calm born of a deep certainty in Me, in My Promises, in My Power to save and keep. Gain this calm, and at all costs keep this calm. Rest in Me. Live in Me. Calm, quiet, assured—at Peace.

Not unto us, O Lord. . .but unto Thy Name be Glory.

My Name. I AM. Existent before all Worlds, changeless through Eternity, changeless in Time.

All I have ever been through the ages I AM.

All that you ever crave I may be to you—I AM.

In a changing world you need to dwell much upon Me, your Master, the Jesus Christ of whom it was said—

"The same yesterday, today and forever."

Then it follows that with you today is The Lord of Creation, Jesus of Nazareth, the Christ of the Cross, the Risen Savior, the Ascended Lord. What a Companionship for the uncertain ways of a changing world.

OCTOBER 4

God Calling: All You Desire

He hath no form nor comeliness; and when we shall see him,
there is no beauty that we should desire him.
ISAIAH 53:2

My children, in this verse My servant Isaiah spoke of the wonderful illumination given to those who were Spirit-guided.

To those who know Me not, there is in Me nothing to appeal to them or to attract them.

To those who know Me there is nothing more to be desired. "No beauty they could desire of Him."

Oh! My children, draw very near to Me. See Me as I really am, that ever you may have the Joy of finding in Me all you could desire. The fulfillment of all you could desire in Master, Lord, or Friend.

God at Eventide: Bright Reality

O Jesus, make Thyself to me
A living, bright reality.

Then will you show Me as a living bright reality?

I died that I might live in you, My followers, and you present Me to the world as a dead Christ.

"I am alive forevermore."

Though you may repeat those words they are not vibrant with Life, here and now. They speak but of My existence in another sphere far removed from this earth and its joys and sorrows, achievement and stress.

Yet in all these daily things I would have My Spirit active in and through you.

How can man so misread My Teaching?

OCTOBER 5

God Calling: No Chance Meetings

The LORD shall preserve thy going out and thy coming
in from this time forth, and even for evermore.
PSALM 121:8

All your movements, your goings and comings, controlled by Me. Every visit, all blessed by Me. Every walk arranged by Me. A blessing on all you do, on every interview.

Every meeting not a chance meeting, but planned by Me. All blessed.

Not only now, in the hour of your difficulty, but from this time forth and for evermore.

Led by the Spirit, a proof of Sonship. "As many as are led by the Spirit of God, they are the Sons of God," and if children then heirs—heirs of God.

What a heritage! Heirs—no prospect of being disinherited. "Heirs of God and joint heirs with Christ: if so be that you suffer with Him that you may be also glorified together."

So your suffering has its purpose. It is a proof of Sonship. It leads to perfection of character (the being glorified), and to Union with Me, God, too. Think of, and dwell upon, the rapture of this.

God at Eventide: One with Me

One with the God of Creation.

One with the Jesus of Calvary.

One with the Risen Christ.

One with His Spirit operating in every corner of the Universe, energizing, renewing, controlling, all-powerful.

Could man ask more? Could thought rise higher?

OCTOBER 6

God Calling: A Child's Hand

Dear Lord, we cling to Thee.

Yes, cling. Your faith shall be rewarded. Do you not know what it means to feel a little trusting hand in yours, to know a child's confidence?

Does that not draw out your Love and desire to protect, to care? Think what My Heart feels, when in your helplessness you turn to Me, clinging, desiring My Love and Protection.

Would you fail that child, faulty and weak as you are? Could I fail you? Just know it is not possible. Know all is well. You must not doubt. You must be sure. There is no miracle I cannot perform, nothing I cannot do. No eleventh-hour rescue I cannot accomplish.

How pitiful man's striving after power when God's Power, with all its mighty possibilities, is there for him did he but know how to obtain it.

To tell one such that this would only be possible for one who has entered My Kingdom of Heaven, might indeed arouse his curiosity.

But tell him the way into that Kingdom is one of self-effacement, obedience to and love of My Will, tell him that he must enter as a little child, that only by spiritual progress can he attain to man's true estate, and that the training might be long, the discipline hard—tell him this and he will turn empty away.

Yet in so doing he will renounce, all unknowing, the victor's prize, the life of peace, and power, and joy.

OCTOBER 7

God Calling: Rejoice at Weakness

> *Savior, breathe forgiveness o'er us.*
> *All our weakness Thou dost know.*

Yes! I know all. Every cry for mercy. Every sigh of weariness. Every plea for help. Every sorrow over failure. Every weakness.

I am with you through all. My tender sympathy is yours. My strength is yours.

Rejoice at your weakness, My children. My strength is made perfect in weakness. When you are weak then am I strong. Strong to help, to cure, to protect.

Trust Me, My children. I know *all*. I am beside you. Strong, strong, strong to save. Lean on My Love, and know that all is well.

Only with Me, and in My Strength will you have Grace and Power to conquer the weakness, the evil, in yourself. Your character-garment is spoiled. Only by applying My Salvation can it to become a wedding garment, fit robe in which to meet the Bridegroom.

The foundation-cleansing of the garment is belief in Me as your Savior, your Redeemer. Thereafter to each fault and evil in your nature must be applied that evil-eradicating Power that can only come from relying on My Strength, and from living with Me, from loving Me, and loving to do My Will.

Mere general belief in Me as Redeemer and Savior is insufficient. Set yourself now to walk steadily the upward way, strong in Me and in the power of My Might.

OCTOBER 8

God Calling: The Dark Places

Jesus, the very thought of Thee with Sweetness fills us.

Yes. Love Me until just to think of Me means Joy and rapture. Gladness at the thought of One very near and dear.

It is the balm for all sorrows, the thought of Me. Healing for all physical, mental, and spiritual ills you can always find in thinking of Me and speaking to Me.

Are doubts and fears in your hearts? Then think of Me, speak to Me. Instead of those fears and doubts there will flow into your hearts and beings such sweet Joy as is beyond any joy of Earth.

This is unfailing. Never doubt it. Courage. Courage. Courage. Fear nothing. Rejoice even in the darkest places. Rejoice.

God at Eventide: "Lord, Save Me"

I will, be thou clean.

Saved from all that tarnishes the purity of your soul.

Saved from harsh judgments.

Saved from disobedience to My Command.

Saved from all that offends My Justice, all that sins against My Love. I will, be thou clean.

OCTOBER 9

God Calling: Love Me More

Jesus, our Lord, we Thee adore.
Oh, make us love Thee more and more.

Yes! I would draw you closer and closer to Me by bonds of Love. The Love of the sinner for the Savior, of the rescued for the Rescuer, of the sheep for the Loving Shepherd, of the child for its Father.

So many ties of Love there are to bind you to Me.

Each experience in your life of Joy, and sorrow, of difficulty or success, of hardship or ease, of danger or safety, each makes its own particular demand upon Me. Each serves to answer the prayer: "Make me love Thee more and more."

God at Eventide: Overcome Desire

The listening ear—

Train the listening ear to hear Me.

The first step is to subdue earth's desires and to want only My Will.

Desire as a control must be overcome.

Then follows the turning within to speak with Me.

Then the listening ear.

OCTOBER 10

God Calling: Extra Work

Our Lord and our God. Help us through poverty to plenty. Through unrest to rest, through sorrow to Joy, through weakness to Power.

I am your Helper. At the end of your present path lie all these blessings. So trust and know that I am leading you.

Step with a firm step of confidence in Me into each unknown day. Take every duty and every interruption as of My appointment.

You are My servant. Serve Me as simply, cheerfully, and readily as you expect others to serve you.

Do you blame the servant who avoids extra work, who complains about being called from one task to do one less liked? Do you feel you are ill served by such a one?

Then what of Me? Is not that how you so often serve Me? Think of this. Lay it to heart and view your day's work in this light.

God at Eventide: Peter's Example

My child, I will never fail you.

My Promise is not dependent upon your perfection, only upon your accepting My Will and striving ever to walk in it.

But, for your happiness, I give you Divine Assurance that though you may fail in achievement, if not in desire, *I* cannot plead human frailty, *so My Promises must be fulfilled*.

When I chose Peter *I* saw in him not only one who after failure and denial, would become a Power for Me in My Strength; I chose him that others, frail and weak, might take courage as they remembered My Love and forgiveness, and his subsequent spiritual progress.

God Calling: Shame and Distress

I will bless the LORD at all times: his praise shall continually be in my mouth. I sought the LORD, and he heard me, and delivered me from all my fears. They looked unto him, and were lightened: and their faces were not ashamed.
PSALM 34:1, 4, 5

See, My children, that even in distress, the first step is *Praise*. Before you cry in your distress, bless the Lord; even when troubles seem to overwhelm you.

That is My Divine order of approach. Observe this always. In the greatest distress, search until you find cause for thankfulness. Then bless and thank.

You have thus established a line of communication between yourself and Me. Along that line let your cry of distress follow.

Thus you will find I do My part, and deliverance will be sure. Oh! the gladness of heart. Lightened you will be, the burden rolled away, as the result of looking to Me.

The shame and distress will be lifted, too. That is always the *second* step. First right with Me, and then you will be righted, too, in the eyes of men.

God at Eventide: All Clear

Love is the great power of understanding. Love explains all, makes all clear.

How *can* you understand Me unless you love Me? How can men see My purposes unless they love Me?

Love is indeed the fulfilling of the law. It is also the understanding of the law.

He that loveth is born of God, because he enters into a

new life in God who is Love. Live in that Love.

Love it is that prepares the ground for My teaching, that softens the hardest heart, that disposes the most indifferent, that creates desire for My Kingdom.

Therefore love. Love Me first. Then love all, and so you link them to Me.

OCTOBER 12

God Calling: You Are My Joy

Thine they were, and thou gavest them me;
and they have kept thy word.
JOHN 17:6

Remember, that just as you thank God for Me, so I thank God for His Gift to Me of you. In that hour of My agony on Earth, one note of Joy thrilled through the pain: the thought of the souls, given Me by My Father, who had kept My Word.

They had not then done great deeds, as they did later, for and in My Name. They were simple doers of My Word, not hearers only. Just in their daily tasks and ways they kept My Word.

You, too, can bring Joy to My Heart by faithful service. Faithful service in the little things. Be faithful.

Do your simple tasks for Me.

God at Eventide: Eyes of the Spirit

You have much to learn.

Life will not be long enough to learn all, but you are gaining that Spirit-Vision which replaces the eyes of your mortal body when you enter into a life of fuller comprehension with My Father and Me.

God Calling: The Sculptor's Skill

Lord, we believe, help Thou our unbelief. Lord,
hear our prayers and let our cries come unto Thee.

Along the road of Praise, as I told you. Yes! I will indeed help your unbelief, and in answer to your prayers grant you so great a Faith, such an increasingly great Faith, that each day you may look back, from the place of your larger vision, and see the Faith of the day before as almost unbelief.

The Beauty of My Kingdom is its growth. In that Kingdom there is always progress, a going on from strength to strength, from glory to glory. Be in My Kingdom and of My Kingdom, and there can be no stagnation. Eternal Life, abundant Life is promised to all in it and of it.

No misspent time over failures and shortcomings. Count the lessons learnt from them but as rungs in the ladder. Step up, and then cast away all thought of the manner of the making of the rung. Fashioned of joy or sorrow, of failure or success, of wounds or healing balm, what matter, My children, so long as it served its purpose?

Learn another lesson. The Sculptor who finds a faulty marble casts it aside. Because it has no fashioning, it may regard itself as perfect; and it may look with scorn upon the marble the Sculptor is cutting and shaping into perfection. From this, My children, learn a lesson for your lives.

God at Eventide: Stories in the Bud

Learn a further lesson from the Two Debtors. . . .

A lesson in forgiving others as you realize My forgiveness of sins committed, lessons slowly learnt, faults and shortcomings so easily condoned, which hinder your progress, and work for Me.

Can you show to others My patience to you?

Can you, too, give to others freely, while you claim *My* unrestricted Bounty? Meditate on this.

A story of Mine is like a bud. Only to the Sun of self-effacement and Spirit-Progress does it unfold.

OCTOBER 14

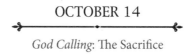

God Calling: The Sacrifice

Behold the Lamb of God, which taketh away the sin of the world.
JOHN 1:29

"Christ our Passover is sacrificed for us." I am the Lamb of God. Lay upon Me your sins, your failures, your shortcomings. My sacrifice has atoned for all. I am the mediator between God and Man, the man Christ Jesus.

Do not dwell upon the past. You make My Sacrifice of no effect.

No! realize that in Me you have all, complete forgiveness, complete companionship, complete healing.

God at Eventide: Receptivity

Only those in close touch with Me, inspired by My Spirit, infected by My Love, impregnated with My Strength, retain a resilience of being and receptivity to new Truth.

The child heart that I enjoined upon My followers is ever ready to be renewed, is ever responsive to all that is prepared for "the new creature in Christ Jesus."

God Calling: Feel Plenty

Live in My Secret Place, and there the feeling is one of full satisfaction. You are to feel plenty. The storehouses of God are full to overflowing, but you must see this in your mind.

Be sure of this before you can realize it in material form.

Think thoughts of plenty. See yourselves as Daughters of a King. I have told you this. Wish plenty for yourselves and all you care for and long to help.

God at Eventide: The Way of the Lord

Always before My coming into a life there must be a time of preparation. This is the work of those who already know Me.

The preparation may differ in each individual case. The Baptist came with his thunder-note of repentance!

In many cases a loving hand of help may be needed before the ground is ready for Me, The Sower.

Prepare My Way:—by loving intercourse, by Spirit-led example, by tender help, by unflinching adherence to Truth and Justice, by ready self-sacrifice, and by much prayer. Prepare ye the Way of the Lord.

OCTOBER 16

God Calling: The Imprisoned God

Our Lord, we praise Thee and bless Thy Name forever.

Yes! Praise. That moment, in the most difficult place, your sorrow is turned to Joy, your fret to Praise, the outward circumstances change from those of disorder to order, of chaos to calm.

The beginning of all reform must be in yourselves. However restricted your circumstances, however little you may be able to remedy financial affairs, you can always turn to yourselves, and seeing something not in order there, seek to right that.

As all reform is from within out, you will always find the outward has improved too. To do this is to release the imprisoned God—Power within you.

That Power, once operative, will immediately perform miracles. Then indeed shall your mourning be turned into Joy.

God at Eventide: In Step

This means endeavoring to suit your steps to Mine. Yet know full well, with the trust that gives security, that I ever suit *My Steps* to your weakness.

Divine restraint springs ever from a tender understanding. With Me beside you there is the hope, the assurance, that the day will come when My firm tread will be yours.

"Keep pace with us," the world says as it rushes by.

But there is One Who knows no feverish haste. He walks with you. Be not afraid.

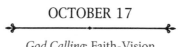

God Calling: Faith-Vision

Turn your eyes to behold Me. Look away from sordid sur-roundings, from lack of beauty, from the imperfections in yourselves and those around you. Then you who have the Faith-Vision will see all you could and do desire in Me.

In your unrest behold My calm, My rest. In your impa-tience, My unfailing patience. In your lack and limitation, My Perfection.

Looking at Me you will grow like Me, until men say to you, too, that you have been with Jesus.

As you grow like Me, you will be enabled to do the things I do, and greater works than these shall ye do because I go unto My Father.

From that place of abiding, limited by none of humani-ty's limitations, I can endue you with the all-conquering, all miracle-working Power of your Divine Brother and Ally.

God at Eventide: See Clearly

Then will you see clearly how to take out the grain of dust from your brother's eye. This is a promise.

You note the fault of another. You long to help.

You need the Spirit-inspired vision for this work. That cannot be granted until all obstruction is removed. Obstruc-tions are caused not by the sins of others but by your own sins and imperfections.

So look within. Seek to conquer those, and so to gain the Spiritual insight which will enable you to help your brother. My Promises are always kept.

OCTOBER 18

God Calling: Loneliness

And they all forsook him, and fled.
MARK 14:50

Down through the ages all the simple acts of steadfast devotion, of obedience in difficulty, of loving service, have been taken by Me as an atonement for the loneliness My humanity suffered by that desertion.

Yet I, who had realized to the full the longing of the Father to save, and His rejection by men, the misunderstanding of His mind and purpose, how could I think that I should not know that desertion too?

Learn, My children, from these words two lessons. Learn first that I know what loneliness, desertion, and solitude mean. Learn that every act of yours of faithfulness is a comfort to My Heart. Learn too that it was to those deserters I gave the task of bringing My Message to mankind. To those deserters, those fearful ones, I gave My Power to heal, to raise to life.

Earth's successes are not the ones I use for the great work of My Kingdom. "They all forsook Him and fled." Learn My tender understanding and pardon of human frailty. Not until man has failed has he learnt true humility. And it is only the humble who can inherit the earth.

God at Eventide: Grace That Transfigures

My Grace is sufficient for you, all-satisfying.

Meditate upon this *grace*. Study what the Scriptures say of it. Learn to value it. Crave it as a gift from Me.

It can be the charm that transfigures all that without it might be sordid or dreary or monotonous. It is the leaven to the dough, the oil to the machine.

It is a priceless gift. Wait with bowed head and heart at that blessing, "The Grace of our Lord Jesus Christ."

OCTOBER 19

God Calling: Hear My Answer

Lord, hear our prayer, and let our cry come unto Thee.

The cry of the human soul is never unheard. It is never that God does not hear the cry, but that man fails to hear the response.

Like parts of a machine, made to fit each into the other, and to work in perfect harmony, so is the human cry and the God-response.

But man treats this cry as if it were a thing alone, to be heard, or not, as it pleased God, not realizing that the response was there in all eternity, awaiting the cry, and only man's failing to heed, or to listen, kept him unaware of the response, and unsaved, unhelped by it.

God at Eventide: A Royal Giver

You tell Me that your hearts are full of gratitude. I do not want from you gratitude as much as the joy of friendship. Realize that I love to give.

As the Scriptures say, "It is your Father's good pleasure to give you the Kingdom." I love to give. The Divine Nature is the Nature of a Royal Giver.

Have you ever thought of My Delight when you are ready to receive? When you long to hear My Words and to receive My Blessings?

God Calling: No Burden Irks

Our Lord and our God.
Be it done unto us according to Thy Word.

Simple acceptance of My Will is the Key to Divine Revelation. It will result in both Holiness and Happiness. The way to the Cross may be a way of sorrow, but at its foot the burdens of sin and Earth-desire are rolled away.

The yoke of My acceptance of My Father's Will in all things is adjusted to My servants' shoulders, and from that moment no burden irks or presses.

But not only in the great decisions of life accept and welcome My Will. Try to see in each interruption, each task, however small, the same fulfillment of Divine intent.

Accept it; say your thanks for it. Do so until this becomes a habit, and the resulting Joy will transfigure and transform your lives.

God at Eventide: Force

My Kingdom must be won by force, that is, by effort. How can you reconcile this with My free gift of Salvation?

My gift is free truly, and is not the reward of any merit on the part of man. But just as God and mammon cannot both be given the overlordship in any one life, so My Kingdom, where I rule as King, cannot be inhabited by one in whom self reigns.

Therefore the violence is that of discipline and self-conquest, together with the intensity of longing for My Kingdom and tireless effort to know and do My Will.

God Calling: A Love Feast

*Behold, I stand at the door, and knock: if any man hear my voice, and open
the door, I will come in to him, and will sup with him, and he with me.*
REVELATION 3:20

See, My children, the knocking rests upon no merit of yours
though it is in response to the longing of your heart for Me.

Keep, keep that listening ear. "If any man will hear My
Voice." Again no merit of yours. Only the ear bent to catch My
tones, and to hear the sound of My gentle knocking.

Then listen: "If any man hear My Voice, and open the
door, I will come in to him, and will sup with him, and he
with Me."

What a feast! You think it would have been Joy to have
been present at the Marriage Feast of Cana of Galilee, or to
have been one of My disciples in the Upper Room, seated
with Me at the Last Supper or one of the two at Emmaus, or
one of the few for whom I prepared that lakeside feast!

But oh! at each of these feasts, God-provided and
God-companioned as they were, you could not have known
the rapture you may know as you hear the knocking and the
Voice, and, opening, bid Me welcome to My Feast.

A Feast of tenderest companionship, of Divine Sustenance, truly a Love Feast.

God at Eventide: Absorb Good

The only way to eradicate evil is to absorb good. This is My
story of the seven other spirits.

This story was to illustrate the vast difference between
the Mosaic Law and My Law. The Pharisees and the Elder
Brother were the observers of the Mosaic Law.

You have proved this in your own life. To pray that you may resist temptation and conquer evil is in itself but useless.

Evil cannot live in My Presence. Live with Me. Absorb My Life, and evil will remain without.

OCTOBER 22

God Calling: Home-Building

You are building up an unshakable faith. Be furnishing the quiet places of your souls now.

Fill them with all that is harmonious and good, beautiful, and enduring.

Home-build in the Spirit now, and the waiting time will be well spent.

God at Eventide: The Peace of God

The Peace of God lies deeper than all knowledge of earth's wisest. In that quiet realm of the Spirit, where dwell all who are controlled by *My* Spirit, there can all secrets be revealed, all Hidden-Kingdom-Truths be shown and learned.

Live there, and *Truth* deeper than all *knowledge* shall be revealed to you.

Their lines are gone out into all the earth—so travels the influence, ever-widening, of those who live near to Me.

Take time to be with Me. Take time in prayer to draw others to Me.

Count all things but loss, so that you may have Me.

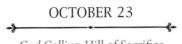

God Calling: Hill of Sacrifice

You must trust to the end. You must be ready to go on trusting to the last hour.

You must know even when you cannot *see*. . . . You must be ready, like My servant Abraham, to climb the very Hill of Sacrifice, to go to the very last moment, before you see My Deliverance.

This final test has to come to all who walk by Faith. You must rely on Me *alone*.

Look to no other arm, look for no other help. Trust in the Spirit Forces of the Unseen, not in those you see. Trust and fear not.

God at Eventide: Passing Understanding

The Peace of God that passeth all understanding.

That Peace that both fills and encircles the soul that trusts in Me. It is born of a long faith-experience that is permeated through and through with the consciousness of the never-failing Love of a Father.

A Father Who supplies and protects, not alone because of His obligations of Fatherhood, but because of a longing, intense, enduring Love, that delights to protect and supply, and that cannot be denied.

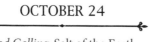

God Calling: Salt of the Earth

Our Lord, we bless Thee and thank Thee for Thy Keeping Power.

Yes! "Kept by the Power of God" is a promise and an assurance that holds Joy and Beauty for the believing soul.

The keeping that means security, safety, is wonderful. There is, too, the keeping that implies Life, freshness, purity, the being "kept unspotted from the world."

Then there is the keeping that I ensure to those of whom I speak as the salt of the earth.

"Ye are the salt of the earth: but if the salt have lost his savour it is henceforth good for nothing, but to be cast out, and to be trodden under foot of men."

Only in very close contact with Me is the keeping Power realized. That keeping Power which maintains the salt at its freshest and best, and also preserves from corruption that portion of the world in which I place it.

What a work! Not by activity in this case, but simply by its existing, by its quality.

God at Eventide: A Special Message

Peace has, for every true disciple, a special meaning and message. It is endeared to him by association. It was the parting gift of his Lord to His followers, bequeathed through them to followers of each succeeding generation. It is not the peace of indifference, of sloth; *that* is mere acquiescence.

No, the Peace I left to My own is vital and strong. It can exist only in the heart of one who lives with Me. It derives from Me that Eternal Life which is Mine, and which makes the Gift ever full of an imperishable beauty, and instinct with Life indeed.

God Calling: No Unemployment

The way of conquest over the material, the temporal, which all My disciples should know, is learned by the conquest of the physical, the self-life, in each of you.

So seek, in all things, to conquer. Take this as a very definite Guidance. Circumstances are adverse. Temporal power, as money, needs to be forthcoming.

Then seek daily more and more to obtain this self-conquest, and you are gaining surely, though you may not see it, conquest over the temporal forces and powers.

Unemployment would cease if man realized this.

If he has not the work, let him make himself a conquering force, beginning with the conquest of all evil in himself, then in his home, then in all round him. He will have become a force that will be needed and must be employed.

There are no idle hours in My Kingdom. Waiting may seem a time of inactivity, as far as the outer world is concerned, but it can, and should, be a time of great activity in the inner life and the surrounding material plane.

God at Eventide: Fullness of Joy

There is a joy of My Kingdom that My followers may know, and that no shadow of the world's pessimism can endanger. It resists all cramping of outward, soulless convention.

Too often My followers fail to see how full of Joy I could be. They see Me, the *Jesus* who beheld the city and wept over it, Who was so touched by the suffering all round Me, and they fail to realize how filled with Joy I could be at the response to My Call.

No shadow of the Cross could darken that Joy. I was as a bridegroom among the friends he had chosen to share his wedding joys.

As such I refused to consider the implied reproof of the Pharisees. We were a band filled with desire to save a world, we were full of hope and enthusiasm. Our Spirits could not be compressed into the outworn bottles of mere pharisaic convention. Ponder this and recognize your Master Who bids you Love and Laugh.

OCTOBER 26

God Calling: Deserters

You must believe utterly. My Love can bear nothing less. I am so often "wounded in the house of My friends." Do you think the spitting and scorn of My enemies, the mocking and reviling hurt me? No!

"They all forsook Him and fled." "I know not the man." These left their scars.

So now, it is not the unbelief of My enemies that hurts, but that My friends, who love and know Me, cannot walk all the way with Me and doubt My Power to do all that I have said.

God at Eventide: Love Is Duty-Free

How human, how earthbound are the thoughts man has of God. He judges of Me and My Father by his own frail impulses and feelings.

There is in Divine Love no compulsion of duty from the loved one to the Lover.

Love draws, certainly, and then love longs to serve and to express one's love.

But no question of duty in *return* for Love.

God Calling: Days of Conquest

I see the loving, striving, not the defects. I see the conquest of your particular battle. I count it victory, a glad victory.

I do not compare it with the strenuous campaigns of My great Saints.

For you it is victory, and the angels rejoice, and your dear ones rejoice, as much as at any conquest noted, and rejoiced over, by Heaven.

My children, count the days of conquest as very blessed days.

God at Eventide: Mysteries

There is only one road that leads to the solving of mysteries, the road of obedience and Love.

But in perfect Love there is no curiosity, only a certainty that when the time has come all will be clear, and that until that time there is no desire to know anything that the Beloved has not chosen to reveal.

Does it matter if no mystery is made plain down here? If you have Me, then in Me you have all. Continue ye in My Love.

OCTOBER 28

God Calling: Glad Surprises

Our Lord, we know that all is well. We trust Thee for all.
We love Thee increasingly. We bow to Thy Will.

Bow not as one who is resigned to some heavy blow about to fall or to the acceptance of some inevitable decision.

Bow as a child bows, in anticipation of a glad surprise being prepared for it by one who loves it.

Bow in *such* a way, just waiting to hear the loving word to raise your head, and see the glory and Joy and wonder of your surprise.

God at Eventide: Growing Young

There will never be a time when you will have conquered all of self. As you mount higher and higher you will see more and more clearly the errors and shortcomings of your character and life.

That is as it should be. Progress means youth. Arrested growth means stagnation. Lack of progress and failure to conquer mean—old age.

In Eternal Life there can be no old age. Eternal Life is Youth-Life, full and abundant Life. "And this is Life Eternal that they may know Thee, the only True God, and *Jesus* Christ, Whom Thou hast sent."

God Calling: Discount Money

Never count success by money gained. That is not the mind of My Kingdom. Your success is the measure of My Will and Mind that you have revealed to those around you.

Your success is the measure of My Will that those around you have seen worked out in your lives.

God at Eventide: Little Difficulties

The secret of true discipleship is service in little things. So rarely do Mine understand this.

They are ready to die for Me, but not to live for Me, in all the small details of this life.

Is not this the way of men, so often, toward those they love in the world? They are so ready to make the big sacrifices, but not the little ones.

Guard against this in service for Me. Suffer little hardships gladly, overcome little proud impulses, little selfishnesses, and little difficulties. Serve Me in the little things. Be My servants of the little ways.

God Calling: The Hardest Lesson

Wait and you shall realize the Joy of the one who can be calm and wait, knowing that all is well. The last, and hardest lesson, is that of waiting. So wait.

I would almost say tonight, "Forgive Me, children, that I allow this extra burden to rest upon you even for so short a time."

I would have you know this, that from the moment you placed all in My Hands, and sought no other aid, from that moment I have taken the quickest way possible to work out your salvation, and to free you.

There is so much you have had to be taught—to avoid future disaster. But the Friend with whom you stand by the grave of failure, of dead ambitions, of relinquished desires, that Friend is a Friend for all time.

Use this waiting time to cement the Friendship with Me and to increase your Knowledge of Me.

God at Eventide: [Untitled]

Again I would stress that the service of My followers must be ever one of Love, not of duty. Temptations can so easily overcome a resolution based on fear, on duty, but against Love temptation has no power. Live in My Spirit, rest in My Love.

Remember, if you look to Me for everything, and trust Me for everything, and if I do not send the full measure you ask, it must not be thought that it is necessarily some sin or weakness that is hindering My Help from flowing into and through you.

In some cases this may be so, but it may be simply My restraining Hand laid on you as I whisper, "Rest, step aside with Me. Come apart and rest awhile."

OCTOBER 31

God Calling: The Voice Again

Thy word is a lamp unto my feet, and a light unto my path.
PSALM 119:105

Yes! My Word, the Scriptures. Read them, study them; store them in your hearts, use them as you use a lamp to guide your footsteps.

But remember, My children, My Word is more even than that. It is the Voice that speaks to your hearts, that inner consciousness that tells of Me.

It is the Voice that speaks to you intimately, personally, in this sacred evening time. It is even more than that. It is I your Lord and Friend.

"And the Word was made flesh and dwelt among us." Truly a lamp to your feet and a light to your path.

God at Eventide: And Seek No Surplus

I would impress upon you again that only as you are channels can I make your supply plentiful and constant.

If you keep all you need, and then intend of your surplus to give to Me and Mine, there will be no surplus. I have promised to supply your need, so that as you impoverish yourselves, I repair that loss. Try and grasp that Truth in all its fullness.

God Calling: Prayer of Joy

Joy is the messenger, dear Lord, that bears our prayers to Thee.

Prayer can be like incense, rising ever higher and higher, or it can be like a low earth-mist

The Eye that sees all, the Ear that hears all, knows every cry.

But the prayer of real faith is the prayer of Joy, that sees and knows the heart of Love it rises to greet and that is so sure of a glad response.

God at Eventide: Joy in November

These things have I spoken. . .that your Joy may be full.

The hallmark of a true follower of Mine is Joy.

Not a surface pleasure at life's happenings, a something that is reflected from without, but a welling up from within of that happiness that can only come from a heart at peace, secure in its friendship with Me.

Joy, strong and calm, attracts men to Me.

How many who claim Me Lord reflect a dull Christ, and wonder that the world turns rather to the glitter and tinsel of that world's pleasures.

Truly My followers deny Me in so doing. I am a Glorified Christ. A Christ of Triumphant Conquest.

Alas! My followers point too often to the grave-clothes of the tomb. Still learn to love and laugh.

God Calling: Spend

Give, give, give. Keep ever an empty vessel for Me to fill. In future use all for Me, and give all *you* cannot use.

How poor die those who leave wealth! Wealth is to use, to spend, for Me.

Use as you go. Delight to use.

God at Eventide: Your Store of Wealth

The stored wealth of the Spirit of Jesus Christ.

The giving out of that Spirit-wealth.

The supply of the Spirit of Jesus Christ.

This, My Spirit, must be absorbed, not in a moment of emergency, but in the quiet alone-times, so that from this store all help and strength can be supplied.

The mistakes My followers often make is that they rely upon this supply being ready for them to claim from Me at need, when the claim should have been made before, and My Spirit in all its fullness have already become a part of them.

My Spirit is not a Spirit of Rescue alone. It is both Builder and Strength, making of My follower that strong soldier ready for the emergency or strong to avoid it, as the need of My Kingdom may demand.

God Calling: No Limit

Unlimited supply, that is My Law. Oh! the unlimited Supply, and oh! the poor, blocked channels! Will you feel this, that there is no limit to My Power?

But man asks, and blasphemes in asking, such poor, mean things. Do you not see how you wrong Me? I desire to give you a gift, and if you are content with the poor and the mean and the sordid, then you are insulting Me, the Giver.

"Ask what ye will and it shall be done unto you." How I can fulfill the promise is My Work, not yours, to consider. . . . Have a big Faith, and expect big things, and you will get big things.

God at Eventide: Up in the Heights

The Sunlight on the Hills of God lures men to seek His Mountain Heights.

Get away from valley prejudices and fears on to the sunlit slopes with Me. Gently at first I will lead, so gently; then as you gain strength we will leave, together, the grassy slopes for the rugged Mountain Heights, where fresh visions are spread out before you, and where I can teach you My Secrets of those Heights.

Life holds in store more wonderful possibilities than you can sense as yet, and ever, more and more, as you go on, will further possibilities reveal themselves.

NOVEMBER 4

God Calling: I Am Beside You

*In thy presence is fulness of joy; at thy right
hand there are pleasures for evermore.*
PSALM 16:11

Do not seek to realize this fullness of Joy as the result of effort.
This cannot be, any more than Joy in a human friend's presence would come as the result of trying to force yourself to
like to have that friend with you.

Call often My Name, "Jesus."

The calling of My Name does not really summon Me. I
am beside you. But it removes, as it were, the scales from your
eyes, and you see Me.

It is, as it were, the pressure of a loved one's hand, that
brings an answering pressure, and a thrill of Joy follows, a
real, and a joyful sense of nearness.

God at Eventide: The Life Beautiful

The Wonder of a life with Thee, dear Lord.

In the Spirit realm Truths reveal themselves in the same varied wonders of color as Nature her beauties.

Experiences, Guidance, Revelation of Truth, these are all,
as it were, the flashing of glorious color-harmonies upon your
inner sight, provoking such a wealth of joy, such a thrill of
ecstasy as is beyond mortal tongue to describe.

That joy is no shimmering beauty of the surface, but
strength-giving and comforting. It furnishes the very
foundation-altar upon which your life yields itself in sacrifice
to Me, and from which your prayers ascend.

317

NOVEMBER 5

God Calling: Second Advent

Jesus, Comforter of all the sorrowing, help us to bring Thy comfort into every heart and life to which Thou art longing to express that comfort through us. Use us, Lord. The years may be many or few. Place us where we can best serve Thee, and influence most for Thee.

The world would be brought to Me so soon, so soon, if only all who acknowledge Me as Lord, as Christ, gave themselves unreservedly to be used by Me.

I could use *each* human body as mightily as I used My own human body as a channel for Divine Love and Power.

I do not delay My second coming. My *followers* delay it.

If each lived for Me, by Me, in Me, allowing Me to live in him, to use him to express the Divine through him, as I expressed it when on Earth, then long ago the world would have been drawn to Me, and I should have come to claim My own.

So seek, My children, to live, knowing no other desire but to express Me, and to show My Love to your world.

God at Eventide: Wine of Life

They have no wine.

Something is lacking at the feast of life.

I only can supply that wonderful Life element that the world lacks. The Joy, the sparkle is Mine to give.

Yours to feel the lack, the soullessness. Yours to say— "They have no wine."

"Whatsoever He saith unto you, do it."

Your task to fill the waterpots with water.

God Calling: God in Action

Power is not such an overwhelming force as it sounds, a some-thing you call to your aid, to intervene in crises. No! *Power is just God in action.*

Therefore, whenever a servant of Mine, however weak he humanly may be, allows God to work through him, then all he does is *powerful*.

Carry this thought with you through the days in which you seem to accomplish little. Try to see it is not you, but the Divine Spirit in you. All you have to do, as I have told you before, is to turn self out. A very powerful ax in a Master Hand accomplishes much. The same in the hand of a weak child, nothing. So see that it is not the instrument, but the Master Hand that wields the instrument, that tells.

Remember no day is lost on which some Spiritual Truth becomes clearer. No day is lost which you have given to Me to use. My use of it may not have been apparent to you. Leave that to Me. Dwell in Me, and I in you; so shall ye bear much fruit. The fruit is not the work of the branches, though proudly the branches may bear it. It is the work of the Vine that sends its life-giving sap through those branches. I am the Vine and ye are the branches.

God at Eventide: Your Garden of Life

Think of Me tonight as the Great Gardener, tending and car-ing for you as a gardener does for his garden.

Pruning here, protecting from frost there, planting, trans-planting. Sowing the seed of this or that truth, safeguarding it with the rich earth, sending My rain and sun to help in its growth, watching so tenderly as it responds to My care.

Lovingly anxious when its first eager green appears. Full

of joy at the site of bud, and when the beauty of flower is seen. The seed and fruit of His pastures.

The Great Gardener. Let Me share with you the tending of your garden of life.

NOVEMBER 7

God Calling: Self Kills Power

Dwelling with Me, desiring only My Will and to do My work, My Spirit cannot fail to pass through the channel of your life into the lives of others.

Many think it is humility to say they do little and are of little value to My world. To think *that* is pride.

What if the pipe were to say, "I do so little; I wish I could be more use." The reply would be, "It is not you, but the water that passes through you, that saves and blesses. All you have to do is to see there is nothing to block the way so that the water cannot flow through."

The only block there can be in *your* channel is self. Keep that out, and know that My Spirit is flowing through. Therefore all must be the better for coming in contact with both of you, because you are channels. See this, and you will think it natural to know they are being helped, not by you, but by My Spirit flowing through you as a channel.

God at Eventide: Lost Opportunities

Think of one who has wrought great evil in the world or in your own life. Then remember there may have been the time when a simple act of obedience to Me by one who crossed his path might have corrected and shown him his wrong before evil mastered him.

Many a sin unconquered, an evil occurrence, could well be traced back to a lack of obedience, perhaps in years long past, of one who professed to serve Me.

Remember this in speaking to those who judge Me by the evil they feel I permit in the world. For yourself now, dwell not on the past, but dwell more with Me, that in future there be no sins of omission or commission.

NOVEMBER 8

God Calling: Wipe the Slate

But this one thing I do, forgetting those things which
are behind, and reaching forth unto those things
which are before, I press toward the mark. . . .
PHILIPPIANS 3:13–14

Forget the past. Remember only its glad days. Wipe the slate of your remembrance with Love, which will erase all that is not confirmed in Love. You must forget *your* failures, your failures and those of others. Wipe them out of the book of your remembrance.

I did not die upon the Cross for man to bear the burdens of his sins himself. "Who His own self bare our sins in His own body on the tree."

If you forget not the sins of others, and I bear them, then you add to My sorrows.

God at Eventide: Your Life-Line

Think of the strong lifeline of Faith and Power. This I have told you is your line of rescue.

It means constant communication between us.

You pray for Faith. I give you Faith. This enables you to test the Power I give, as your Faith goes back to me in ever-increasing strength. My Power and your Faith ever inter-changing. The one calling forth the other, each dependent upon the other, until *My Faith* in *you* is justified indeed by the Power you exercise.

NOVEMBER 9

God Calling: Wonderful Friendship

Think of Me as a Friend, but realize, too, the wonder of the Friendship. As soon as man gives Me not only worship and honor, obedience, allegiance, but loving understanding, then he becomes My Friend, even as I am his.

What I can do for you. Yes! but also what we can do for each other. What you can do for Me.

Your service becomes so different when you feel I count on your great friendship to do this or that for Me. . . .

Dwell more, dwell much, on this thought of you as My friends, and of the sweetness of My knowing where I can turn for Love, for understanding, for help.

God at Eventide: The Glowing Heart

Think of the walk to Emmaus, think of the feast of Revelation that followed, of the understanding Friendship that was the result. How much I, their Lord, their Risen Lord, had explained to My two disciples during that walk. So much that was mystery to them became clear as we went along the way.

Yet not as their Master did I become known, until in the Breaking of Bread I revealed Myself. In speaking of Me afterwards they said, "Did not our hearts burn within us when He talked with us by the way?"

So do not fret if all that I can be to you is not yet revealed. Walk with Me, talk with Me, invite Me to be your guest, and leave to Me My moment of self-Revelation. I want each day to be a walk with Me.

Do you not feel, even now, your hearts burn within you, as if with the glow of anticipation?

NOVEMBER 10

God Calling: New Forces

Remember that life's difficulties and troubles are not intended to arrest your progress, but to increase your speed. You must call new forces, new powers into action.

Whatever it is must be surmounted, overcome. Remember this.

It is as a race. Nothing must daunt you. Do not let a difficulty conquer you. You must conquer it.

My strength will be there awaiting you. Bring all your thought, all your power, into action. Nothing is too *small* to be faced and overcome. To push small difficulties aside is to be preparing big troubles.

Rise to conquer. It is the path of victory I would have you tread. There can be no failure with Me.

"Now unto him that is able to keep you from falling, and to present you faultless before the presence of his glory with exceeding joy. . ."

God at Eventide: Rest for the Weary

This weariness must compel you to sink back, a tired child, to rest in My Love. *There* remain, until that Love so permeates your being that you are supported by it, and, so strengthened, arise.

Until you feel that this is so, remain inactive, conscious of My Presence. Yours is a big work, and you must refresh yourself and only approach it again after periods of repose.

The activity on the Spirit-plane is so great, so wonderful,

that but for the times of enforced rest and prayer, you would be stirred to an emotional activity on the physical plane that defeats My ends.

NOVEMBER 11

God Calling: Heaven's Colors

Looking back you will see that every step was planned. Leave all to Me. Each stone in the mosaic fits into the perfect pattern, designed by the Master Artist.

It is all so wonderful!

But the colors are of Heaven's hues, so that your eyes could not bear to gaze on the whole until you are beyond the veil.

So, stone by stone, you see and trust the pattern to the Designer.

God at Eventide: A Noble House

Though I was a Son yet learnt I obedience.

This was to teach My followers that allegiance to Me meant no immunity from discipline.

The house of your spirit is fashioned brick by brick— Love, Obedience, Truth. There is a plan, and each action of yours is a brick in its building.

Think. A misguided act, a neglected duty, or a failure to carry out My wishes would mean not only a missing brick but a faulty edifice.

How many an otherwise noble character is spoilt thus. Build now for eternity.

God Calling: The Voiceless Cry

Jesus, hear us, and let our cry come unto Thee.

That voiceless cry that comes from anguished hearts is heard above all the music of Heaven.

It is not the arguments of theologians that solve the problems of a questioning heart, but the cry of that heart to Me, and the certainty that I have heard.

God at Eventide: Heaven's Music

To glorify Me is to reflect, in praise, My character in your lives. To mount up with wings as eagles, higher and higher, to soar ever nearer to Me.

To praise Me is to sing, to let your hearts thrill. To glorify Me is to express exactly the same, but through the medium of your whole beings, your whole lives. When I say, "Rejoice, rejoice," I am training you to express this in your whole natures.

That is the Music of Heaven, the glorifying Me through sanctified lives and devoted hearts of Love.

NOVEMBER 13

God Calling: Every Problem Solved

Man has such strange ideas of the meaning of My invitation "Come unto Me." Too often has it been interpreted as an urge to pay a duty owed to a Creator or a debt owed to a Savior.

The "Come unto Me" holds in it a wealth of meaning far surpassing even that. "Come unto Me" for the solution of every problem, for the calming of every fear, for all you need—physical, mental, spiritual.

Sick, come to Me for health. Homeless, ask Me for a home. Friendless, claim a friend. Hopeless, a refuge.

"Come unto Me" for everything.

God at Eventide: A Lonely Road

To Me each one of My children is an individual with varying characteristics and varying needs. To one and all the way to the highest must be a lonely road, as far as human help and understanding are concerned.

None other can feel the same needs and desires, or explain the inner self in the same way. That is why man needs Divine Companionship. The Companionship that alone can understand each heart and need.

God Calling: Devious Ways

Life is not easy, My children. Man has made of it not what My Father meant it to be.

Ways that were meant to be straight paths have been made by man into ways devious and evil, filled with obstacles and stones of difficulty.

God at Eventide: Joy Is Yours

The future is not your concern, that is Mine. The past you have handed back to Me, and you have no right to dwell on that.

Only the present is My gift to you, and of that only each day as it comes. But, if unto that day you crowd past sorrows and resentments and failures, as well as the possible anxieties of the years that may be left to you here—what brain and spirit could bear that strain.

For this I never promised My Spirit and Comfort and Help.

NOVEMBER 15

God Calling: By My Spirit

Man is apt to think that once in time only was My Miracle-working Power in action. That is not so. Wherever man trusts wholly in Me, and leaves to Me the choosing of the very day and hour, then there is My miracle-working Power as manifest, as marvelously manifest today, as ever it was when I was on Earth, as ever it was to set My apostles free or to work miracles of wonder and healing through them.

Trust in Me. Have a boundless faith in Me, and you will see, and, seeing, will give Me all the glory. Remember, and say often to yourselves, "Not by might, nor by Power, but by My Spirit, saith the LORD."

Dwell much in thought upon all I accomplished on earth, and then say to yourselves, "He, our Lord, our Friend, could accomplish this now in our lives."

Apply these miracles to your present-day need, and know that your Help and Salvation are sure.

God at Eventide: Sharing With Me

Not by life's difficulties and trials are you trained and taught as much as by the times of withdrawal to be alone with Me.

Difficulties and trials alone are not remedial, are not of spiritual value.

That value is only gained by contact with Me. Joy shared with Me, or sorrow and difficulty shared with Me, both can prove of great spiritual value, but that is gained by the *sharing with Me*. Share all with Me.

Remember in true friendship sharing is mutual, so as you share with Me, do I in ever-increasing measure share with you—My Love, My Grace, My Joy, My Secrets, My Power. My Manifold Blessings.

NOVEMBER 16

God Calling: Union Is Power

*For where two or three are gathered together
in my name, there am I in the midst of them.*
MATTHEW 18:20

Claim that promise always. Know it true that when two of My lovers meet, I am the Third. Never limit that promise.

When you two are together in My Name, united by one bond in My Spirit, I am there. Not only when you meet to greet Me and to hear My Voice.

Think what this means in Power. It is again the lesson of the Power that follows *two united to serve Me*.

God at Eventide: All Are Worthy

Treat all as those about whom I care.

You would visit the poor, the sick or those in prison, knowing full well I would see it as done unto Me.

I want you now to go still further along the way of my Kingdom. You contact many who are not poor, not sick, not in prison.

They may be opposed to you. They may disregard much that you consider of value, they may not seem to need your help. Can you treat these, too, as you would wish to treat Me? They may be in need greater than the others you long to aid.

To you their aims may seem unworthy, their self-seeking may antagonize you. When I said, "Judge not," was I not including them, too?

Can you limit My words to suit your own inclinations?

This is not an easy task I set you, but your way is the Way of Obedience. I did not suggest to My followers one they could take or not as they willed. My "Judge not" was imperative, and a new *commandment* I gave unto them that they should love.

For those who do not yet name Me Lord, Love is the only magnet that will draw them to Me.

Be true, be strong, be loving.

NOVEMBER 17

God Calling: Quiet Lives

Well done, thou good and faithful servant. . .
enter thou into the joy of thy lord.
MATTHEW 25:21

These words are whispered in the ears of many whom the world would pass by unrecognizing. Not to the great, and the world-famed, are these words said so often, but to the quiet followers who serve Me unobtrusively, yet faithfully, who bear their cross bravely, with a smiling face to the world. Thank Me for the quiet lives.

These words speak not only of the passing into that fuller Spirit Life. Duty faithfully done for Me does mean entrance into a Life of Joy—My Joy, the Joy of your Lord. The world may never see it, the humble, patient, quiet service, but I see it, and My reward is not Earth's fame, Earth's wealth, Earth's pleasures, but the Joy Divine.

Whether here or there, in the earth-world or in the Spirit-world, this is My reward. Joy. The Joy that carries an exquisite thrill in the midst of pain and poverty and suffering. That Joy of which I said no man could take it from you. Earth has no pleasure, no reward, that can give man *that* Joy. It is known only to My lovers and My friends.

This Joy may come, not as the reward of activity in My service. It may be the reward of patient suffering, bravely borne.

Suffering, borne with Me, must in time bring Joy, as does all real contact with Me.

God at Eventide: Union with God

True religion is that which binds the soul to God, and supplicatory prayer binds the soul less than any other form of approach.

It is necessary, how necessary, but how often it can fail to bind truly. Meditation and Communion are of infinitely more value.

Meditation is man's line thrown out. It links the soul to God. Communion is God's line thrown out. It draws and unites the soul to Him.

NOVEMBER 18

God Calling: Dazzling Glory

Arise, shine; for thy light is come,
and the glory of the LORD is risen upon thee.
ISAIAH 60:1

The glory of the Lord is the Beauty of His Character. It is risen upon you when you realize it, even though on earth you can do so only in part.

The Beauty of the Purity and Love of God is too dazzling for mortals to see in full.

The Glory of the Lord is also risen upon you when you reflect that Glory in your lives, when in Love, Patience, Service, Purity, whatever it may be, you reveal to the world something of the Father, an assurance that you have been with Me, your Lord and Savior.

Trust in Me. Do more than trust. Joy in Me. If you really trust, you cannot fail to Joy. The wonder of My Care, Protection and Provision is so transcendingly beautiful, as your trust reveals it to you, that your whole heart must sing with the Joy of it.

It is that Joy that will, and does, renew your youth. That source of your Joy and Courage.

Truly did I not know what I was enjoining when I said, "Love and Laugh." But—your attitude must be right, not only with Me, but with those around you.

NOVEMBER 19

God Calling: Hills of the Lord

I will lift up mine eyes unto the hills, from whence cometh my help.
My help cometh from the Lord, which made heaven and earth.
Psalm 121:1–2

Yes! always raise your eyes, from Earth's sordid and mean and false, to the Hills of the Lord. From poverty, lift your eyes to the Help of the Lord.

In moments of weakness, lift your eyes to the Hills of the Lord.

Train your sight by constantly getting this long view. Train it to see more and more, further and further, until distant peaks seem familiar.

The Hills of the Lord. The Hills whence comes your help. A parched earth looks to the Hills for its rivers, its streams, its life. So look you to the Hills. From those Hills comes Help. Help from the Lord—who made Heaven and Earth.

So, for all your spiritual needs, look to the Lord, who made Heaven, and for all your temporal needs, look to Me, owner of all this, the Lord who made the earth.

Turn out all of your self that would rebel against My sway. Know no other rule.

Check your actions and motives habitually. Those that are actuated by self-esteem or self-pity—condemn.

Discipline yourself ruthlessly rather than let self gain any ascendancy. Your aim is to oust it, and to serve and follow Me only.

NOVEMBER 20

God Calling: Mysteries

Your Hope is in the Lord. More and more set your hopes on Me. Know that whatever the future may hold it will hold more and more of Me. It cannot but be glad and full of Joy. So in Heaven, or on Earth, wherever you may be, your way must be truly one of delight.

Do not try to find answers to the mysteries of the world. Learn to know Me more and more, and in that Knowledge you will have all the answers you need here, and when you see Me face-to-face, in that purely Spiritual world, you will find no need to ask. There again all your answers will be in Me.

Remember, I was the answer in time to all man's questions about My Father and His Laws. Know no theology. Know Me. I was *the Word* of God. All you need to know about God you know in Me. If a man knows Me not, all your explanations will fall on an unresponsive heart.

Wait before Me, in humble, silent anticipation. Wait in entire and childlike obedience. Wait as a servant anticipating his master's orders and wants.

Wait as a lover eager to note the first suggestions of a need, and to hasten to supply it. Wait for My orders and commands. Wait for My Guidance, My Supply.

Well indeed in such a life may you be of good cheer. Can a life be dull and dreary when always there is that watchful expectancy, always that anticipation of glad surprise, always wonder of fulfillment, Joy of supply?

NOVEMBER 21

God Calling: Radiate Joy

Not only must you rejoice, but your Joy must be made manifest. "Known unto all men." A candle must not be set under a bushel, but on a candlestick, that it may give light to all who are in the house.

Men must see and know your Joy, and seeing it, know, without any doubt, that it springs from trust in Me, from living with Me.

The hard dull way of resignation is not *My* Way. When I entered Jerusalem, knowing well that scorn and reviling and death awaited Me, it was with cries of Hosanna and with a triumphal procession. Not just a few "Lost Cause" followers creeping with Me into the city. There was no note of sadness in My Last Supper talk with My disciples, and "when we had sung an hymn" we went out unto the Mount of Olives.

So trust, so conquer, so joy. Love colors the way. Love takes the sting out of the wind of adversity.

Love. Love. Love of Me. The consciousness of My Presence, and that of My Father, we are One, and He—God—is Love.

Wait before Me with a song of praise in your hearts. Sing unto Me a new song. There will always be something in each day for which to thank Me.

Acknowledge every little happening as a revelation of My Love and thought for you. Praise has the power to wash away the bitterness of life. Be glad in the Lord.

Rejoice evermore. Great is the heart's "Thank You." As you learn to thank Me more and more you will more and more see Me in the little happenings, and increasingly see much about which to rejoice. Praise and thanksgiving are the preservers of youth.

NOVEMBER 22

God Calling: Only Love Lasts

Though I speak with the tongues of men and of angels, and have not charity, I am become as sounding brass, or a tinkling cymbal.
1 CORINTHIANS 13:1

See that only Love tells. Only what is done in Love lasts, for God is Love, and only the work of God remains.

The fame of the world, the applause given to the one who speaks with the tongues of men and of angels, who attracts admiration and compels attention, it is all given to what is passing, is really worthless, if it lacks that God-quality, Love.

Think how a smile or word of Love goes winged on its way, a God-Power, simple though it may seem, while the mighty words of an orator can fall fruitless to the ground. The test of all true work and words is—are they inspired by Love?

If man only saw how vain is so much of his activity! So much work done in My Name is not acknowledged by Me. As for Love: Turn out from your hearts and lives all that is not loving, so shall ye bear much fruit, and by this shall all men know ye are My disciples, because ye have Love one toward another.

God at Eventide: The Look of the Lover

How few *wait* on Me.

Many pray to Me.

They come into My Presence feverish with wants and distress, but few wait there for that calm and strength that contact with Me would give.

Look unto Me and be ye saved. But the look was not meant to be a hurried glance. It was to be the look into My face of the lover beholding the Beloved.

NOVEMBER 23

God Calling: Earth's Furies

In the world ye shall have tribulation: but be of good cheer; I have overcome the world.
JOHN 16:33

Then you may ask why have you, My children, to have tribulation if I have overcome the world.

My overcoming was never, you know, for Myself, but for you, for My children. Each temptation, each difficulty, I overcame as it presented itself.

The powers of evil were strained to their utmost to devise means to break Me. They failed, but how they failed was known only to Me, and to My Father, who could read My undaunted Spirit. The world, even My own followers, would see a Lost Cause. Reviled, spat upon, scourged, they would deem Me conquered. How could they know My Spirit was free, unbroken, unharmed?

And so, as I had come to show man God, I must show him God unconquered, unharmed, untouched by evil and its power. *Man* could not see My Spirit untouched, risen above these Earth furies and hates, into the Secret Place of the Father. But man could see My Risen Body and learn by that, that even the last attempt of man had been powerless to touch Me.

Take heart from that, for you must share My tribulations.

And in *My* conquering Power you walk unharmed today.

God at Eventide: When Misunderstood

Wait upon Me.

Wait until My strength has filled your being, and you are no longer weak, petty, "misunderstood."

Rise above any fret as to how others may judge you. Leave Me to explain what I will of you and your actions.

Would you seek to follow a Christ Who had wasted His God-Power on fruitless explanations?

So with you. Leave Me to vindicate you, and to be your Advocate, or trust My silence in this as in all else.

NOVEMBER 24

God Calling: Suffer to Save

Take each day's happenings as work you can do for Me. In that Spirit a blessing will attend all you do. Offering your day's service thus to Me, you are sharing in My Life-work and therefore helping Me to save My world.

You may not see it, but the power of vicarious sacrifice is redemptive beyond man's power of understanding here on Earth.

Remember that you live in Eternity, not time. Let there be no rush to do this or that.

It follows that for each task Eternity is yours.

How often, and how sadly, impotent haste has hindered not hastened the work of My Kingdom.

Live more quietly, bathed in the calm of Eternity. Feel this before you leave My Presence.

No fevered haste to work My Will. You must go forth in God's Great Calm.

There was no haste in His Creative Plan. Do you not feel the Strength of Calmness that lies behind God's work in Nature? Rest and know.

NOVEMBER 25

God Calling: The Heavenly Beggar

Behold, I stand at the door, and knock.
Revelation 3:20

Oh, ponder again these words and learn from them My great humility.

There is that gracious invitation, too, for those who yearn to realize a happiness, a rest, a satisfaction they have never found in the world and its pursuits. To them the pleading answer to their quest is "Come to Me and I will give you rest."

But to those who do not feel their need of Me, who obstinately reject Me, who shut the doors of their hearts so that I may not enter, to these I go, in tender, humble longing. Even when I find all closed, all barred, I stand a Beggar, knocking, knocking. The Heavenly Beggar in His Great Humility.

Never think of those who have shut you out or forgotten you that now they must wait, you have no need of them.

No! remember *that*, the Heavenly Beggar, and learn of Me, humility.

Learn, too, the value of each man's happiness and Peace and rest, to Me, his God; and learn, and learning pray to copy the Divine Unrest until a soul finds rest and peace in Me.

God at Eventide: Green Pastures

Walk in My Pastures. The eye will be rested and the spirit restored by the soft green of their verdure. The ear soothed and then enchanted by the sound of My Waters of Comfort.

No stones will impede your progress.

The soft haze over all will speak of unrevealed mysteries, while the wonder of life about you will tell of My ever-active, creative and protective Power, and you will be filled with a content that will merge into a strange yearning for a spirit-oneness with Me.

Then—you will know I am there.

NOVEMBER 26

God Calling: My Beauty

The prophet realized the Truth of My later saying, "He that hath ears to hear let him hear," which might be rendered, "He that hath eyes to see let him see."

The God who was to be born upon Earth was not to be housed in a body so beautiful that men would follow and adore for the beauty of His Countenance.

No! He was to be as one whom the world would despise, but to the seeing eye, the Spirit that dwelt in that body should be so beautiful as to lack nothing. "Yet when we shall see Him, there is no Beauty that we should desire Him."

Pray for the seeing eye, to see the Beauty of My Character,

of My Spirit. Nay, more, as faith saw the Beauty of the God-head in One who had no form nor comeliness, so pray to have that faith to see the Beauty of My Love in My dealings with you, in My actions. Till, in what the world will distort into cruelty and harshness, you, with the eyes of faith, will see all that you could desire.

Know Me. Talk to Me. Let Me talk to you, so that I may make clear to your loving hearts what seems mysterious now and purposeless ("having no form nor comeliness").

God at Eventide: Complete Obedience

Walk in My Way.

My Way is that of *doing*, not only of *accepting*, the Father's Will.

Submitting to that Will, however gladly you may do so, is not enough.

Your work and influence for Me are hindered if your life is not one of complete obedience. "By the obedience of one shall many be made righteous."

Where would your salvation have been had I faltered and wavered in MY task?

It was by the obedience of My earth-life I saved; and so must it be with you.

NOVEMBER 27

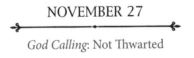

God Calling: Not Thwarted

Not our wills but Thine, O Lord.

Man has so misunderstood Me in this. I want no will laid grudgingly upon My Altar. I want you to desire and love My Will, because therein lies your happiness and Spirit-rest.

Whenever you feel that you cannot leave the choice to Me, then pray, not to be able to accept My Will, but to know and love Me more. With that knowledge, and the Love, will come the certainty that I know best, and that I want only the best for you and yours.

How little those know Me who think I wish to thwart them. How often I am answering their own prayers in the best and quickest way.

God at Eventide: Spirit of Adventure

The path has been tried, every step has been planned with a view to your progress. Never test your work by what others can accomplish, or by what they leave undone. Yours to master the task I have set *you*. Go forward in My Strength and in the Spirit of Adventure.

Undreamed of heights can be attained in this way. Never question your capability. That has been for Me to decide. No experienced Leader would set a follower a task beyond his Power. Trust Me, your Leader.

The World would have been won for Me ere this had My followers been dauntless, inspired by their faith in Me. It is not humility to hesitate to do the great task I set. It is a lack of faith in *Me*.

To wait to feel strong is cowardly. My strength is provided for the task, but I do not provide it for the period of hesitancy before you begin.

How much of My Work goes undone through lack of faith. Again and again might it be said—

"He did not many mighty works through this follower's unbelief."

NOVEMBER 28

God Calling: The Way of the Spirit

Jesus, we come to Thee with Joy.

The Joy of meeting Me should more and more fill your lives. It will. Your lives must first of all be narrowed down, more and more, into an inner circle life with Me (the three of us), and then, as that friendship becomes more and more engrossing, more and more binding, then, gradually, the circle of your interests will widen.

For the present do not think of it as a narrow life. I have My Purpose, My Loving Purpose, in cutting you away from other work and interests, for the time.

To work from large interests and a desire for great activities and world movements, to the inner circle life with Me, is really the wrong way. That is why so often, when, through all these activities and interests, a soul finds Me, I have to begin our Friendship by cutting away the ties that bind it to the outer and wider circle. When it has gained strength and learned its lesson in the inner circle, it can then widen its life, working this time from within out, taking then to each contact, each friendship, the inner circle influence.

And this is to be your way of life.

This is the way of the Spirit. Man so often misunderstands this.

God at Eventide: Active but Alert

Walk very carefully in life. It is a wonderful thing to be known as one who loves Me and seeks to follow Me, but it is also a very great responsibility.

So much that you may do, in which you are not guided by Me, may be condemned as unworthy, and a slur be cast upon

My followers and My Church.

There are no moments in your life from now on in which you can be free from great responsibility. Never forget this. My soldiers are ever on active service.

NOVEMBER 29

God Calling: When Two Agree

If two of you shall agree.

I am the Truth. Every word of Mine is true. Every promise of Mine shall be fulfilled.

First, "gathered together in My Name," bound by a common loyalty to Me, desirous only of doing My Will.

Then, when this is so, I am present, too, a self-invited guest, and when I am there and one with you, voicing the same petition, making your demands Mine, then it follows the request is granted.

But what man has failed perhaps to realize is *all* that lies behind the words. For two to agree about the wisdom of a request, to be certain it *should* be granted, and will be granted (if it should be), is not the same as two agreeing to pray that request.

God at Eventide: Miracles I Could Not Do

What emphasis has been laid upon the wonder of My walking upon the Sea, and upon My feeding the multitudes. In the eyes of Heaven those were miracles of small importance.

Nature was My servant, the creation of the Father; and the Father and I are one. Over her and over the material world I had complete control. My acts were natural, spontaneous, requiring no premeditation, beyond the selection of a suitable moment for their performance.

But My real Miracle work was in the hearts of men, because there I was limited by the Father's gift of Free-will to man. I could not command man as I could the waves. I was subject to the limitations the Father had set. No man must be coerced into My Kingdom.

Think of all that My restraint cost Me. I could have forced the world to accept Me, but I should then have broken faith with all mankind.

NOVEMBER 30

God Calling: From Self to God

The eternal God is thy refuge.
DEUTERONOMY 33:27

A place to flee to, a sanctuary. An escape from misunderstanding, *from yourself*. You can get away from others into the quiet of your own being, but from yourself, from the sense of your failure, your weakness, your sins and shortcomings, whither can you flee?

To the Eternal God your refuge. Till in His Immensity you forget your smallness, meanness, limitations.

Till the relief of safety merges into Joy of appreciation of your refuge, and you absorb the Divine, and absorbing gain strength to conquer.

God at Eventide: Fly the Flag

In your life and on your home you have unfurled the flag of My Kingship. Keep that flag flying.

Depression, disobedience, and want of faith, these are the

half-masts of My Kingdom's flag.

Full and free, above earth's fogs and smokes, *keep My flag flying high.*

"The King is there, they serve the King," should be upon the lips and in the hearts of all who see it. Those who know you must, too, join those who fly My Flag.

DECEMBER 1

God Calling: Responsibility

I am beside you. A very human Jesus, who understands all your weaknesses, and sees too your struggles and conquests.

Remember, I was the Companion of the Weak. Ready to supply their hunger. Teaching My followers their responsibility toward all, not only those near and dear to them, but to the multitude.

"Lord, send them away that they may go into the villages and buy themselves victuals," said My disciples, with no sympathy for the fainting, exhausted men, women, and children.

But I taught that Divine Sympathy includes responsibility. "Give ye them to eat" was My reply. I taught that pity, without a remedy for the evil, or the need, is worthless.

"Give ye them to eat." Wherever your sympathy goes, you must go too, if possible. Remember *that* in thinking of your own needs. Claim from Me the same attitude now.

The servant is not above his Master, certainly not in Spiritual attainments, and what I taught My disciples, I do.

So fainting and needy, by the lakeside of life, know that I will supply your need, not grudgingly, but in full measure.

When you long for your prayer to be answered, when your need is great and you ask great things, then your way is so clear.

Take the next simple duty that lies to your hand and seek to do that thoroughly. . .and so with the next.

As you do it, remember My Promise.

Be faithful in that which is least, and I will make thee ruler over many things.

DECEMBER 2

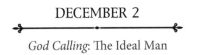

God Calling: The Ideal Man

Draw nigh, shoes off thy feet, in silent awe and adoration. Draw nigh, as Moses drew near to the burning bush.

I give you the loving intimacy of a Friend, but I am God too, and the wonder of our intercourse, the miracle of your intimacy with Me, will mean the more to you if sometimes you see the Majestic Figure of the Son of God.

Draw nigh in the utter confidence that is the sublimest prayer. Draw nigh. No far-off pleading, even to a God clothed with majesty of fire. Draw nigh. Draw nigh, not as a suppliant, but as a listener. I am the Suppliant, as I make known to you My wishes. For this Majestic God is Brother too, longing so intensely that you should serve your brother-man, and longing even more intensely that you should be true to that Vision He has of you.

You speak of your fellow man as disappointing you, as falling short of the ideal you had of him. But what of Me? For every man there is the ideal man I see in him. The man he could be, the man I would have him be.

Judge of My Heart when he fails to fulfill that promise. The disappointments of man may be great and many, but they are nothing as compared with My disappointments. Remember this, and strive to be the friend I see in My Vision of you.

God at Eventide: Learning Times

In performing the simple duty, and in the restraint you achieve in doing it, and not in the feverish looking for the answer to your prayer for the big thing—maybe you learn the one thing needful before I entrust you with what you desire.

With Me, and in obedience to My Will, you have now become suited for that answer.

These are learning-times, rather than testing-times.

DECEMBER 3

God Calling: A Journey with Me

Fret not your souls with puzzles that you cannot solve. The solution may never be shown you until you have left this flesh-life.

Remember what I have so often told you, "I have yet many things to say unto you, but ye cannot bear them now." Only step by step and stage by stage can you proceed in your journey upward.

The one thing to be sure of is that it is a journey with Me. There does come a Joy known to those who suffer with Me. But that is not the result of the suffering, but the result of the close intimacy with Me, to which suffering drove you.

"Whom do men say that I am?" That is the first question I put to each man. My Claim, and the world's interpretation of My Mission and its culmination must be a matter of consideration.

Then comes My second question, and upon the answer to this depends the man's whole future. Here we have left the realm of the mind. Conviction must be of the heart. "Whom do *you* say that I am?"

"Thou art the Christ, the Son of the Living God," was Simon's answer. Then, and not till then, was it possible, without infringement of man's right of Free Will, to add to that profession of faith, the confirmation of My Father, "This is My Beloved Son."

I had lived My Life naturally, as a man among men. But always with the Longing that those I had chosen might have the eyes to see, the faith to penetrate the Mystery of Incarnation, and to see Me, the God revealed.

The faith of a personal conviction is always cemented by the assurance of My Father. It is that which makes the faith of My true followers so unshakable.

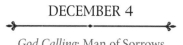

God Calling: Man of Sorrows

*He is despised and rejected of men; a man of sorrows,
and acquainted with grief: and we hid as it were our faces
from him; he was despised, and we esteemed him not.*
ISAIAH 53:3

That these words strike a note of Beauty in the hearts of those attuned to hear the Beautiful shows truly that the heart recognizes the need for the Man of *Sorrows*. That it sees nothing contemptible in One despised by the world.

One of the things My disciples must ever seek to do is to set aside the valuation of the world and judge only according to the values of Heaven. Do not seek the praise and the notice of men. You follow a despised Christ. See, the mob is hooting, throwing stones, jeering, and yet in that quiet little throng, there is a happiness and Joy the reviling crowds could never know.

In your dark hours, when human help fails, keep very close to the Man of Sorrows. Feel My Hand of Love press yours in silent but complete understanding. I, too, was acquainted with grief. No heart can ache without My heart aching, too. "He was despised, and we esteemed Him not."

God at Eventide: Withdraw Yourself

It is not in the crowd that lovers learn to know and cherish each other. It is in the quiet times alone.

So with My own and Me. It is in the tender alone-times that they learn all that I can be to each.

Shut out the world with its all-too-insistent claims. Then, because of the power and the peace and the joy that come to you, you will crave to be alone with Me.

DECEMBER 5

God Calling: Law of Supply

The first law of giving is of the Spirit world. Give to all you meet, or whose lives touch yours, of your prayers, your time, yourselves, your love, your thought. You must practice *this* giving first.

Then give of this world's goods and money, as you have them given to you. To give money and material things, without having first made the habit daily, hourly, ever increasingly, of giving on the higher plane, is wrong.

Give, give, give all your best to all who need it.

Be great givers—great givers. Give as I said My Father in Heaven gives. He who makes His sun to shine on the evil and on the good, and sendeth rain on the just and on the unjust. Remember, as I have told you before, give according to need, never according to desert. In giving, with the thought of supplying a real need you most closely resemble that Father in Heaven, the Great Giver.

As you receive, you must supply the needs of those I bring to you. Not questioning, not limiting. Their nearness to you, their relationship, must never count. Only their need is to guide you. Pray to become great givers.

God at Eventide: Perfect Achievement

Yield to My demands.

Obey My Will, that is God's Will, for My *meat* was ever to do the Will of Him that sent Me. Obeying that Will, making it yours, all you will *must* be granted.

That Will is creative, secures perfect achievement, and being of God (One and indivisible), secures all that is of God—Love, Peace, Joy, Power, in the measure that one of His creatures can absorb them.

DECEMBER 6

God Calling: Expect Temptation

Lord, give us Power to conquer temptation
as Thou didst in the wilderness.

The very first step toward conquering temptation is to see it as temptation. To dissociate yourself from it.

Not to think of it as something resulting from your tiredness, or illness, or poverty, or nerve-strain, when you feel you might well excuse yourself for yielding, but first to realize very fully that when you have heard My voice ("the Heavens opened," as it were) and are going to fulfill your mission to work for me and to draw souls to me, you must expect a mighty onslaught from the evil one, who will endeavor with all his might to frustrate you and to prevent your good work. Expect that.

Then when these little temptations, or big ones, come, you will recognize them as planned by evil to thwart Me. Then for very love of Me you will conquer.

God at Eventide: A New Song

You are being led forth. You have crossed the Red Sea. Your wilderness wanderings are nearly over. Behold I make all things new.

A new birth, a new heart, a new life, a new song.

Let this time be to you a time of renewal.

Cast away all that is dead. Truly live the Risen Life. In mind and spirit turn out all that offends.

God Calling: Food of Life

Those were My words to My disciples in the early days of My Ministry. Later I was to lead them on to a fuller understanding of that Majestic Union of a soul with God in which strength, life,

Meat is to sustain the body. To do the Will of God is the very strength and support of Life. Feed on that Food.

Soul-starvation comes from the failing to do, and to delight in doing, My Will. How busy the world is in talking of bodies that are undernourished! What of the souls that are undernourished?

Make it indeed your meat to do My Will. Strength and Power will indeed come to you from that.

God at Eventide: Secret Service

You are blessed, very richly blessed. Never forget that you have My Love and Protection. No Treasures of the world can mean to you what that can.

Never forget, too, that you are guided. Every word, every letter, every meeting, God-planned and God-blessed. Just feel that, know that.

You are not a stray and uncared for. You belong to the Secret Service of Heaven. There are privileges and protections for you all along the Way.

God Calling: My Kingdom

And greater works than these shall ye do, because I go unto My Father.

While I was on the earth, to those with whom I came in contact, Mine was a lost cause. Even My disciples only believed, half-doubting, half-wondering. When they all forsook Me and fled, it was not so much fear of My enemies as the certainty that My Mission, however beautiful they thought it, had failed.

In spite of all I had taught them, in spite of the revelation of the Last Supper, they had secretly felt sure that when the final moment came and the hatred of the Pharisees was declared against Me, I should sound some call to action, and that I should lead My many followers and found My earthly kingdom. Even the disciples who had eyes to see My Spiritual Kingdom had thought material forces had proved too strong for Me.

But with My Resurrection came hope. Faith revived. They would remind each other of all I had said. They would have the assurance of My Divinity, Messiahship. And they would have all My Power in the Unseen—the Holy Spirit—to help them.

Those who lived in the Kingdom were to do the work—greater works than I was able to do. Not a greater Power shown, not a greater Life lived, but, as men recognized My Godhead, opportunities for works in My Name would increase.

You are Mine. Mine to control, to lead, to cherish. Trust Me for all.

In thinking of and dealing with others realize that whatever their sin, you would be as they are but for My protection, but for My tender forgiveness.

Remember, too, that My Command of "Judge not" was as explicit as that of "Thou shalt do no murder," "Thou shalt not commit adultery." Obey Me in all.

DECEMBER 9

God Calling: Your Search Rewarded

Lord, all men seek for Thee.

All men seek for Me, but all men do not know what they want. They are seeking because they are dissatisfied without realizing that I am the Object of their quest.

Count it your greatest Joy to be the means, by your lives, sufferings, words, and love, to prove to the questing ones you know that their search would end when they saw Me.

Profit by My Example. I left My Work—seemingly the greatest work—that of saving souls, to seek communion with My Father. Did I know perhaps that with many it was idle curiosity? Did I know that there must be no rush into the Kingdom, that the still small voice, not the shoutings of a mob, would alone persuade men I was the Son of God?

Why be surrounded by multitudes if the multitudes were not really desiring to learn from, and to follow, Me? Follow the Christ into the quiet places of prayer.

God at Eventide: Power to Help

Not so much on what you say as on your willingness to let My Influence flow through you, will your power to help others depend.

The Power of My Father is summoned by you to the aid of those whom you desire to help.

Live in the consciousness of My Presence, and your thoughts of Love, anxiety, and even interest will let loose a flood of Power to save.

DECEMBER 10

God Calling: The Quiet Time

There may be many times when I reveal nothing, command nothing, give no guidance. But your path is clear, and your task, to grow daily more and more into the knowledge of Me. That this quiet time with Me will enable you to do.

I may ask you to sit silent before Me, and I may speak no word that you could *write*. All the same that waiting *with* Me will bring comfort and Peace. Only friends who understand and love each other can wait silent in each other's presence.

And it may be that I shall prove our friendship by asking you to wait in silence while I rest with you, assured of your Love and understanding. So wait, so love, so joy.

God at Eventide: Successful Failures

You grieve that you have failed Me. Remember it was for the failures that I hung on Calvary's Cross. It was a failure I greeted first in the Easter Garden.

It was to one of the failures I entrusted My Church, My Lambs, My Sheep.

It was to one who had thwarted and despised Me, who had tortured and murdered My followers that I gave My great world Mission to the Gentiles.

But each had first to learn to know Me as Savior and Lord by a bitter consciousness of having failed Me.

If you would work for Me, then you must be ready for the valley of humiliation through which all My followers have to pass.

DECEMBER 11

God Calling: A Sunrise Gift

To those whose lives have been full of struggle and care, who have felt as you both have, the tragedy of living, the pity of an agonized heart for My poor world—to those of My followers I give that Peace and Joy that bring to age its second Spring, the youth they sacrificed for Me and for My world. . . .

Take each day now as a joyous sunrise gift from Me. Your simple daily tasks done in My Strength and Love will bring the consciousness of all your highest hopes. Expect great things. Expect great things.

God at Eventide: Help Is Here

You have been told to end all prayer upon a note of praise. That note of praise is not only faith rising up through difficulties to greet Me. It is more.

It is the echo in the heart of the sound borne on Spirit waves—of that Help upon the way. It is given to those who love and trust Me to sense this approach. So rejoice for truly your redemption draweth nigh.

God Calling: Carefree

Perfect love casteth out fear.

Love and fear cannot dwell together. By their very natures they cannot exist side by side. Evil is powerful, and fear is one of evil's most potent forces.

Therefore a weak, vacillating love can be soon routed by fear, whereas a perfect Love, a trusting Love, is immediately the Conqueror, and fear, vanquished, flees in confusion.

But I am Love because God is Love, and I and the Father are One. So the only way to obtain this perfect Love, that dispels fear, is to have Me more and more in your lives. You can only banish fear by My Presence and My Name.

Fear of the future—Jesus will be with us.

Fear of poverty—Jesus will provide. (And so to all the temptations of fear.)

You must not allow fear to enter. Talk to Me. Think of Me. Talk of Me. Love Me. And that sense of My Power will so possess you that no fear can possess your mind. Be strong in this My Love.

God at Eventide: Prove Me Now

You have to prove Me. To come to Me walking upon the water. No sure, accustomed earth beneath you. But remember He to Whom you come is Son of God and Son of Man.

He knows your needs. He knows how difficult it must be for mortal to learn to live more and more a life that is not of the senses. To know that when I say, "Come," I asked no impossibility.

Seeing the waves Peter was afraid.

Refuse to look at the waves. Know that with your eyes

on Me you can override all storm. It is not what happens that matters, but where your gaze is fixed.

DECEMBER 13

God Calling: Perpetual Guidance

Fullness of Joy. The Joy of Perpetual Guidance. The Joy of knowing that every detail of your lives is planned by Me, but planned with a wealth of tenderness and Love.

Wait for Guidance in every step. Wait to be shown My Way. The thought of this loving leading should give you great Joy. All the responsibility of Life taken off your shoulders. All its business worry taken off your shoulders. It is indeed a Joy for you to feel so free and yet so planned for.

Oh! the wonder of this God-guided life. To think anything impossible in such circumstances is to say it cannot be done by Me. To say that is surely a denial of Me.

God at Eventide: The Narrow Way

You must obey My Will unhesitatingly if you would realize My Blessings. It is a straight and narrow way that leads into the Kingdom.

If man turns aside to follow his own will he may be in bypaths where My fruits of the Spirit do not grow, where My blessings are not outpoured.

You must remember that you have longed to help a world, the sorrows of which have eaten into your very souls. Do you not understand that I am answering your prayers?

The world is not always helped by the one who walks in sunlight on a flower-strewn path. Patient suffering, trials bravely borne, these show men a courage that could only be maintained by Help Divine.

DECEMBER 14

God Calling: Storms

Our loving Lord, we thank
Thee for Thy marvelous keeping Power.

There is no miracle so wonderful as the miracle of a soul being kept by My Power. Forces of evil batter and storm but are powerless. Tempests rage unavailingly.

It is like a cool garden with sweet flowers and bees and butterflies and trees and playing fountains set in the midst of a mighty roaring city. Try to see your lives as that.

Not only as calm and unmoved, but as breathing fragrance, expressing beauty. Expect storms. Know this—you cannot be united in your great friendship and bond to do My Work, and in your great Love for Me, and not excite the envy, hatred, and malice of all whom you meet who are not on My side.

Where does the enemy attack? The fortress, the stronghold, not the desert waste.

God at Eventide: Songs of Rejoicing

You must pray about all you plan to meet. Pray that you may leave them the braver, better and happier for having seen and talked with you.

Life is so serious, let nothing turn you from your desire to serve and help. Realize all you are able to accomplish in your moments of highest prayer and service, and then think that, were your desire as intense always what could you not accomplish?

Rejoice in Me. The Joy of the Lord must indeed be your strength. You must step aside, and wait until the Joy floods all your being if you wish to serve.

Let Joy keep your hearts and minds lifted above frets and cares. If you want the walls of the city to fall down you must go round it with songs of rejoicing.

DECEMBER 15

God Calling: My Shadow

Learn that each day must be lived in My Power, and in the consciousness of My Presence, even if the thrill of Joy seems to be absent. Remember that if sometimes there seems a shadow on your lives, it is not the withdrawal of My Presence. It is My shadow as I stand between you and your foes.

Even with your nearest and dearest there are the quiet days. You do not doubt *their* Love because you do not hear their laughter, and feel thrill of Joy at their nearness.

The quiet gray days are the days for duty. Work in the calm certainty that I am with you.

God at Eventide: Excess of Joy

Your life is full of Joy. You realize now that though I was the Man of Sorrows in My deep Experience of life, yet companionship with Me means an excess of Joy such as nothing else can give.

Age may have its physical limitations, but, with the soul content to dwell with Me, age has no power to limit the thrill of Love, the ecstasy of Joy-giving Life.

Reflect this Joy that it may be seen by souls weary of life, chafing at its limitations, lonely and sad, as the door closes on so many activities. They will learn by this reflection something of the Joys that Eternal Life here and hereafter brings to those who know and love Me.

So Joy.

God Calling: What Joy Is

Lord, give us Thy Joy, that Joy that no man, no poverty,
no circumstances, no conditions can take from us.

You shall have My Joy. But Life just now for you both is a march—a toilsome march. . . . The Joy will come, but for the moment do not think of that, think simply of the march. Joy is the reward. . . .

Between My Promise of the Gift of Joy to My disciples and their realization of that Joy came sense of failure, disappointment, denial, desertion, hopelessness, then hope, waiting, and courage in the face of danger.

Joy is the reward of patiently seeing Me in the dull dark days, of trusting when you cannot see. . . . Joy is as it were your heart's response to My smile of recognition of your faithfulness. . . .

Stop thinking your lives are all wrong if you do not feel it. . . . Remember you may not yet be joyous, but you are brave, and courage and unselfish thought for others are as sure signs of true discipleship as Joy.

God at Eventide: Varied Delights

Poor indeed is the life that does not know the riches of the Kingdom. A life that has to depend on the excitement of the senses, that does not know, and could not realize, that delight, Joy, expectation, wonder and satisfaction can be truly obtained only in the Spirit.

Live to bring men to the realization of all they can find in Me. I, Who change not, can supply the soul of man with Joys and delights so varied as to bring ever changing scenes of beauty before him.

I am truly the same, yesterday, today, and forever; but man, changing as he is led nearer and nearer to the realization of all I can mean to him, sees in Me new wonders daily. There can be no lack of glad adventure in a life lived with Me.

DECEMBER 17

God Calling: Conditions of Blessing

Jesus, we love Thee. We see that all things are planned by Thee. We rejoice in that vision.

Rejoice in the fact that you are Mine. The privileges of the members of My Kingdom are many. When I said of My Father, "He maketh His Sun to rise on the evil and on the good, and sendeth rain on the just and on the unjust," you will notice it was of temporal and material blessings I spoke.

I did not mean that believer and unbeliever could be treated alike. That is not possible; I can send rain and sunshine and money and worldly blessings equally to both, but of the blessing of the Kingdom that would be impossible.

There are conditions that control the bestowal of these. My followers do not always understand this, and it is necessary they should do so if they are remembering My injunction which followed—"Be ye therefore perfect even as your Father in Heaven is perfect."

To attempt to bestow on all alike your Love and Understanding and interchange of thought would be impossible. But temporal blessings you too bestow, as does My Father. All must be done in Love and in the spirit of true forgiveness.

Praise. Pray until you praise. That is the note upon which you have been told to end all prayer. Such marvels, truly such marvels are here.

Have no fear. Live in My Love. Draw nearer and nearer to Me. I will teach you. You shall see.

Before you could pass on to the Vision of Delights, you had to be taught the foundation Truths of honesty, trustworthiness, order and perseverance. All is very well. Have no fear.

DECEMBER 18

God Calling: See Wonders

Think your thought-way into the very heart of My Kingdom. See there the abundance of delights in my storehouse, and lay eager hands on them.

See wonders, ask wonders, bear wonders away with you. Remember this beautiful Earth on which you are was once only a thought of Divine Mind. Think how from your thought one corner of it could grow and become a Garden of the Lord, a Bethany-Home for your Master, a place to which I have a right to bring My friends, My needy ones, for talk and rest with Me.

God at Eventide: Watch Me

Pray ever with watchful eyes on Me, your Master, your Giver, your Example. "As the eyes of servants are on the hands of their master, so are our eyes unto the Lord our God."

Ever look unto Me. From Me comes your help, your all. The servant watches for support, for wages, for everything. Life is for him in the hands of his master.

So look to Me for all. Intent, gazing with a look of complete faith and surrender that draws all it needs towards you. Not merely faith, but intent regard. You must watch the bestowal, so that you may bestow.

DECEMBER 19

God Calling: Perfect Love

Our Lord, give us that Perfect Love of Thee that casts out all fear.

Never let yourselves fear anybody or anything. No fear of My failing you. No fear that your faith will fail you. No fear of poverty or loneliness. No fear of not knowing the way. No fear of others. No fear of their misunderstanding.

But, My children, this absolute casting out of fear is the result of a Perfect Love, a Perfect Love of Me and My Father. Speak to Me about everything. Listen to Me at all times. Feel My tender nearness, substituting at once some thought of Me for the fear.

The powers of evil watch you as a besieging force would watch a guarded city—the object being always to find some weak spot, attack that, and so gain an entrance. So evil lurks around you, and seeks to surprise you in some fear.

The fear may have been but a small one, but it affords evil a weak spot of attack and entrance, and then in come rushing despondency, doubt of Me, and so many other sins. Pray, My beloved children, for that Perfect Love of Me that indeed casts out all fear.

God at Eventide: Spiritual Practice

Pray without ceasing until every thought and every wish is a prayer. This can only be so by following the plan of recollection which I have set you.

How rarely My followers realize that Spiritual Practice is as necessary as any practice to become perfect in any art or work.

It is by the drudgery of the little steps of practice that you will ascend to Spiritual Attainment.

DECEMBER 20

God Calling: Depression

Fight fear as you would fight a plague. Fight it in My Name . . . . Fear, even the smallest fear, is the hacking at the cords of Love that bind you to Me.

However small the impression, in time those cords will wear thin, and then one disappointment or shock and they snap. But for the little fears the cords of Love would have held.

Fight fear.

Depression is a state of fear. Fight that, too. Fight. Fight. Depression is the impression left by fear. Fight and conquer, and oh! for Love of Me, for the sake of My tender, never-failing Love of you, fight and love and win.

God at Eventide: Make His Paths Straight

Prepare ye the way of the Lord, make straight His Path. Must you not do this before you see His Coming? Must you not be content to clear a way for Me, leaving it to Me to pass along it when I will?

This is My way and work for you, one of silent, unapplauded preparation.

Preparation not for your work but for Mine.

Your feet shod with the Gospel of Peace.

Yes, the preparation must first be made in your own heart. If unrest is there, nothing can make you well-shod.

DECEMBER 21

God Calling: Smile Indulgently

Children, take every moment as of My Planning and ordering. Remember your Master is the Lord of the day's little happenings. In all the small things yield to My gentle pressure on your arm. Stay or go, as that pressure, Love's pressure, indicates.

The Lord of the moments, Creator of the snowdrop and the mighty oak. More tender with the snowdrop than the oak.

And when things do not fall out according to your plan, then smile at Me indulgently, a smile of Love, and say, as you would to a human loved one, "Have Your way then"—knowing that My loving response will be to make that way as easy for your feet as it can be.

God at Eventide: Adore Him

Prove your adoration in your life. All should be calm and joy. Calm and joy are the outward expressions of adoration.

Adoration is that welling up of the whole being in Love's wonder-praise to Me.

If you truly adored, your whole life would be in harmony with that adoration, expressing as far as you were able, in all its varied manifestations, that Beauty of the Lord Whom you adore.

DECEMBER 22

God Calling: Practice Protection

Fear no evil because I have conquered evil. It has power to hurt only those who do not place themselves under My Protection. This is not a question of feeling; it is an assured fact.

All you have to do is to say with assurance that whatever it is cannot harm you, as I have conquered it. Children, in not only the big, but the little things of life, be sure of My conquering Power. Know that all is well. Be sure of it. Practice this. Learn it until it is unfailing and instinctive with you.

But practice it in the quite small things, and then you will find you will do it easily, naturally, lovingly, trustingly in the big things of life.

God at Eventide: All Loves Apart

A hush fell on the earth at My first coming. In the still hours of night I came. A silence broken only by the angels' song of praise.

So in the fret and turmoil of the world's day let that hush fall. A hush so complete that the soft footfall of your Master may not pass unnoticed. Forget the blows of life, and its adverse conditions, so that you may be ever sensitive to the touch of My Hand on your brow.

For a time you may put aside the loves of earth, and your human friendships, so that the vibrations from the heart of the Eternal may stir your hearts, and strengthen your lives.

God Calling: The World's Song

*Bless us, O Lord, we beseech Thee and show us
the way in which Thou wouldst have us walk.*

Walk with Me in the way of Peace. Shed Peace, not discord, wherever you go. But it must be My Peace.

Never a Peace that is a truce with the power of evil. Never harmony if that means your life-music being adapted to the mood and music of the world.

My disciples so often make the mistake of thinking all must be harmonious. No! Not when it means singing the song of the world.

I, the Prince of Peace, said that I came "not to bring Peace but a sword."

God at Eventide: Welcome the Interruption

I went to prepare a place for you, but I still need My Bethany Homes and My Upper Rooms. These can be prepared only by loving hearts.

When you have prepared your home, My Home, you must be prepared to receive any whom I may send. Be ready for any interruption. Treat it as from Me.

You know neither the day nor the hour when your Lord will come. You know not the guise in which He will come, in that of a prince or in that of a beggar.

See in the unwanted your Much-desired Lord.

DECEMBER 24

God Calling: He Is Coming

Our Lord, Thou art here. Let us feel Thy nearness.

Yes! but remember the first Hail must be that of the Magi in the Bethlehem stable. Not as King and Lord in Heavenly triumph must you first hail Me. But as amongst the lowliest, bereft of Earth's pomp like the Magi.

So to the humble the worship of humility—the Bethlehem Babe—must be the first Hail.

Then the worship of repentance. As Earth's sinner, you stand by Me in the Jordan, baptized of John, worshiping Me, the Friend and Servant of sinners.

Dwell much on My Life. Step out beside Me. Share it with Me. Humility, Service, Worship, Sacrifice, Sanctification—Steps in the Christian Life.

God at Eventide: Eve of Christmas

"A virgin shall conceive and bear a son and shall call his name Immanuel."

"Unto us a child is born, unto us a son is given. . .his name shall be called Wonderful, Counselor, the Mighty God . . .the Prince of Peace."

"And the Angel said unto her, 'Fear not, Mary. . .behold thou shalt bring forth a son and shalt call his name Jesus. . . .' "

" 'The Holy Ghost shall come upon thee, and the power of the Highest shall overshadow thee: therefore also that holy thing, which shall be born of thee, shall be called the Son of God.' "

God Calling: Babe of Bethlehem

Kneel before the Babe of Bethlehem. Accept the truth that the Kingdom of Heaven is for the lowly, the simple.

Bring to Me, the Christ-child, your gifts, truly the gifts of Earth's wisest.

The Gold—your money.

Frankincense—the adoration of a consecrated life.

Myrrh—your sharing in My sorrows and those of the world.

"And they presented unto Him gifts: gold, frankincense and myrrh."

God at Eventide: Miracle of the Ages

"And the Word was made flesh."

Word proceeding from the Father, the thought. Dwell this evening upon this miracle of all ages. This stupendous fact of all mankind's history:—

God made man.

I came to restore to man his lost dignity. To show him that his physical and mental being could only be maintained at their intended height and power by constant communion with the Maker of man's being.

I came, God, to live with man, *to show man how to live with God.*

DECEMBER 26

God Calling: Health and Wealth

Be not afraid; health and wealth are coming to you both. My wealth which is sufficiency for your needs, and for My Work you long to do.

Money, as some call wealth, to hoard, to display, you know is not for My disciples.

Journey through this world simply seeking the means to do My Will and Work. Never keep anything you are not using. Remember all I give you will be Mine, only given to you to use. Could you think of Me hoarding My Treasures? You must never do it. Rely on Me.

To store for the future is to *fear* and to doubt Me. Check every doubt of Me at once. Live in the Joy of My constant Presence. Yield every moment to Me. Perform every task, however humble, as at My gentle bidding, and for Me, for love of Me. So live, so love, so work.

You are the Apostles of the Little Services.

God at Eventide: Perfect Rest

Even My Perfection could be no place of rest for weary souls. Rest in My Love. No true rest but that.

How much of earth's weariness is sin-caused. Contact with My Perfection would but make your sin seem the greater. The sight of it might truly spur you on to further effort, to further emulation, but rest—? No. And so with other attributes of Divinity.

But in My Love! in that you *can* rest. Pillowed like a tired child, a happily tired child. Pillowed in security, cradled in a Love, tireless and limitless. In a Love that will not only care for the weary, and rest the weary, but will rest you until in the very strength of Love you can face your life again.

Rest in My Love. Here alone is perfect Rest. Rest for Spirit, mind and body.

DECEMBER 27

God Calling: Glorious Work

I have stripped you of much, that it should be truly a life of well-being. Build up stone by stone upon a firm foundation, and that Rock is your Master—that Rock is Christ.

A life of discipline and of joyous fulfillment is to be yours. . . . Never lose sight of the glorious work to which you have been called.

Let no riches, no ease entice you from the path of miracle-working with Me upon which your feet are set. Love and Laugh. Trust and pray. Ride on now in a loving humility to victory.

God at Eventide: When Evil Smiles

Remember that the forces of evil are always ranged against you. They know the power you can become as a channel for God-Power.

I had to conquer them in the wilderness before *My* Life of Healing and Helpfulness could be all-powerful.

Not by great falls but by little stumbles does evil seek the downfall of My friends. Your Mountain of Transfiguration can only come after your conquest in the wilderness. Temptations at which your whole nature would shudder are no temptations for you.

Beware the smiling face of evil, its seeming innocence, its hand of friendliness.

Fail Me not. Will you not walk the path I trod?

God Calling: Signs and Feelings

Our Lord, Thou art here. Let us feel Thy nearness.

I am here. Do not need *feeling* too much. To ask for feeling too much is to ask for a sign, and then the answer is the same as that I gave when on Earth. "There shall no sign be given but the sign of the prophet Jonas. . . . For as Jonas was three days and three nights. . .so shall the Son of Man be three days and three nights in the heart of the earth."

Veiled from sight to the unbeliever. To the believer the veiling is only temporary, to be followed by a glorious Resurrection. . . .

What does it matter what you feel? What matters is what I am, was, and ever shall be to you—A Risen Lord. . . . The *feeling* that I am with you may depend upon any passing mood of yours—upon a change of circumstances, upon a mere trifle.

I am uninfluenced by circumstances. . . . My Promise given is kept. I am here, one with you in tender loving friendship.

God at Eventide: Still Seek Me

Softly I speak to the tired and the distressed, yet in My quiet Voice there is healing and strength.

A healing for the sores and sickness of spirit, mind and body and a bracing strength that bids those who come to Me rise to battle for Me and My Kingdom.

Search until you find *Me,* not merely the Truth about Me. None ever sought Me in vain.

God Calling: Work and Prayer

Work and prayer represent the two forces that will ensure you success. Your work and My Work.

For prayer, believing prayer, is based on the certainty that I am working for you and with you and in you.

Go forward gladly and unafraid. I am with you. With men your task may be impossible, but with God all things are possible.

God at Eventide: Safe at the Last

Safe amid storms, calm amid a world-unrest, certain amid insecurity. Safely through the year.

The only safe way is the sure way of Divine Guidance. Not the advice of others, not the urgings of your own hearts and wills. Just My Guidance.

Think more of its wonder. Dwell more on its rest. Know that you are safe, secure.

DECEMBER 30

God Calling: Fishers of Men

When you think of those of whom you read who are in anguish, do you ever think how My Heart must ache with the woe of it, with the anguish of it?

If I beheld the city and wept over it, how much more should I weep over the agony of these troubled hearts, over lives that seek to live without My sustaining Power.

"They will not come unto Me that they might have Life."

Live to bring others to *Me*, the only Source of Happiness and Heart-Peace.

So silently I teach, and that silent teaching depends upon your approach.

Let every discipline, every joy, every difficulty, every fresh interest serve to draw you nearer, serve to render you more receptive to My word, serve to make you more sensitive, more spiritually aware.

It is this sensitiveness that is the prelude to the joy I give you. The sweetest harmony can be played on a sensitive instrument.

Those who fail to hear think Me far off. I am ever ready to speak but they have missed the power of discipline, the wonder of Communion with Me.

DECEMBER 31

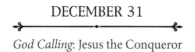

God Calling: Jesus the Conqueror

Jesus. That is the Name by which you conquer. Jesus. Not as cringing suppliants but as those recognizing a Friend, say My Name—Jesus. "Thou shall call His Name Jesus, for He shall save His people from their sins."

And in that word "sins" read not only vice and degradation, but doubts, fears, tempers, despondencies, impatience, lack of Love in big and little things. Jesus. "He shall save His people from their sins." The very uttering of the Name lifts the soul away from petty valley-irritations to mountain heights.

"He shall save His people from their sins." Savior and Friend, Joy-bringer and Rescuer, Leader and Guide—Jesus. Do you need delivering from cowardice, from adverse circumstances, from poverty, from failure, from weakness?

"There is none other Name. . .whereby you can be saved"—*Jesus*. Say it often. Claim the Power it brings.

Bring to Me this eventide the past year with its sins, its failures, its lost opportunities.

Leave that past with Me, your Savior today as ever, and go into the New Year forgiven, unladen, free.

Bring to Me your youth or age, your powers, your love—and I, as your God-guide through the year to come, will bring My agelessness, My powers, My love.

So shall we share the burdens and the joys, and the work of the days that lie ahead.

NOTES

NOTES

_____

_____

_____

_____

_____

_____

_____

_____

_____

_____

_____

_____

_____

_____

_____

_____

_____

_____

NOTES

NOTES

NOTES

NOTES

_____

_____

_____

_____

_____

_____

_____

_____

_____

_____

_____

_____

_____

_____

_____

_____

_____

NOTES

NOTES